NECESSARY KNOWLEDGE

Necessary Knowledge
Piagetian Perspectives on Constructivism

Leslie Smith
Department of Educational Research
Lancaster University

LAWRENCE ERLBAUM ASSOCIATES, PUBLISHERS
Hove (UK)   Hillsdale (USA)

Lawrence Erlbaum Associates Ltd., Publishers
27 Palmeira Mansions
Church Road
Hove
East Sussex, BN3 2FA
U.K.

British Library Cataloguing in Publication Data
Smith, Leslie
    Necessary Knowledge: Piagetian
    Perspectives on Constructivism. —
    (Essays in Developmental Psychology,
    ISSN 0959-3977)
    I. Title II. Series
    155

    ISBN 0-86377-270-6 (Hbk)

Printed in Great Britain by Redwood Books, Trowbridge, Wiltshire

For Rose - for all the years salvo amore

"Although we had contemplated building a tower which would reach to the heavens, the supply of materials suffices only for a dwelling-house, just sufficiently commodious for our business on the level of experience, and just sufficiently high to allow of our overlooking it. The bold undertaking that we had designed is thus bound to fail through lack of material—not to mention the babel of tongues, which inevitably gives rise to disputes among the workers in regard to the plan to be followed, and which must end by scattering them all over the world, leaving each to erect a separate building for himself, according to his own design."

(Kant, 1787/1933, A707).

Contents

Jean Piaget *circa* 1925.
From J.J. Ducret (1990) *Jean Piaget: Biographie et parcours intellectuel*, published by Editions Delachaux et Niestlé, Lausanne.

Preface
or
Hill-climbing with
Jean Piaget

"As soon as vacation time comes, I withdraw to the mountains in the wild regions of the Valais and write" (Piaget, 1952/1976, p.255/20).

The noble view that human knowledge is a towering structure, reaching to the heavens, was sympathetically regarded by Immanuel Kant as a vain illusion. Changing the analogy to hill-climbing may provide a better way to represent Jean Piaget's view about human knowing.

A common view of Piaget's writings is that they make hard reading, since they are a fine example of an up-hill struggle. There is something in this view, especially if the identity of the mountain is unknown and the route to be followed is uncertain. Hill-climbing can be hazardous since there is ample scope for walking in a circle, losing the way and even falling so severely that a rescue service must be called out. But mountains have arresting features too. Hill-climbing is difficult because of steepness and height. Yet one attraction of the Matterhorn is the steepness of its symmetrically angular slopes. And height confers distinct advantage, not merely in a panoramic view from the summit but also in the progressively encompassing views of a notable ascent. The question to ask about hill-climbing is not whether it is hard work but whether it is worthwhile. The question to ask is not whether Piagetian writings are difficult but rather whether they have value on rational or empirical grounds.

A test case is provided by questions about the growth of necessary knowledge. The concept of necessity is a fundamental concept and it is for precisely this reason that it has been at the centre of philosophical discussions for more than two millennia. This means that it is a problematic concept, defying easy empirical use. Piaget set out to show how normative questions in epistemology can be addressed empirically. His questions are central to philosophy with a basis in rational thought. But Piaget changed these philosophical questions. His genetic, or constructivist, epistemology was conceived by him to provide a rationale for the systematic study of the how knowledge develops, one which is neutral to specific answers to these transformed, epistemological questions. A normative question such as "What is knowledge?" cannot, of course, be answered empirically. The advance is to show that the transformed question "How does knowledge develop?" is open to empirical investigation. This is an achievement in itself, not because Piaget was the first genetic epistemologist but rather because of his demonstration of how such a study could take place with respect to a range of epistemological questions. The list is well known, covering the fundamental categories of human thinking. Piaget's account provides some guidance as to the features that a minimally adequate answer to this question should possess. Even if Piaget did not successfully resolve this formidable question, there is a case for claiming that his account is the best available account.

In my discussion, I have not set out systematically to survey Piaget's own writings, still less the Piagetian literature. Nor is new evidence provided with a relevance to the development of modal understanding. Rather, my main aim has been to try to make sense of both Piaget's writings and Piagetian commentary with reference to the question of the construction of necessary knowledge. My discussion is deliberately selective and is an attempt to take stock by a survey of alternatives. This strategy has the compensation that it could lead to the identification and assessment of a promising route up one Piagetian mountain, one in which necessary knowledge is a construction from non-necessary precursors. Its obvious defect is that it ignores other mountains and their attendant routes of ascent.

Piaget's output was regularly formidable over a period of sixty years with posthumous publications continuing to appear in the decade after his death in 1980. He was the author and editor of some sixty books and five hundred papers. This vast corpus of published writings has been catalogued by the Fondation Archives Jean Piaget (1989) and a breakdown of these works is shown in Table 1.

There are three striking features of these works. One is the commitment to a rational model of empirical research. A paradigm

TABLE 1
Number[1] of Published Works (*italics*) and Pages (**bold**) by Piaget[2]
based on Publications[3] in the Period 1896–1990[4]

AGE	PERIOD	PAPERS		BOOKS		TOTAL
1-18	1896-1914	*31*	**595**	*0*	**0**	595
19-22	1915-1918	*4*	**174**	*2*	**278**	492
23-25	1919-1921	*7*	**213**	*0*	**0**	213
26-29	1922-1925	*16*	**675**	*2*	**426**	1101
30-33	1928-1929	*16*	**557**	*2*	**814**	1371
34-43	1930-1939	*33*	**488**	*3*	**1316**	1804
44-54	1940-1950	*64*	**1251**	*11*	**4686**	5937
55-70	1951-1966	*178*	**4293**	*9*	**2531**	6824
71-80	1967-1976	*102*	**1678**	*19*	**4003**	5681
81-84	1977-1980	*27*	**195**	*4*	**1033**	1228
	1981-1990	*5*	**38**	*5*	**1099**	1137
TOTAL	1896-1990	*483*	**10157**	*57*	**16186**	26343

[1]Adapted from information available from The Librarian, Fondation Archives Jean Piaget, Geneva
[2]Jean Piaget (1896–1980)
[3]Excluding 40 reports International Bureau of Education
[4]Using ages indicated in Piaget's autobiography for the years 1896–1976

example is Piaget's logical description of operational thought in advance of its empirical investigation. A second is his use of a variety of available, formal models, ranging from Boolean algebra during the early part of his work to the entailment logic of the 1970s in recent studies. This prodigality is insightful. A third feature is that Piaget's writings are demanding. It is now common ground that they act as an essential reference point in discussions of the construction of knowledge, even though there are competing evaluations of their acceptability. However, this reference point has attracted an enormous Piagetian literature, which is itself expanding, interdisciplinary, and erudite. It makes more, not less, demands on developmentalists and, as such, is more demanding still. This literature is compulsively interesting and has independent value (Smith, 1992a). But in two respects it is questionable whether the Piagetian literature can provide a self-sufficient introduction to Piaget's work. First, this literature invariably rests on an interpretation of Piaget's position. The point is that there are several on offer. Yet it is rare for the comparative merits of the alternatives to be explicitly discussed. Second, there are considerable variations in the relevance and strength of the criticisms of Piaget's position. The only approach to recommend is one that requires the joint examination of issues in Piagetian theory through Piagetian research and vice versa. Curiously, many guides typically imply that Piagetian commentary provides the best, and self-sufficient, route for the understanding and evaluation of Piagetian theory. This cannot be right—one might as easily suppose that a book of literary quotations and criticism is sufficient for an adequate appreciation of the plays of Shakespeare. We need the Piagetian commentary, which is essential, but we also need to read Piaget's writings to find his answers to the questions he set. Reading these texts may not be easy since Piaget wrote for himself, to clarify his own thinking, rather than for anyone else, to clarify theirs.

Since Piaget wrote in French, I have used French editions rather than their English counterparts for two reasons. One is that not all of Piaget's writings are available in English editions, including some of his more important papers and monographs. The second is that some English editions embody mistranslation. Here's an example, taken from the first English version of Piaget's (1975/1978, p.149/*155) text on equilibration: "a child of three, for example, will ask if a new *orange*, separated from a preceding one by a long interval, is the same *orange*". This is an odd, almost ridiculous claim. In fact, the key French term is *orage*, whose standard meaning *storm*, is used in the completely revised translation (Piaget, 1975/1985, p.123). A child's question about when one storm ends, and another begins, is a meaningful and intriguing question. Note that this example of mistranslation is simple, whilst other examples can be more subtle, including the claim—see [19]—which is often quoted in English commentary but whose basis in the French text is deficient.

My procedure here has been to refer to Piagetian texts using dual dates, usually to French and English editions such as (Piaget, 1977/1986) but also to successive French editions such as (Piaget, 1950/1973). Single page references are to the English edition alone, for example (Piaget, 1961/1966, p.132). Dual pages references are given where there are minor discrepancies between editions, for example (Piaget, 1981/1987, p.186/152). Serious discrepancies between editions are indicated with an asterisk, for example (Piaget & Szeminska, 1941/1952, p.17/*4).

Quotations from the following texts are used with the permission of the relevant publishers as follows:

Basil Blackwell:
S. Kripke, *Naming and necessity*

Cambridge University Press:
G. Leibniz, *New essays on human understanding*

Edinburgh University Press:
J. Piaget, *Biology and knowledge*

Editions Dunod:
J. Piaget, *Essai de logique opératoire*

Fondation Archives Jean Piaget:
Table 1 in the Preface

Oxford University Press:
J. Piaget, "Le développement intellectuel chez les jeunes enfants" *Mind* (1932)

Penguin Group:
J. Piaget, *Psychology and epistemology*

Presses Universitaires de France:
J. Piaget, *Introduction à l'épistémologie génétique*

Routledge:
H.I. Brown, *Rationality*
J. Piaget, *The child's conception of number.*

My thanks are also due to the following publishers for the use of material in my own previously published papers:

Basil Blackwell:
"On Piaget on necessity" (1987) in J. Russell, *Philosophical perspectives on developmental psychology*

British Psychological Society:
"Class inclusion and conclusions about Piaget's theory" (1982) *British Journal of Psychology*
"General transferable ability: an interpretation of formal operational thinking" (1986) *British Journal of Developmental Psychology*
"Changing perspectives in developmental psychology" in C. Desforges, *Early childhood education*
"Judgments and justifications as criteria for the attribution of children's knowledge" (1992) *British Journal of Developmental Psychology*

Karger:
"Children's knowledge: a meta-analysis of Piaget's theory" (1986) *Human Development*
"Essay on necessity" (1986) *Human Development*
"The infant's Copernican revolution" (1987) *Human Development*
"A constructivist interpretation of formal operations" (1987) *Human Development*

Lawrence Erlbaum Associates Inc.:
"Age, ability and intellectual development in Piagetian theory" (1991) in M. Chandler & M. Chapman, *Criteria for competence.*

Finally, sections 19 and 26 of this book form the basis of my paper "Reasoning models and intellectual development" to be published by

Elsevier in *Mind reasoning and intelligence: Structure and development"* edited by A. Demetriou.

I naturally want to thank David Wood and the editors of the Essays in Developmental Psychology Series for the invitation to write this book. The writing itself was made very much easier by the help given to me by several organisations. These include the British Academy and the British Council for travel grants; the Fondation Archives Jean Piaget, University of Geneva for its generosity in making possible a study visit during the summer of 1991; the Jean Piaget Society: Society for the Study of Knowledge and Development for its continuing commitment to the critical discussion of both rational and empirical issues in developmental theory and research; and Lancaster University for both study grants and the study leave leading to the completion of this text. Both Jane Charman and Melanie Tarrant at Lawrence Erlbaum have been unfailingly helpful, attentive and efficient in their supervision of the production of this book. My biggest debt is to the many individuals who have contributed to the improvement of this text, including Michael Chapman for his support and the distinctive example that he set. Michael's untimely death coincided with the writing of this book. My warm thanks are given for either personal conversations or comments on different sections of the text to Mark Bickhard, Trevor Bond, Robert Campbell, Sylvain Dionnet, Rémy Droz, Gerry Finn, Christiane Gillièron, Bärbel Inhelder, Henry Markovits, Danielle Maurice, Jacques Montangero, Jim Murphy, Anne-Nelly Perret-Clermont, Silvia Parrat-Dayan, Anastasia Tryphon, Ewald Vervaet, and Jacques Vonèche. My special thanks are given to Peter Bryant, Wolfe Mays, Michael Shayer and Peter Tomlinson for their penetrating and assiduous commentary on the first draft of the entire text. Suffice to say that I made almost all the minor changes that have been suggested but am still having further thoughts about some of the major ones. Suffice also to say what this means—the shortcomings that remain are all my own.

CHAPTER ONE

Towards an Epistemology of Necessary Knowledge

"We are careful in particular to recognise our personal debt in this respect, that almost all the questions that we have studied in psychology had a philosophical inspiration" (Piaget, 1975a, p.18).

[1] INTRODUCTION

Piaget has given an exact formulation of the problem which he takes to be central when questions about the development of knowledge arise.

> The main problem of any epistemology, but principally of any genetic epistemology, is in fact to understand how the mind succeeds in *constructing necessary relationships*, which appear to be "independent of time", if the instruments of thought are merely psychological *operations that are subject to evolution and are constituted in time* (Piaget, 1950, p.23; my emphasis).

This problem concerns the construction during time of necessary knowledge that is true throughout time. According to Piaget, necessary knowledge is a constitutive feature of rationality and also a human construction. Several initial comments can be made about this position. Firstly, Piaget's problem has been one main problem in philosophy since it concerns the distinction between the origins of knowledge and the legitimation of knowledge in the light of the standards of rationality. In traditional epistemology, this distinction is forcefully stated by Hume (1739/1965, p. 165). It re-appears in the distinction between the empirical basis of knowledge and its rational validity (Kant, 1787/1933, B3-4), or in the distinction between the origins of mathematical ideas and their proof (Frege, 1888/1980, p.vi), or in the distinction between the origins of human beliefs and the reasons for those beliefs (Sainsbury, 1991, p.5). Secondly, some version of Piaget's problem continues to be regarded as one of the principal, unresolved problems in contemporary epistemology (Kitchener, 1986, p.99). Philosophers issue the reminder that questions such as "What, exactly, distinguishes logical from psychological study of reasoning ... What has logic to tell us about rationality?" (Haack, 1978, p.242) or the problem of "explaining how a physical organism can be subject to the norms of rationality" (McGinn, 1991, p.23) are intriguing, important but unresolved. Thirdly, Piaget's main proposal is that questions about the development of necessary knowledge bear upon both its psycho-social origins and its rational legitimation in the human mind. On this view, an answer to Piaget's main problem would have to include both empirical and rational elements which would be reducible neither to empirical psychology nor to a priori epistemology.

The interpretation of Piaget's account that is outlined here assigns a key role to the notion of necessity which is used in three ways. Piaget's account is taken to lay down empirically necessary conditions of the understanding of logical necessity through a process of constructive necessity (Smith, 1987a). Allied to this interpretation are three main claims: one philosophical, a second psychological, and a third epistemological.

The philosophical claim states that the concepts (categories, relations, structures) that are central to research in developmental psychology and empirical epistemology have both defining and non-defining properties. Defining properties are necessary properties that lay down all-and-only the properties which must be possessed for a case to fall under that concept. The non-defining properties of a concept are contingent and so are not necessary in this sense, even though cases that fall under the concept may commonly possess them. Necessary properties lay down both why something is, and has to be, what it is and why it is not, and cannot be, something else. A simple statistical example is provided by the notion of an average score. The (common sense) notion of an average is not well defined, unlike the statistical notions of median and mean. The third score in a series of five scores is not always the mean, even if it is the median. Further, even when the third score is the mean, that score is not on that account the mean, since the properties of being the middle score and being the mean score are distinct. Thus knowing that a score is the middle score may coincide with knowledge of the mean of the scores, even though the former is not the latter. This logical claim has been at centre stage in epistemological discussions from Plato to the present day. One implication of this logical claim is that intellectual development can be successful only if an understanding of necessity is attained.

The psychological claim states that, in fact, children typically gain their initial knowledge by use of the non-defining properties of the concepts at their disposal. There are an indefinite number of ways in which this may occur and psychological accounts are advanced as to how the process of acquisition takes place. In turn, psychological research has the role of systematically investigating the local contingencies that operate in a social context and which help to shape human understanding. Knowledge based on non-defining properties is, of course, knowledge. Further, it may sometimes coincide with knowledge based on the defining properties of the concept, and thus psychological research which is directed to its characterisation and explanation is valid in its own right. Yet necessary knowledge is always distinguishable from empirical knowledge and the understanding of proportionality is, according to Spinoza (1660/1963), an illustrious case in point. It is psychologically interesting that street-trading children have developed their own way of understanding proportionality (Saxe, 1991; Carraher, 1991). It is also epistemologically important to ascertain the extent to which their way amounts to rational understanding which has the Kantian properties of universality and necessity. The modal concepts of necessity and possibility are important just because their use is required in the acquisition of all forms of conceptual knowledge. Such concepts are invariably used throughout intellectual development, even though they have variable exemplifications at different developmental points.

The epistemological claim states that progress occurs as a process of differentiation whereby properties which are initially conflated are severally demarcated and ultimately coordinated into a coherent system of thought. Intellectual development is a search for coherence, marked by the progressive construction and conservation of the categories of thought. This search is required because of the conflation of the necessary and empirical properties of concepts. Reverting to a statistical analogy relating to significance testing, modal errors occur either as type I (false-positive) or as type II (false-negative) errors. The growth of knowledge in children is a special case of epistemic search, which is activated by the occurrence of modal errors in understanding and whose successful completion can never be attained, since necessary properties are always co-instantiated with empirical properties in the human understanding. The growth of necessary knowledge is a process that is both co-extensive with all intelligent life and which is never complete. There are however degrees of success which occur as the progressive attainment of rationality. Intellectual search directed towards coherence is an epistemological process, since it bears on the formal characteristics of knowledge which are universally and atemporally valid. That is, these characteristics apply to all knowledge everywhere and always apply without exception. But this epistemic search has its origin in psychological functioning which is constrained by context and contingency. That is, the characteristics of these psychological forms of knowledge are situationally specific and dependent on the particular factors at work. An adequate account of intellectual development will have to do justice to both epistemological and psychological dimensions. If more attention has been given to the former in Piaget's account, and to the latter in Piagetian research, a minimally adequate account is still awaited. It is for this fundamental reason that Piagetian hill-climbing is difficult.

[2] PIAGET'S PROBLEM: THE CONSTRUCTION OF NECESSARY KNOWLEDGE

Four introductory comments can be made about Piaget's problem, which is a central and epistemological one but neither the sole nor a resolved problem in his work. First, the problem has been central throughout Piaget's work. Second, it is one essential problem that developmentalists must address. Third, it is not the sole problem in human development. Finally, Piaget's problem has its basis in epistemology.

First, the construction of necessary knowledge was one of Piaget's central concerns in his early, empirical studies (Piaget, 1922, p.222, my emphasis): "I call *formal reasoning* the reasoning which, from one or several propositions, draws a conclusion to which *the mind assents with certainty, without thereby having recourse to observation*. What is beyond dispute is that *such reasoning exists*". In this paper, the empirical question is to ascertain whether formal reasoning, which is logically necessary, is present in children's thinking. Piaget's question has normative presuppositions since a norm—in this case, *necessity*—is required to identify the species of knowledge. But the question is posed as one to which an empirical answer can be given. Traditionally, normative questions have been the concern of philosophers. Piaget set out to show that his question can be investigated empirically, even though it also embodies a normative component. Because Piaget's findings indicated that not all children do display formal reasoning, the problem of how such necessary knowledge is constructed is posed, as Piaget assumes that such reasoning is present in the thinking of adults.

The same interest is evident throughout Piaget's work, including his final papers. One statement (Piaget, 1967a, p.391; cf. 1977/1986) of this problem is that "the manifestation of logical necessity constitutes the central problem of the psycho-genesis of operational structures". His epistemological interests are stated to lie in accounting for the actual construction of new knowledge, in which process the construction of new necessities would play an essential role. Thus the construction of necessary knowledge has been one of Piaget's concerns for almost the whole of his work.

Second, Piaget claimed that the construction of necessary knowledge is the principal problem in epistemology. This is a strong claim in two respects. There are other epistemological problems which demand equal priority. There are other problems which gain equal attention in Piaget's work, such as the construction of knowledge *tout court* (Kitchener, 1986, p.175) or the origin of universal ideas in individual thinking (Chapman, 1988, p.5). A more modest proposal is that the construction of necessary knowledge is one of the essential problems which will have to be tackled in any minimally adequate epistemology. Necessary knowledge is one species of knowledge. This species of knowledge is important, and so essential, on four counts. First, necessary knowledge is a paradigm example of knowledge because such knowledge is true and atemporally so. Second, such knowledge is a constitutive feature of knowledge in certain domains, such as mathematics. Third, necessary knowledge is a pervasive feature of every domain where necessary conclusions permit the knower to go beyond the information given. Fourth, necessary knowledge has a biological origin. However in the present discussion it is sufficient to state that necessary knowledge has its origins in non-necessary knowledge. The importance of necessary knowledge to developmental theory has been noticed (Campbell & Bickhard, 1986; Chapman, 1988; Kitchener, 1986; Moshman, 1990; Murray, 1990; Smith, 1992a).

Third, the problem of how necessary knowledge is constructed could not be the sole problem that an account of human development would have to address. To be sure, Piaget's problem is far-reaching because *necessity* is domain independent. But necessary knowledge is a sub-species of knowledge which is itself a sub-species of mental states. An account of the human construction of necessary knowledge could not be a comprehensive account of the person. Of course, Piaget never claimed that his position could be comprehensive in this sense. The positions attributed to him in Piagetian commentary are another matter.

Fourth, even if Piaget has clearly stated what he takes his principal problem to be, this is not to say that the full nature of this problem is clear, still less clearly answerable. On the contrary: the problem is a formidable problem in epistemology. Although Piaget (1970, p.25) stated that "all the problems I have attacked are epistemological", there is continuing controversy about the extent to which, and the respects in which these problems have a psychological component. In his *chef d'oeuvre*, Piaget (1950) took his work primarily to be a contribution to genetic epistemology. There are two points to notice here. In one respect, Piaget's work is a contribution to methodology as he outlines and defends proposals about the main elements in any theory of the development of knowledge. In this sense, Piaget's work is a contribution to the philosophy of science, which is further noted in [10]. But there is a different respect to consider as well, since specific accounts of how the construction of knowledge occurs are also elaborated by Piaget. In this sense, Piaget's work is a contribution to empirical epistemology, which accords joint recognition to both rational and empirical issues.

In the present volume, the discussion of Piaget's work has three strands. One strand is philosophical and concerns the importance of normative issues when epistemological questions arise [3]–[7]. A second strand is psychological and concerns the extent to which Piaget's position is vulnerable to psychological challenges [9]–[22]. The third strand is epistemological and concerns the respects in which Piaget's position is an intelligible position relevant to his main question [8], [23]–[26]. An overview of the whole discussion, which could also serve as an introduction, is provided in [27]. A guide to, and commentary on, current research on the development of necessary knowledge is offered in [28].

The primary aim of sections [3]–[10] of Chapters 1–2 is twofold. One aim is to illustrate some of the theoretical issues that have arisen in philosophical discussions of knowledge and necessity. This first aim has two dependent objectives. First, the illustrations in [3.1] are designed to show that problems of knowledge and necessity have been a central preoccupation in philosophical epistemology for two millennia. The second objective is to show that these problems are not merely of antique interest but continue to occupy a central place in current philosophical discussion. Illustrative use is made of the work of Karl Popper and Saul Kripke in [3.2] followed by a selection of case studies in [4] and [5]. The implied conclusion in these sections is that the complexity of these problems resists a facile resolution through over-hasty operational-isation in empirical research. The second aim is to show that Piaget's genetic epistemology addresses epistemological problems of knowledge and necessity by the express introduction of an empirical control. His argument is that there are empirical, and not merely rational, issues to confront when problems of the development of necessary knowledge arise. The central presumption of Piagetian epistemology is that both the derogation of the empirical issues on philosophical grounds, and the derogation of rational issues on methodological grounds, are equally unacceptable. It is for this reason that Piaget takes his position to offer a mediating, middle course, a *tertium quid*. Piaget's argument for this mediating position is reviewed in [7]. A sketch of the general features of Piaget's position is given in [8]. It is this sketch that is later elaborated in [23]–[26] of Chapter 7. The main implication of the discussion in sections [3]–[8] is that a minimally adequate theory of the development of necessary knowledge must be both empirically and rationally acceptable. The argument in [9] is that psychological research on intellectual development should be evaluated with this implication in mind.

In fact, this main implication has been so far out of sight in some psychological research that it appears never to be in view at all. The case for this last claim is elaborated in section [10]–[22] of Chapters 3–6. Although some readers might prefer to address this case directly, either because they prefer to leave the consideration of rational issues to others or because their interest lies exclusively in empirical considerations, they are welcome to by-pass sections [3]–[8] only if prior credence is given to the main implication, that rational and empirical issues require joint consideration. Readers who neither accept this main implication nor the case against certain types of psychological research outlined in [10]–[22] are not in a good position to by-pass sections [3]–[8] completely.

[3] NECESSITY IN PHILOSOPHICAL EPISTEMOLOGY

As a guide to the discussion, Piaget's objection to philosophical epistemology can be stated at the outset (Piaget, 1970/1977, pp.12/*5; my translation and emphasis):

> Platonic, rationalist or apriorist epistemologies suppose themselves to have found some fundamental instrument of knowledge that is extraneous, superior or prior to experience ... Such doctrines, though careful to characterise the properties which they attribute to this instrument ... have omitted to verify that *it was actually at the subject's disposal. Here, whether we like it or not, is a question of fact.*

The objection is that some philosophical questions about human understanding have an empirical component. An exclusively a priori approach is stated to be unacceptable because of its neglect of the facts.

The objection is a denial neither of the importance nor of the relevance of the philosophical questions. The objection is instead that an a priori approach will not lead to their resolution. There is also the implied suggestion that an empirical approach will fare better in this respect. Furthermore, one of the central claims made by Piaget is that the logic embedded in the process of construction in the child's mind is the same as the logic of mature thought. In his review of the study of children's thinking undertaken by Bruner, Olver, & Greenfield (1966), Piaget makes this point in the challenge which is addressed to Bruner in person (Piaget & Voyat, 1968, p.74, my emphasis): "If a logic of some sort therefore exists in *his works* (and it would be awkward if he contested that), it is also necessary to admit that it exists in *his thinking*". Although there are normative considerations to heed, Piaget's central claim also has an empirical element. In consequence, a decision could be made to concentrate on the empirical issues which have been neglected in normative epistemology. According to Piaget (1963, p.viii), some developmentalists appear to have taken just such a decision.

The aims of this section are twofold. One aim is to show that the notion of necessity has occupied a central place in philosophical discussions from Plato onwards. A second aim is to show that similar philosophical disputes continue today. The discussion will be selective with respect to both aims; it aspires to be an exhaustive treatment neither of this fundamental topic in philosophical epistemology nor of those philosophers whose positions are used in its exemplification.

[3.1] Necessity in Traditional Epistemology

In stating his criticism, Piaget referred to three types of epistemological positions in which an epistemic instrument, or the means by which knowledge is made possible, is "extraneous, superior or prior to experience". This claim can be interpreted as a reference to Platonic, Rationalist, and Kantian epistemologies respectively. Since Piaget assumes that necessary knowledge is possessed, the objection does not mention a fourth epistemological position—Humean Empiricism— which is a denial that necessary knowledge is possible at all. Each of these four positions is now reviewed with reference to Piaget's criticism.

In Plato's *Republic* (nd/1941), four central claims with a relevance to Piaget's criticism can be noticed. The first claim is a commitment to essentialism: that there are forms, or ideal types, or essences, which are the defining and constitutive features corresponding to such notions as goodness, truth, number, and similarly fundamental categories of the world. These ideal types provide the reason why anything is what it is.

Thus the number two is a number, and not something else, and is that specific number, rather than any other, just because it is an exemplification of the corresponding ideal type ($507[1]). The second claim is ontological. Ideal types exist in an intelligible world which is distinct from the world of everyday experience ($509). In consequence, human understanding which is located in the mind of a person who lives in the everyday, not the intelligible, world is radically different from its objects, which are these ideal types ($508). The third claim is epistemological because Plato presents a sceptical argument that is a denial that perceptual knowledge could, in principle, provide such knowledge, which has the characteristics of certainty, necessity, and truth ($510, 522). "There can be no knowledge of sensible things" ($529). Thus some account is needed to show how a person in the world of everyday experience gains knowledge that has these characteristics. This is the fourth and psycho-educational claim, as Plato contends that access to the intelligible world of ideal types, and so to knowledge, is the outcome of a process of education which is directed towards the rational justification of human understanding ($531) and dialectical enquiry ($533). This process, which culminates in necessary knowledge, is reckoned not to be for young minds but is rather within the grasp of those aged 30 years or more ($539). In short, because knowledge is directed on an intelligible world of ideal types, that world is external to human understanding, which is directed on the everyday (sensible) world. Thus some extraneous epistemic instrument is needed, one that permits access to this world, and so to the proper objects of knowledge.

The objection offered by Piaget is that Plato's position is vulnerable because of its neglect of empirical issues that are germane to it. His objection, then, is primarily directed towards the fourth claim, namely that—as a matter of fact—children do acquire and possess the necessary knowledge that, according to Plato is confined to adults at the terminal stages of a long process of advanced education. In turn, consequential changes would have to be made to some of the other claims as well, notably the second, ontological claim. In this way Piaget sees his empirically based and constructivist epistemology as a genuine alternative to a normative and a priori epistemology.

It is worth noting that even if contemporary philosophers are disinclined to accept Plato's theory, platonism continues to be a tenable position (Quine 1961, p.1). The ontological question as to what exists is fundamental. The vacuous answer 'everything' requires supplementation so that reasonable decisions can be made as to whether minds, numbers,

---

[1] The $ used in this context represents a reference to either a numbered section or a notional page in the "standard" reference texts.

classes, and universals exist and not merely physical objects.

Questions about what exists are fundamental—witness the denial by the last, British, female Prime Minister that there is any such thing as society. The point is that the seemingly innocent question as to what exists continues to generate divergent answers. According to Lewis (1986) in his analysis of modal logics, each-and-every element in all of the infinite number of 'possible worlds' exists. The world in which an apple hit Newton on the head exists as just one of the infinite number of worlds where an apple hit some other part of his anatomy, or some other object hit his head, and so on. Other logicians offer specific criteria of the existence of abstract objects, for example Hale (1987). One of his criteria allows an abstract object to exist just in case singular terms which refer to it occur in a true statement made about it (Hale, 1987, p.11). The other concerns mind-independence whereby such true statements hold, independently of "our (or any) thought and talk about them" (Hale, 1987, p.165). The point to retain is that these analyses represent diverse proposals made in resolution of outstanding problems. In this respect, Piaget's main problem is similar. According to platonism, necessity is an abstract object, awaiting discovery by the use of rational ability. According to constructivism, necessity is a rational invention arising from the use of human ability. This is an important difference, notably for the argument in [21] about the social construction of knowledge.

The second type of epistemology mentioned in Piaget's objection is Rationalist epistemology, of which three claims made by Leibniz are illustrative. The first claim is a re-statement of the Platonic distinction between intelligible–sensible worlds into an epistemological counter-part. This re-statement is not so much a denial of the Platonic claims about essence and existence but is rather an assertion of the greater importance of epistemic claims about the knowing subject. The preferred distinction is between necessary truths of reason and contingent truths of fact (Leibniz, 1686/1973, pp.96–7). Mathematical and logical truths are subsumed by the former, whereas factual understanding based on the senses, memory, or the imagination corresponds to the latter. The key difference is that mathematical truths are stated to be necessary in a way in which factual truths are not. A second claim concerns the basis of such truths in human understanding. As Leibniz stated (1765/1981, I.1.5): "our mind is capable of knowing truths of both sorts, but it is the source of the former (necessary truths)". This position is clarified by the contention (Leibniz, 1765/1981, I.1.11; my amended translation) that: "intellectual ideas, from which necessary truths arise, do not come from the senses; rather you recognise that some ideas arise from the mind's reflection when it reflects on itself". The point that lies behind such claims is that necessary knowledge could not arise from experience and so could have only one other source, namely from within the mind of the knowing subject. The third claim concerns the stock of innate ideas that is a human possession (Leibniz, 1765/1981, II.1.2; my amended translation):

> Experience is necessary, I admit, if the soul is to be given such and such thoughts, and if it is to take heed of the ideas that are within us. But how could experience and the senses provide the ideas … Someone will confront me with this accepted philosophical maxim that there is nothing in the soul which does not come from the senses. But an exception must be made of the soul itself and its states. *Nihil est in intellectu, quod non fuerit in sensu, excipe: nisi ipse intellectus.* Now the soul includes being, substance, unity, identity, causality, perception, reasoning and many other notions which the senses cannot provide.

In this passage, Leibniz stated that he accepts the traditional maxim *there is nothing in the understanding which will not previously have been in the senses* with one qualification, namely *with the exception of the understanding itself*. His view is that the understanding embodies innate ideas together with organising principles for their transformation. Such ideas include the fundamental categories of experience, because they are the constitutive elements of every intellectual domain. However, the dispositional character of innate ideas is specifically stressed. They are in the human soul and so are implicitly in the mind, awaiting explicit discovery through learning during experience (Leibniz, 1765/1981, I.1.20–23). In short, in Rationalist epistemology, the stock of innate ideas is the epistemic instrument that is superior to experience, and that is the available basis on which necessary knowledge depends.

Piaget's debt to Rationalism is extensive, expecially with regard to its concern with the epistemic subject of knowledge, namely the *ipse intellectus* of Leibniz (Piaget, 1936/1953, p.2). Piaget also retained some version of the Rationalist distinction between truths of reason and truths of fact, shown in his contrast of inferential, coordinatory knowledge, which is necessary, with observable knowledge, which is not necessary in this sense (Piaget, 1975/1985, p.37). However, Piaget (1970/1983) denied that necessary knowledge is innate. Rather, it is taken to be a later construction of the developing mind. Thus the same objection is made, that a position in philosophical epistemology, which has a subtle, normative specification, is defective through its neglect of psychological facts about developing minds.

Humean Empiricism is a third epistemological position to take into account. Although this position is not explicitly mentioned in Piaget's objection, he is well aware of it (cf. Piaget, 1965/1972, p.53). Three claims can be noticed. First, Hume shared with the Rationalist philosophers an epistemological concern with the mind of the knowing subject. Second, Hume also accepted the Rationalist distinction between two types of understanding, which he characterises in terms of constituent relations. One type of relation, such as identity or number, concerns the recombination of ideas. The other type of relation, such as causality, is not based solely on ideas since the relation may vary with the prevailing facts (Hume, 1739/1965, I.III.I). The relation of causality is discussed for two reasons. One is its applicability to scientific reasoning. The other is the prevailing philosophical assumption that causal relations are necessary. The third claim is that, according to Hume, there are no innate ideas in the human understanding, which instead consists in combinations of ideas that are ultimately derived from sense impressions (Hume, 1739/1965, I.I.I). On this view, and contrary to the position held by Leibniz, the mind of the knowing subject is not the source of the truths based on recombinations of ideas. The devastating conclusion that Hume derived is an uncomprising scepticism. Sense impressions are copies of the external world. But there can be no sense impression of necessity and so no idea of necessity (Hume, 1777/1966, $64):

> Our idea, therefore, of necessity and causation arises entirely from the uniformity observable in the operation of nature, where similar objects are constantly conjoined together, and the mind is determined by custom to infer the one from the appearance of the other. These two circumstances form the whole of that necessity, which we ascribe to matter. Beyond the constant *conjunction* of similar objects, and the consequent *inference* from one to the other, we have no notion of any necessary connexion.

In this passage, Hume denied that we have any idea of necessity arising from the external world. Thus any inference that purports to be necessary is a fiction, since it is ultimately based on regularity and conjunction. That is, although human understanding may appear to include necessary knowledge, such knowledge does not extend beyond the circle of ideas which, in the last analysis, have no foundation. A necessary inference is unwarranted because a regular and general sequence is not thereby a necessary sequence. In consequence, Hume (1739/1965, pp.165–66) contrasted two questions that can be raised about a necessary belief. One question concerns its causal origin and empirical formation in experience. The other question concerns the notion of necessity which does not owe its origin to causal experience. Even though a belief—including a belief in necessity—may have a causal origin in past experience, the content of that belief makes use of the notion of necessity and that notion does not have a similar origin. Whereas it is always possible for an empirical regularity to have exceptions, this is never possible with necessary truths. Thus there is no empirical basis for exceptionless, necessary truths.

Piaget shared with Empiricist philosophers the view that necessary knowledge cannot have an experiential basis. He also invoked the Humean distinction between general and necessary relationships (Piaget, 1983/1987, pp.37–38). But Piaget did not accept the sceptical conclusions which, according to Hume, follow from these admissions. Piaget made a clear commitment to there being necessary knowledge, which he regarded as a major characteristic of advanced forms of knowledge (Piaget, 1950). Indeed, the starting-point of Piaget's empirical (genetic) epistemology is to show what Hume argued could not be shown, namely how necessary knowledge can be constructed out of knowledge that is not necessary.

A fourth epistemological position to which Piaget makes reference is that of Kant. Three claims can be noticed. First, Kant demarcated his position from both Rationalism and Empiricism by stating (Kant, 1787/1933, B1) that although "all our knowledge begins with experience ... it does not follow that it all arises out of experience". Kant's point is that although there can be no knowledge that is acquired at some time prior to experience, there can be knowledge that is logically prior to its actual display in experience. The latter knowledge cannot, therefore, be due to experience. One interpretation of this claim is to notice that if X is logically prior to Y, it is logically impossible for Y to occur without X. But that still leaves open two possibilities. One is that X precedes Y in time . The other is that X and Y co-occur in time. The latter possibility leads to Kant's second claim (Kant 1800/1963, p.170) that "the understanding, in particular, is governed in its actions by rules which we can investigate". The intellectual rules that Kant took to be fundamental to all knowledge are those logical rules that are embodied in a priori categories. Knowledge that is due to the use of such categories has two distinguishing criteria since (Kant, 1787/1933, B4) "necessity and universality are ... sure criteria of a priori knowledge". According to Kant, the logical rules which underpin the exercise of the understanding provide the form of human knowledge. That is, they are the organising principles that are stated both to make human knowledge possible at all and to confer on knowledge the characteristics of universality and necessity. On this issue, Kant adopted the same position as Hume, manifest in his claim (Kant, 1783/1953, p.52) that "experience does indeed teach me what exists and what it is like, but never that it must necessarily be so and not otherwise". According to Kant, the notion of necessity will have its formation in experience even though it could not be derived from experience. The notion of necessity could not be derived from experience since it is not an empirical notion.

However, Kant's third claim is a denial of Humean scepticism, since he regards certain intellectual rules as objectively valid principles of knowledge. Although some intellectual rules are contingent, and so are due to experience, the logical rules that are identifiable through the twin criteria of universality and necessity are not (Kant, 1800/1963, p.171): "The science, therefore, which contains these universal and necessary laws is simply a science of thought". The claim is that logic is not an organon but is rather a canon of thought. Logic is not an organon, a set of rules for the enlargement of human knowledge in specific domains such as mathematics or science. Rather, logic is a canon, since it provides the standard for the criticism and correction of knowledge in any specific domain (Kant, 1800/1963, p.172). As an example, Kant (1787/1933, B741) cited the construction of a triangle, whether as a mental image or on paper, "in both cases completely a priori, without having borrowed the pattern from experience. The single figure which we draw is empirical, and yet it serves to express the concept, without impairing its universality". There are an infinite number of ways in which this construction can actually be carried out but, even so, the defining criteria have to be met for any such construction to result in a figure that counts as a triangle. These criteria include, although they are not exhausted by, universality and necessity. In short, it is Kant's view that there are intellectual rules that are universal and necessary. These rules underpin all knowledge and confer on that knowledge its universal and necessary character.

Piaget expressed a clear commitment to Kant's position (Piaget, 1979/1980, p.150): "I consider myself to be profoundly Kantian, but of a Kantianism that is not static, that is, the categories are not there at the outset; it is rather a Kantianism that is dynamic". That is, Piaget endorses the second and third claims attributed to Kant, that exercises of the human understanding are guided by logical rules, which are universal and necessary. However, Piaget did not accept the first claim, as he denied that such rules are present, and available for use, at the outset of experience. This denial is empirical. According to Piaget, an epistemic instrument that Kant takes to be logically prior to experience is not, as a matter of fact, available for human use at the outset of experience. Piaget's epistemology retains the Kantian criteria of universality and necessity but, unlike that of Kant, is stated to be empirical (Piaget, 1967/1971, §20.III).

The conclusions to draw from this brief survey of traditional epistemology are threefold. First, it is accepted in each of the four positions that knowledge based on experience is an inadequate basis for necessary knowledge. Second, Piaget rejected all exclusively philosophical answers to his question by virtue of their neglect of empirical matters. Third, Piaget claimed that, even so, his problem owes its formulation to normative epistemology, namely the problem of showing how the *a priori ad quem* is constructed as an outcome, even though there is no *a priori a quo* at the outset, of development (Piaget, 1965/1972, p.57). This is, of course, exactly the problem that was stated at the outset of this chapter.

[3.2] Necessity in Contemporary Epistemology

It might be contended that traditional epistemology has merely historical interest and that Piaget's objection is consequently limited in its scope. The aim of the discussion in this section is to show why this contention is misplaced.

As a general reply, there are several areas in contemporary epistemology where philosophical problems of necessity and knowledge continue to abound. First, a family of distinctions, such as necessity–contingency, analytic–synthetic truth, *a priori–a posteriori* knowledge, require attention because the grounds on which each of these distinctions rests merit re-evaluation, clarification, and correction (Grayling, 1982; Haack, 1978). Second, underlying all logical systems are meta-logical concepts, such as entailment. One of the defining criteria of entailment is its necessity. Yet the concept of entailment resists easy analysis (Anderson & Belnap, 1975; Piéraut-Le Bonniec, 1974/1980; von Wright, 1957). Third, modal logic presents a special case, since modal logic is the logic of possibility and necessity. Questions about the technical design of modal systems raise almost no problems in relation to the problematic issues that arise in their interpretation (Carnap, 1947/1956; Kripke, 1980; Lewis, 1986; Lewis & Langford, 1932/1959; Quine, 1961; Sainsbury, 1991). Fourth, questions about human rationality lead to the postulation of a range of questions which bear on the nature of, scope for, and limits of, deductive understanding in science (H.I. Brown, 1988; Kuhn, 1970; Lakatos, 1974; Laudan, 1977, 1984; Nagel, 1961; Popper, 1979). In general, normative problems of necessity and knowledge constitute fundamental and outstanding problems.

Two such cases are now reviewed in more detail. One example arises from the work of Popper (1979) which provides an epistemology of scientific knowledge. The other is based on that of Kripke (1980), who discusses epistemological principles relevant to logical knowledge. As in the previous section, exegesis is selective and does not aspire to provide an overview of these positions. Rather, the aim is to bring out the importance of certain normative issues because of their relevance to Piaget's problem.

Six features of Popper's (1979) position can be noticed, namely (i) the 'three worlds', (ii) evolutionary epistemology, (iii) normative standards, (iv) epistemic contexts of discovery and justification, (v) the process of intellectual growth and (vi) deductive justification.

First, a distinction between 'three worlds' is central to Popper's epistemology, that is, the world of physical objects, the world of mental states and the world of the objective contents of thought (Popper, 1979, p.106). Popper explicitly makes an ontological claim about the autonomous existence of each of the three worlds, which are strictly independent (1979, p.118). Evidently, Popper is committed to some form of platonism. So viewed, this ontological commitment is an expression of the problematic nature of the (normative) questions that Popper addresses.

Second, Popper states (1979, p.347) that his aim to is to show how there can be an evolutionary—rather than a developmental—epistemology, since "there is, as it were, only one step from the amoeba to Einstein". But this claim could mislead. The notions of evolution and development are different. The evolution of different species of plants and animals, not to mention human societies, does not embody the suggestion that any one species is *better* than any other. By contrast, the notion of development embodies exactly the suggestion that, intellectually speaking, some forms of knowledge are *better* than others (Kohlberg, 1987; Smith, 1991; van Haften, 1990). The key issue is not whether some human activities, for example intellectual activities, are better than others but rather whether, with respect to a specific activity such as the pursuit of knowledge, some forms of knowledge are better than others. The reason why Popper is committed to an evolutionary theory is because he denies that (scientific) truth can be attained, even though the evolution of scientific theories is a process leading away from error. The literal implication appears to be that all errors are open to equal objection and that the evolution of any scientific theory is as good as that of any other. Yet it is evident that Popper (1979), and not merely Piaget (1950), regards certain theories, such as Einstein's, as better than others. Thus Popper's evolutionary epistemology does include a developmental component.

The third claim brings out why Popper is not committed to this implication, as he offers more than a merely evolutionary epistemology.

He claims that scientific theories belong to the 'third world'. Since psychological claims belong to the 'second world', they are simply irrelevant to the former. Psychological claims about the biographies of Newton and Einstein have no purchase on epistemological questions about the explanatory adequacy of the associated theories. Rather, Popper states (1979, p.53) "a theory is the bolder the greater is its content". By this, Popper means that his epistemology provides a quantitative and logical criterion by whose use scientific *progress* in the 'third world' can be judged. The suggestion is that the logical scrutiny of the 'third world' alone makes possible a rational process of decision, whereby Einstein's theory is deemed to be an advance over that of Newton. Yet the notions of *advance* and *progress* are normative. Popper is assuming that a better theory is one whose content is greater than a rival. This is a normative position which goes beyond the mere description of the contents of the 'third world'.

Fourth, considerations arising from the 'second world' are denied to be necessary to this rational process of scientific decision-making. Popper (1934/1968, p.31) is an avowed opponent of psychologism since he argues that factual questions about how a scientist thinks are independent of, and so irrelevant to, questions about the validity of scientific theories. Rather, decision-making is a rational procedure the rules of which are analogous to the rules of a game (1934/1968, pp.53, 110). An acceptable epistemology will steer clear of the psychological processes by which new ideas arise and will instead focus exclusively on the logical process by which available ideas are tested. Following Reichenbach (1938/1961), the context of discovery is the province of psychology, but not logic, whereas the context of justification is the province of logic, but not psychology. In Popper's epistemology (1934/1968, pp.31–2), the rational reconstruction of knowledge is distinct from the empiricial construction of knowledge.

Fifth, a characteristic process underlies the growth of knowledge. A problem is formulated; a tentative theory is outlined to resolve it; the errors in that theory are successively eliminated; finally a new problem is formulated leading to a new epistemological cycle (Popper, 1979, p.119). According to Popper, Hume was in error to regard the principle of induction as the ultimate basis of scientific knowledge, in error because that principle has no logical basis (Popper, 1979, p.11).

This leads to the sixth claim, that deductive logic—and notably the use of *modus tollens*—does permit the detection of falsity as a contributory factor in the human search for truth (Popper, 1934/1968, $18).

Piaget could not accept Popper's epistemology on four counts. First, whereas Piaget (1950, pp.25–32) accepts the intelligibility of platonic realism, a version of which is exemplified in Popper's 'third world', constructivism is taken to be a preferred alternative. (See [21] for an elaboration of this point.) Second, Piaget & Garcia (1983/1989, p.293) point out that a constructivist epistemology must address the question of how any theory leads to the *construction of a better* theory. This question is not addressed in an evolutionary epistemology which addresses the different question of showing that one of two *available* theories is superior to another. Third, Piaget (1961/1966, p.132) explicitly denies that his position embodies psychologism because his concern is with the epistemic subject. In turn, Piaget & Garcia (1983/1989, p.35) challenge the empiricist assumption that there can be no logic of discovery. This is because the question that is central to a constructivist epistemology concerns the development of *necessary* knowledge, which is neither due to preformation nor the outcome of chance (Piaget, 1967/1971). Fourth, Piaget can press the empirical objection which was reviewed in the previous section. According to Popper, *modus tollens* is the principle of deductive reasoning that is a constitutive rule in theory-testing. Presumably other logical principles are equally required as well (cf. Popper, 1934/1968). But factual claims are implicated here as a check on, first, whether such logical principles are available for human use and, second, how such principles came into our possession. Popper (1979, ch.1) would presumably deny that they are learned inductively. Yet his evolutionary epistemology apparently has no answer to questions about the emergence of such principles in lower forms of biological life. As Piaget (1979/1980, p.150) put it: "I have a difficult time believing that Cantor's theories or today's theories of categories are already preformed in bacteria or viruses". In short, Popper's epistemology addresses its own stock of questions but makes empirical assumptions which, according to Piaget, certainly require verification and possibly revision.

A second contemporary contribution to philosophical epistemology arises from the work of Kripke (1980), five of whose claims are now reviewed, namely (i) the interpretability of modal systems, (ii) 'possible worlds', (iii) essential and accidental properties, (iv) reference and trans-world identity, (v) necessary, *a posteriori* knowledge.

First, Kripke (1963) is committed to the view that quantified modal logic is interpretable, and so his position is incompatible with that of Quine (1960; 1961). The latter has argued that the presence of failures of reference based on principles of extensional logic—notably that of identity—indicate the problematic nature of the logic of modal systems. Commentary on these arguments is to hand (Haack, 1978; Linsky, 1971; Loux, 1979; Sainsbury, 1991). A central notion is that of 'possible worlds'. An individual exists in the actual world but there are an infinite number of other worlds in which that individual both could have existed and yet could have been different. One normative problem is to clarify the commitments that are embodied in such claims. Unlike Lewis (1986), who explicitly states that each of the infinite number of possible worlds exists in exactly the same way that the actual world exists, Kripke (1980, pp.15, 43) denies that 'possible worlds' are like distant planets. That is, Kripke denies that modality requires any commitment to platonic realism.

Second, Kripke's (1980, p.16) own explication of the notion of a 'possible world' is based on an analogy. Using two dice (A, B), it is evident that there are different possible ways in which a specified outcome can occur. Thus a total score of eleven can be gained in two ways (A=6, B=5; A=5, B=6). If both dice are thrown once and show the former pattern, the latter pattern is still a possibility. The latter pattern is analogous to a 'possible world'. That is (Kripke, 1980, p.44, his emphasis), "a possible world is *given by the descriptive conditions we associate with it* … 'Possible worlds' are *stipulated*, not *discovered*".

Third, a 'possible world' is, on this view, conceptual rather than realistic. It follows that the descriptions used to refer to individuals and their properties in such worlds are fundamental. However, Kripke also makes claims which imply that modality is not merely a characteristic of the way in which an individual is described (modality *de dicto*) but is instead a characteristic of that individual (modality *de re*). That is, he invokes the essentialist distinction between the defining, and so necessary, properties of an individual and the accidental, and so contingent, properties which may vary with changes in prevailing factors in different 'possible worlds'. Using his example (Kripke, 1980, p.45), Humphrey did not win the Presidential Election in the actual world in 1970, although he—that is, Humphrey himself—might have done so in some other world. But this very claim implies that a distinction can be drawn between the essential properties, by virtue of which reference can be made to the unique individual, Humphrey, and his accidental properties which may vary in the different worlds. Evidently, the property of being a Presidential Election loser is not one of Humphrey's essential properties. This example shows the importance of trans-world identification, when modal references are made.

Fourth, Kripke proposes a distinction between rigid and non-rigid designation so that trans-world identification can be secured. A term is a *rigid designator* (Kripke, 1980, p.48) "if in every possible world it designates the same object, a *nonrigid or accidental designator* if that is not the case". According to Kripke, the names of individuals and terms describing natural kinds are rigid designators (1980, pp.48, 134) because they fix the reference through all, and not merely some, of the 'possible worlds' to which they are applicable; (Kripke, 1980, p.48) "Although someone other than the US President in 1970 might have been the US President in 1970 (e.g. Humphrey might have been), no one other than Nixon might have been Nixon". One consequence of this proposal is that identity statements are necessary statements. The statement that "Nixon is Nixon" is true in all possible worlds by virtue of the rigid designators that are used to make it. Hence there is no world in which it could have been false, and so it is necessarily true.

A second consequence leads to a fifth claim. As a non-rigid designator—such as "winner of the 1970 Presidential Election"—may be used to refer to Nixon, the statement "Nixon is the winner of the 1970 Presidential Election" is not necessary due to the cross-modality of the two modes of designation. It therefore follows that the necessary properties of individuals, and of natural kinds, can be discovered on the basis of empirical evidence. On this view, not all necessary knowledge is acquired a priori (Kripke, 1980, pp.35, 128, 140–2). In fact, reference is typically mediated in that (Kripke, 1980, p.159) "one can learn a mathematical truth *a posteriori* by consulting a computing machine, or even by asking a mathematician".

Kripke has presented a distinctive position which commands the attention of epistemologists. In view of its recency, it is not a position to which Piaget has made a specific reply. Even so, four general comments can be made. One is that Kripke's commitment to the importance of modal notions would be compatible with an empirical epistemology in which the development of modal understanding is central (Piaget, 1977/1986; 1981/1987; 1983/1987). A second comment is that Kripke's concern is with ideal rationality, unlike Piaget's concern with minimal forms of rationality. Whereas Kripke provides an explication of the notion of modality the understanding of which is simply assumed to be available, Piaget addresses issues relating to the construction of modal understanding. This difference is apparent is the use of *accessibility* and *access*. Kripke (1963) proposes that accessibility is a relation that holds between the actual world and any other world which is possible relative to it. This is an essentialist claim about the semantics of modality as the relation holds independently of any specific understanding of it. Piaget (1977/1986) views access (*ouverture*) as an intellectual process whereby new forms of modal understanding arise in the mind of a specific individual. This is a constructivist claim related to Piaget's main problem. A third comment concerns the several manifestations of this general difference between essentialism and constructivism. Thus Kripke simply assumes that the logical principle of identity is at the individual's disposal. By contrast, Piaget & Voyat (1968, p.2; cf. [16]) contend that this principle is, ironically, the principle that remains least self-identical through its construction in children's minds. This point is applicable to conservation, as the number of objects in an array remains self-identical through all *possible* transformations of the array (see [25.2]). Yet Kripke (1980, p.19) merely states that "in practice, no one who cannot understand the idea of possibility is likely to understand that of a 'possible world' either". Finally, although Kripke simply assumes that an understanding of the combinatorial system is instantiated in his example of the two dice, it is exactly this form of understanding which Piaget & Inhelder (1951/1975) suggest is open to construction. In short, whatever the normative merits of Kripke's position, it is vulnerable to the charge that it neglects the empirical issues about the availability of modal notions to the mind of the knowing subject.

In sum, if the review in this section is a guide, recent contributions to normative epistemology are vulnerable to exactly the same objection that Piaget has used in connection with traditional contributions. Of course, two examples are simply examples and so the charge is not that all recent contributions are similarly vulnerable in this respect. It is, however, worth stating that Piaget's objection does generalise from traditional to contemporary epistemology. Further, it generalises to include substantial contributions to normative epistemology, as the contributions of Popper and Kripke are, by any standard, notable. The conclusion to draw is not, then, that such contributions are of no consequence, nor that the questions that are addressed in them can simply be set aside. Rather, the conclusion is that any epistemological contribution which by-passes factual issues that are germane to it must be partial. It is Piaget's specific contention that genetic (empirical) epistemology will address such factual issues without losing sight of the normative considerations that have been the central concern in philosophical epistemology.

[4]   LOGICAL NORMS

Empirically minded developmentalists could be tempted into making an interesting intervention at this point. They could say that Piaget's empirical objection to normative epistemology is well taken. It is for this reason that the science of psychology provides a better base from which to pursue empirical questions about intellectual development.

Such an intervention can appear in either of two versions. The weak version states that empirical issues will have to be added to the normative issues to be addressed with the construction of necessity in mind. The strong version states that the normative issues can be noted and set aside, so that attention can settle on the empirical issues that are decisive. Developmentalists who make this stronger intervention could say that Piaget's challenge (see p.8) to Bruner contains the valid point that logical intuition is a pervasive capacity which makes human thinking possible and respectable. The empirical issues can, then, be addressed with due allowance to the reliability of logical intuition.

But the stronger intervention is too strong. Four examples follow, with the aim of identifying some of the reasons why intellectual norms are present, and are important, when questions are raised about necessary knowledge. In thinking about these examples, a question to keep in mind is: which of the examples embodies a necessary relation? In cases of necessary knowledge, the object of knowledge must itself be necessary. So prior agreement is neeeded as to what does, and what does not, count as necessary. This is a normative matter. Such issues are important since the defining principles and criteria which are constitutive of the phenomena in a domain are normative, and so not empirical, in character. Thus normative issues will have to be reckoned with since they provide an essential reference point which cannot be ignored by those who address problems within any domain to which those norms are applicable.

[4.1] Different Norms

The first example is a variant of that paradigm of syllogistic reasoning:

(1) All women are immortal,
(2) Socrates is a woman,
(3) Socrates is immortal.

Is conclusion (3) a necessary consequence of premises (1) and (2)? The point about this question is that it does not ask whether each of propositions (1), (2), and (3) is true, but rather whether proposition (3) would have to be true, if propositions (1) and (2) were true. Clearly, each of the three propositions is false. But the truth-value of these propositions has no bearing on the validity of an inference from (1) and (2) to (3). This example brings out the point that validity is distinct from truth-value, since these are two distinct norms. However one of these norms has priority over the other when questions are asked about the presence of necessary relationships between propositions. When questions about the validity of the relation between premises (1) and (2) and conclusion (3) arise, the truth-value of the three propositions is irrelevant to the answer. This is a normative distinction, which is based on the difference between form and content. Thus there is conservation of the formal relation that links these propositions through changes in their content. Changing the content of propositions (1), (2) and (3)—for example, by substituting 'men' for 'women' in (1) and (2) and by substituting 'mortal' for 'immortal' in (1) and (3)—leaves the form of the relation unchanged. Thus the content of these propositions is, for certain purposes, unimportant. It is for this reason that a logical model focuses attention on the key features that clarify formal properties (Lemmon, 1966; Quine, 1972). The importance of this normative distinction carries implications for empirical investigations about the immortality of women and the gender of Socrates. Such investigations could, of course, be undertaken by anyone with interests in such questions. However, such investigations would be beside the point with respect to questions about inferential validity. Different norms are different and so embody different implications for empirical investigations arising from their acceptance. Logical systems are designed to make explicit the differences that arise when distinct norms (truth, validity) are co-instantiated in specific cases. Logical intuition is not, then, homogeneous, as such differences have to be respected. Further, the use of explicit, logical models provides an unambiguous way to justify the differing judgments that arise from the implicit use of such norms.

A second example illustrates the point that different logical models can make a difference to reasoning. Thus models that set out to capture the formal features of 'all' and 'some' analyse their inter-relations differently. It has been claimed that if everything has a certain property:

(4) All x is F,

then something does:

(5) Some x is F.

In this example, F symbolises any property, for example the property 'being a unicorn', and x refers to any object in a universe of discourse. The question to ask is not whether (4) and (5) are true, but rather whether (5) is a necessary consequence of (4). According to the traditional model of syllogistic logic, these propositions have the logical form which is characterised as A (all x has the property F) in the case of (4), and as I (some x has the property F) in the case of (5). In the traditional model, "A entails I" (Strawson, 1952, p.158) and so (5) is a necessary consequence of (4). However, the traditional model is not the only model to be applied to such reasoning. In the present century, predicate logic has been designed to capture the formal properties embodied in the relation between 'all' and 'some'. But in predicate logic, (5) is not entailed by (4) (H.I. Brown, 1988, p.72; Guttenplan, 1986, pp.185–6; Lewis & Langford, 1932/1959, p.276), and so (5) is not a necessary consequence of (4). This is because the logical forms of universal quantification in (4) and existential quantification in (5) are different.

[4.2] Problematic Norms

Not all normative claims are clear-cut. Two further examples now follow, relating to the problematic status of some normative claims about knowledge and necessity. Normative issues do not on that account have negligible relevance but rather can have intractable features that exclude easy resolution.

Identity is a paradigm example of a logical relation, as anything is identical with itself. Adapting an argument due to Frege (1980, p.57), in extensional logic, transformations due to the substitutivity of identity are truth-preserving and can be undertaken *salva veritate*, for example:

(6) morning star = Venus,
(7) morning star = evening star,
so
(8) evening star = Venus.

If (6) and (7) are true, then so is (8). But not all contexts are extensional, shown by the failure of the substitutivity of identity. Consider a young European child called Jean, who has limited knowledge of astronomy, and the inference:

(9) Jean knows that the morning star = morning star,
so
(10) Jean knows that the morning star = evening star.

Supposing that Jean knows nothing (6), (7) and (8), then (9) can be true with (10) false. Thus truth is not conserved in this inference. It is for this reason that epistemic contexts are intensional, in that principles of extensional logic fail in them. Further, Quine (1961, pp. 141–50) has extended this argument, first, by noting that modal contexts are similarly intensional and, second, by showing that other extensional principles such as existential generalisation fail in both epistemic and modal contexts. In short, extensional logic is not universally applicable to all contexts. (See Haack, 1978, and Sainsbury, 1991 for discussion of the Frege-Quine argument.)

This is a powerful conclusion which would apply with a vengeance to Piagetian claims about the development of necessary knowledge. Such claims are doubly intensional since they are both epistemic and modal. However, the force of this conclusion is open to the challenge that not all logic is extensional. Indeed, intensional logics have been designed specifically to capture both epistemic (Hintikka, 1962; Hintikka &

Hintikka, 1989) and modal (Hughes & Creswell, 1972; Kripke, 1963) inferences. A common feature of these intensional systems is the commitment to 'possible worlds' semantics. But any such claim raises a range of unresolved questions, a notable example of which concerns trans-world identity and the logical status of the individuals in such worlds. Consider two people, Jean and Jean such that Jean is male and unmarried, whilst Jean is female and married (world 1). Now consider three possible worlds, corresponding to some of the ways in which they could have been different: in one possible world, Jean is male and married, whilst Jean is female and unmarried (world 2); in another possible world, Jean is female and unmarried, whilst Jean is male and married (world 3); in yet another possible world, Jean is female and married, whilst Jean is male and unmarried (world 4). One question to ask is: to how many individuals has reference been made in these four worlds? For example, since the inhabitants of world 2 and world 3 are indistinguishable, which Jean is which? A related question is: what are the individuating properties of any individual to which reference has been made in these four worlds? Easy resolution of such questions has proved hard to find and yet they are central questions about the validity of 'possible world' semantics (Lewis, 1986; Linksy, 1971; Loux, 1979).

The point to notice here is that intensional logicians can provide a rival reply to the Frege-Quine argument only by postulating the validity of 'possible worlds' semantics. Thus Hintikka & Hintikka (1989, p.51) propose that (10) is implied by (6) and (9), provided that the context of (6), which is the actual world, is differentiated from that of (9), which is a possible world corresponding to the knowledge possessed by Jean. If this latter world includes the knowledge corresponding to (6), then the inference is valid. Manifestly, this proposal presupposes the intelligibility of 'possible worlds' and so the resolution of questions about trans-world identity.

The dilemma is acute. Extensional logic is clear, but does not apply to epistemic and modal contexts. Intensional logic does apply to such contexts, but is not similarly clear. This dilemma has its basis in normative dispute.

As a final example, normative disputes can beset logical proofs where explicit arguments are given for contrary positions. Question: does a contradiction entail any proposition? According to Lewis & Langford (1932/1959), the answer can be *shown* to be affirmative; according to Anderson & Belnap (1975), it can be *shown* to be negative. Further, each answer is based on a well defined modal system (strict implication and entailment logic respectively).

The proof that a contradiction does entail any proposition requires the explicit specification of the intermediate steps between this premise and the conclusion. Lewis & Langford (1932/1959, pp.248–51) have attended to this task.

(11) p & $-p$,
(12) p,
(13) $p \vee q$,
(14) $-p$,
(15) q.

The impossible premise is (11): whatever p may be, the conjunction of p with its negation is a contradiction. But (15) is the conclusion, stating any proposition, q, which is other than p. Lewis & Langford argue that (11) does entail (15), provided the three further premises are accepted. But each of these is entirely acceptable, when they are judged by the standards of extensional logic. The elimination rule for conjunction can be applied to (11) to yield (12), because it is valid to infer one of the conjuncts from a conjunction. The introduction rule for disjunction can be applied to (12) to yield (13), because if one disjunct is true, (12), then its disjunction with any other proposition is so as well, (13). The re-application of the elimination rule for conjunction to (11) yields (14). Finally, the inference rule for the disjunctive syllogism can be applied to (13) and (14) to yield (15): given a disjunction, and the falsity of one disjunct, the other disjunct must be true. Thus (15) is entailed by (11).

This same conclusion has been specifically denied by Anderson & Belnap (1975, pp.163–67). The rational way to reject the proof that a contradiction entails any proposition is to reject one of the three intermediate steps. The third step in the proof is the one that Anderson & Belnap deny. Their argument is that the so-called proof trades on ambiguity. The step from (12) to (13) is dependent on an extensional reading of disjunction (the logical connective v), unlike that from (13) and (14) to (15) which is dependent on an intensional reading of this same connective. Anderson & Belnap do not deny that any proposition can be disjoined with any other, but they do deny that necessary deductions can be made from any set of irrelevantly related propositions. Their argument is that the failure to limit disjunction introduction has, in the argument provided, led Lewis & Langford to commit a fallacy of relevance. Thus they propose (Anderson & Belnap, 1975, p.165) to limit the scope of the disjunctive syllogism because the argument offered by Lewis & Langford embodies "a simple inferential mistake, such as only a dog would make".

This dispute is important. The disjunctive syllogism is a fundamental principle of extensional logic (Quine, 1972) and natural logic (Braine &

O'Brien, 1991). Further, many logicians agree with Lewis & Langford that it is a fundamental principle of modal logic (Bradley & Swartz, 1979; Hughes & Cresswell, 1972). Crucially, acceptance of the system of entailment logic requires that some inference principles, including *modus ponens*, are not valid. Although Anderson & Belnap (1975, p.259) are willing to accept this severe limitation, other logicians would rather reject the system of entailment logic than curtail the validity of standard principles of extensional logic (Hughes & Cresswell, 1972, p.338). Further, objections have been raised about the necessity of the relevance criterion that Anderson & Belnap regard as central to entailment logic (Iseminger, 1980). This issue is not pursued here (though see [26] for discussion of this dispute in relation to Piagetian epistemology).

The main point which lies behind the four examples is that intellectual norms are important even though they can be open to rational disagreement. The common feature of the examples is that the application of a norm makes a difference to the permissible modes of interpretation of the phenomena in its domain. This would be a welcome conclusion, if normative claims were clear-cut. As this is not the case, objections can arise about the status of normative claims. Two objections are now discussed.

[5] LOGICAL INTUITION

One objection is that intellectual norms are often so opaque that their application in empirical investigation is impossible. The second objection is that logical intuition is sufficient to guide empirical investigations. Even though intellectual norms are important, their explicit specification in formal models is not.

[5.1] Different Intuitions

The first objection is that, of course, normative issues are important but that developmentalists who undertake empirical studies of human understanding often have to make an unwelcome choice. On the one hand, methodological norms are relatively clear and precise, and so due recognisance can be paid to them. On the other hand, intellectual norms are often opaque and embody no obvious empirical implications. Faced with such a choice, it is no surprise to find that the latter norms are derogated in favour of the former. The point behind this objection is valid, namely that normative problems often have a long, unsettled history. But the force of this point is limited for three reasons.

First, disputes about the merits of normative positions on the problem of necessity are likely to continue. But commentators concur as to what are the currently available answers (see [3.2] and [4.2]). But a proposed answer is better than no answer at all, and a decision not to take sides is effectively to have no view.

Second, a position that has some strengths and some weaknesses is better than the total absence of a position. Dispute makes the selection of a preferred position difficult, but that does not exclude selection altogether. Endemic dispute has not prevented philosophers from making decisions as to which position—in their view—is better than its rivals. Further, the rationality of this stance has been well made in connection with scientific progress. A scientific theory is constituted by its ontological and methodological norms which lay down what counts as the phenomena in the domain of the theory and the means by which they may be investigated (Laudan 1977, p.80). So viewed, empirical science has a normative element which is indispensable, since fact-finding is trivial and leads to instant rationality that is of little value, especially when scientific advances take their time—the owl of Minerva flies at dusk (Lakatos, 1974, pp.157, 177). Scientific progress occurs as a comparative test between different theories, one of which may provide a *better* explanation that its rivals (Lakatos, 1974, p.130; Laudan, 1984, p.27). This conclusion applies, *mutatis mutandis*, to all normative disputes.

Third, human fallibilism must be taken into account (Cherniak, 1986, pp.5–9; Haack, 1978, pp.232-35; McGinn, 1991, p.9). There is no reason to suppose that what is knowable is equivalent to what we can know. The point is not the truism that we now know much less than what people in the future will know, but rather that human rationality is less than ideal rationality. Thus the truths of logic are necessarily true, even though there may be, and in fact are, disputes about the ways in which they can be formulated and understood. Modal error is pervasive (see [25.2]). What is necessarily so is necessarily so, but whether a person understands that necessity is quite another matter. Further, something may be accepted as true, even necessarily true, even when it is not, and could not be so. But a fallibilist position is still a position, one which could be expected to be compatible with progress in a developing science that is still in its infancy.

[5.2] Problematic Intuition

A different objection is that, even though intellectual norms are important, their explicit formulation in logical models is not necessary. Indeed, it was noticed in the previous section that the untutored intuition of literate adults suffices to show that there are distinct norms of truth and validity, or that modal operators may vary in their scope. Using an antique terminology (Gellatly, 1989; Haack, 1978, p.16), *logica utens* (unreflective judgment) is the basis of *logica docens* (rigorous judgment). As Bob Dylan might have put it, we do not really need a weather-man to show which the way the wind is blowing. Philosophers draw a distinction between common sense judgments and their rational reconstruction (cf. Lakatos, 1974; Putnam, 1988). Thus a formal, logical model can be viewed as a rational reconstruction of common sense logical intuition. The reconstruction does not share all the features of the latter, as the reconstruction is usually designed to be a clearer version of its founding intuition. But that is exactly the point: it is a reconstruction of the intuition by reference to which it must ultimately be judged. Thus an intuition has priority over its reconstruction.

Indeed, the objection can be generalised because the developmental perspectives that are currently dominant make a common commitment to the biological origins of human understanding (Chomsky 1980, p.80; Piaget 1967/1971, p.478; Popper 1979, p.261). If intellectual development has a biological basis, formal models could not be a constitutive feature of the process of development as such.

The short response to this objection is that it overlooks the presence of epistemic fallibility: the best minds provide ample illustration of the logical errors to which humans are vulnerable. The conclusion to draw is not that these thinkers are guilty of crass error. Rather, if the *best* minds can display logical error, it is fanciful to suggest that the logical intuition of *any* person is a completely reliable guide in empirical investigation. Three examples now follow which show that logical contradiction is present in the thinking of talented minds.

The first example is Russell's detection of the antinomy in Frege's logical theory of number. Russell (1919, p.25) was the first to acknowledge the substantial contribution that Frege had made to mathematical logic. Even so, he argued that Frege's theory was inconsistent because it embodied the notion of the class of classes which are not members of themselves. When the question is raised "Is such a class a member of itself?", the elegance of Russell's demonstration is exemplary (Russell, 1919, p.136):

> If it is, it is one of those classes that are not members of themselves, i.e. it is not a member of itself. If it is not, it is not one of those classes that are not members of themselves, i.e. it is a member of itself. Thus of the two hypotheses—that it is, and that it is not, a member of itself—each implies its contradictory. This is a contradiction.

Frege (1980, p.214) acknowledged the potency of this contradiction. There are three points to notice about this case. First, it is evident that it is not unique, since the history of logic is littered with similar examples

(Haack, 1978). Second, it carries the implication that if the best logicians can make logical mistakes in formulating logical theories, the intuitions of creative minds are not always to be relied on. Frege had outlined a logical theory of mathematics and this theory was taken by Russell to be the best available theory. But Frege's commitment to this theory was revealed by Russell to be a judgment based on misleading intuition. Finally, Russell provided an explicit demonstration of his paradox, which is not simply the judgment "Foul", and this demonstration required the use of creative intuition to a high degree. This issue is further discussed in [24].

The second example is that of the Indian mathematician Ramanujan. There are three points to notice. One is that the mathematical talent, which Ramanujan undoubtedly possessed, was not noticed by all of the (literate) adults with whom he was in contact. His 'discovery' depended largely on a Cambridge Professor of Mathematics. People cannot be relied on to realise the logical acumen of others. Second, as stated in Hardy, 1959 (p.16), the latter was percipient enough to notice that intuition or "imagination is a very unreliable guide. In particular, this is so in the analytic theory of numbers, where even Ramanujan's imagination led him seriously astray". Third, the mathematical claims which Ramanujan made could not be accepted just because of his authority. As is quoted by H.I. Brown (1988, p.32): "All his results, new or old, right or wrong, had been arrived at by a process of mingled argument, intuition, and induction, of which he was entirely unable to give any coherent account". This case underscores the general point that the acceptability of a belief owes less to personal qualities, however exceptional, than to its standing when appropriate rules are applied to it. The application of such rules, which are normative, requires their prior specification.

A third example concerns Darwin's theory of evolution. By all accounts, Darwin was a creative individual. But Gruber & Barrett (1974, p.127) have documented successive drafts of this theory, as they appeared in Darwin's copious notebooks. They argue that the early formulations of the theory made commitments that are incompatible with the final formulations. Further (Gruber & Barrett, 1974, p.148), this inconsistency remained undetected in much of Darwin's own thinking. "The theory of evolution through natural selection is subtle and elusive. It eluded Darwin the first time he seemed to have had it in his grasp". The conclusion is disturbing for those who attach too much credence to logical intuition. On the one hand, Darwin could be expected to have taken special care in formulating his famous theory. On the other hand, it is evident that he unwittingly lapsed into inconsistency when doing precisely that.

The conclusions to draw from these examples are threefold. First, the examples are not confined to any one domain, as they arise across the formal and natural sciences. Second, the examples refer to contradictions and so to normative errors. Such errors are important not because of the fact of their occurrence but rather due to the reasons why they are there at all. As Wittgenstein (1978, p.370) commented, Russell's paradox "is disquieting, not because it is a contradiction, but because the whole growth culminating in it is a cancerous growth". The fact that a contradiction has occurred is of little consequence in itself, if it is due to trivial reasons. The contradiction in

(16) The first day of 1993 is a Friday,
(17) The first day of 1993 is not a Friday,

can easily be eliminated by checking a diary. Rather, the reasons that lie behind the manifestation of a contradictions show the extent to which a contradiction is important, especially when there are apparently good reasons for retaining both of a pair of incompatible propositions. Third, the way to deal with normative errors is not to regard their complete elimination as a minimum prerequisite of progress. Rather, it is to have an agreed strategy for dealing with their presence on detection. Formal models are intellectual resources in just this sense because they provide defining principles and criteria by the application of which contributions to the removal of these errors can be made. Intuition is not a superior form of knowledge (Cohen, 1986, p.75) and is sometimes not a form of knowledge at all, as the examples given earlier show. But exactly the same can be said about logical models, and the pervasive presence of normative disagreement—which is frequently manifest in contradictions—is testimony to their fallibility. Both logical intuition and logical models are necessary in a fallibilist epistemology.

Fallibilism is the denial that knowlege has self-evident, indubitable, unrevisable, justified foundations. This does not mean that no knowledge is possible at all. The possibility that all epistemic principles are revisable does not mean that all of them are wrong, still less that any individual principle, under a specific formulation, actually is incorrect. Revisions may well have to occur in the *characterisation* of epistemic principles, because these characterisations are due to human proposal, based either on intuition or on some model. Fallibilism is the reminder that human proposals can be misleading and even wrong. In particular, necessary truths are, by definition, necessary, but from this it does not follow at all that any proposed characterisation of such a truth is necessary. As Haack (1978, p.234) puts it: "even if the laws of logic are not possibly false, this by no means guarantees that we are not liable to hold false logical beliefs". In short, faced with fundamental human disagreements, with respect both to logical intuitions and to logical models, the welcome conclusion is that both can, and should, be retained. The resolution of such disputes does not require a commitment to one of these to the exclusion of the other, but rather to their dual use as the sole way to make progress. Making progress may be difficult when logical intuitions do not cohere in a comprehensive system, and this difficulty is exacerbated when logical systems are themselves contradictory. Difficulty is not, however, impossibility.

[6] CONCLUSION

The discussion in this chapter can be summarised by three claims, concerning Piaget's problem, normative approaches to it, and their consequences for empirical epistemology.

First, Piaget's problem concerns the temporal construction of necessary knowledge. This is, of course, merely the bald statement of a problem whose more detailed description is undertaken in [8] and [25]. It is, however, a statement that serves to identify the *explanandum* of Piaget's theory.

Second, problems of knowledge and necessity have preoccupied philosophers in the past and continue to do so in the present. This is a potent omen. It would be simplistic to dismiss these normative contributions, which bring out why such problems are difficult to resolve. One major distinction concerns necessary truths, of which mathematical truths are a paradigm example, and contingent truths, which are due to experience. Thus if human knowledge does extend to include both types of truths, some special account is required to show how the knowledge of necessity is possible. Such an account would have to postulate an epistemic instrument by whose use necessary knowledge would be realised in actual minds. This instrument could cover the knowledge of contingent truths, arising from experience, but it could not, in principle, be exhaustively specified by reference to contingent knowledge. An epistemic instrument for necessary knowledge would have to be sensitive to the special features of necessary truths, and would have to show how such truths can be accessed by the human mind. A symptom of the complexity of this problem is shown by the normative commitments that are made in past and contemporary philosophical positions. Although there is no agreed, normative answer to problems of necessity and knowledge, they command attention because of their fundamental place in human rationality.

The third claim concerns empirical epistemology, which is now widely accepted as a valid species of epistemology, whether it is styled genetic

(Baldwin, 1911), naturalised (Kornblith, 1985), evolutionary (Callebaut & Pinxten, 1987)) or plain cognitive science (Hunt, 1989). The proposal is that epistemological problems should be tackled empirically, including the problem of necessary knowledge. In turn, this proposal requires the positivist distinction between the contexts of discovery and justification to be revised.

According to Reichenbach (1938/1961, pp.7, 383), the context of discovery is the actual (empirical) construction whereby new beliefs and knowledge arise in a person's mind. The context of justification is their rational reconstruction consisting in deductive appraisal. This distinction is clarified in the work of Popper (1934/1968), who regards empirical construction as a matter for psychology, but not logic; unlike rational reconstruction which is a matter of logic, not psychology. Some analogue of this distinction underpins certain versions of cognitive science, which is directed on the search for the causal explanation of mental processes (Hunt, 1989). However, not all empirical epistemology is viewed in this way, as the claim is made that there is both continuity and inter-dependence between causally produced procedures and logically embodied structures (Leiser & Gillièron, 1990). This position has been elaborated in Piaget's (1967/1971) genetic epistemology, in that intellectual functioning is taken to be an outcome of biological functioning.

In short, certain forms of empirical epistemology are committed to there being a unified explanation of a process of construction that is both causal and rational. This commitment is incompatible with the positivist distinction in two respects. First, the commitment requires that the context of discovery could not be exclusively causal for reasons elaborated in the learning paradox (see [22]). A causal process, which is not necessary, could not result in an intellectual state that is necessary knowledge. Second, the commitment requires that the context of justification could not be exclusively rational for reasons given in the dismissal of ideal rationality (Cherniak, 1986; Kornblith, 1985). It is just such a dismissal that underpins Piaget's (1970/1977) rejection of normative epistemology (see [3]).

Thus an epistemological study that is directed on 'normative facts' (Piaget, 1961/1966, p.132) of necessary knowledge, embodies both an empirical and a normative component. Piaget's problem has its starting-point in philosophical epistemology, whereas its resolution is taken by him to reside in empirical epistemology.

CHAPTER TWO

Piaget's Empirical Epistemology

"In Professor Flavell's opinion, there is too wide a gap between the findings I describe and the theories I invoke—it could be argued that the differences between us stem from the fact that his approach is perhaps too exclusively psychological and insufficiently epistemological, while the converse is true for me" (Piaget, 1963, pp.viii-ix).

[7] PIAGET'S *TERTIUM QUID*

Philosophical epistemology deals with such questions as "What is knowledge?" and "How is knowledge possible?". Obviously, Piaget does not claim that constructivist epistemology can resolve such questions directly. It would be to strain credulity to suppose both that these questions are empirical and that philosophers from Plato to Popper had simply taken them to be normative. Rather, Piaget's strategy is to tranform philosophical into empirical questions. For example, Plato's normative question "What is knowledge?" is a standard request for the defining features which all-and-only cases of knowledge possess. By contrast, Piaget assumes that mature cases of knowledge are identifiable. Armed with this assumption, he transforms the normative question into an empirical successor "How do the different types of knowledge succeed in growing with respect both to their intensions and to their extensions?" (Piaget, 1950/1973, p.9). Again, Kant's normative question "How is knowledge possible" is transformed by Piaget into the empirical question "How do the different types of knowledge become possible?" (Piaget, 1950/1973, p.9). The analogous shift concerning necessary knowledge leads away from the normative question "What is necessary knowledge?" to the transformed question "How does the actual process of construction result in atemporal norms?" (cf. Piaget, 1950, p.34).

A tempting conclusion to draw is that the normative–empirical distinction is co-extensive with the distinction between philosophy and psychology, that a question is either one for philosophy, or one for psychology, but not for both. Not so. It is Piaget's claim that his transformed questions are empirical and epistemological. His position is outlined in an early discussion of the relation of scientific psychology and religious values. Piaget (1923, p.57) claims that *the study of true reasoning* can generate three types of inquiry. One type is normative, concerning why a conclusion is entailed by a set of premises. This is the province of logic with its concern with formal systems of inference (cf. Quine, 1972). A second type is empirical, concerning how children succeed in mastering and learning to use the deductive reasoning abilities at their disposal. This is the province of psychology with its concerns for testable laws of learning (cf. Johnson-Laird, 1983) With these two types of inquiry in mind, Piaget (1953, pp.1-2; 1961/1966, p.132) is well aware that both logicism and psychologism must be avoided. Logicism arises when human reasoning is viewed as a formal system, i.e. using a normative approach to investigate an empirical issue. Psychologism arises when the validation of logical laws is taken to be dependent on how humans do reason, i.e. using empirical inquiry to ground a normative principle. But Piaget (1923, p.56) contends that a third type of inquiry is possible, namely "how the idea of truth arrives in the child's mind at all—is that a question for logic or for psychology?". Clearly, this question can be generalised. It could be broadened to cover other fundamental categories, such as identity, number or causality. It could be narrowed to focus on other characteristic features of reasoning, such as validity or necessity. This is the province of Piaget's constructivist (genetic) epistemology. In short, Piaget views his epistemology as a *tertium quid*, which is reducible neither to logic nor to psychology. The aim in constructivist epistemology, so conceived, is to use some logical system as the template so that the construction of its fundamental notions could be investigated empirically, both in children's development and in the history of science.

The *tertium quid* that Piaget has in mind leads straight back to the normative discussions of philosophers in [3.1]. All of these philosophical positions assume that the idea of necessity is either in the mind, or it is not. That is, they are committed to some version of idealised rationality

(Cherniak, 1986). By contrast, Piaget is committed to some version of minimal rationality, according to which there is a continuum of levels extending to a limit of idealised rationality. This is an epistemological commitment. Further, it carries an empirical commitment, as the only way to ascertain the specific level of rationality in some population—say, the mentally deranged, primitive people or children in Western society (cf. Piaget, 1923, p.56)—is through empirical verification. In short, Piaget's question is both normative and empirical (cf. Kitchener, 1986, p.174).

There is scope, then, for a constructivist epistemology which has the following characteristics. First, it is normative because, with respect to a nominated domain of knowledge, the first task is to draw up a catalogue of the defining notions and principles which are constitutive of that domain (Piaget, 1950). Second, it is empirical because a factual check has to be undertaken to establish the extent to which those (normatively identified) features have been used in some population. Piaget (1950, p.15) indicates two possible ways in which this empirical control can be carried through, namely through historico-critical studies in the history of science (cf. Piaget & Garcia, 1983/1989) and psycho-genetical studies of the development of children's thinking (cf. Piaget, Henriques, & Ascher, 1990). Third, an account of intellectual construction, based on the empirical control but directed on normatively identified problems, is required. It is worth noticing that Piaget (1918; 1950; 1979) has constantly stressed that the questions arising from his constructivist epistemology cannot be resolved by reference to the perspectives in any one domain, such as psychology. Fourth, the implications of this account for normative epistemology can be surveyed and evaluated (Piaget, 1965/1972; 1968/1971).

It is then reasonable to envisage an inquiry in which the construction of adult logic from children's logic is seen as lawful (Piaget, 1921b, p.150). If one outcome of intellectual development is the emergence of atemporally true norms of reason, that process could not be exclusively contingent (cf. Bickhard, 1988). Of course, this is exactly Piaget's (1936/1953, p.403; 1967/1971, pp.312–13) position. If the process was random, a contingency would have to yield a necessity. But this is impossible since the contingency could be false unlike the necessity which must be true. So it is Piaget's view that, if the process is not random, there must be a lawful process of construction, because adult thinking does eventually emerge from children's thinking which was different from it. It is, then, reasonable to ascertain the laws of intellectual construction. But such laws cannot be exclusively empirical, as they bear on the construction of necessary, and so non-empirical, knowledge.

[8] KNOWING AS A RELATIONAL PROCESS

Despite the reminders of some commentators (cf. Chapman, 1988; Gruber & Vonèche, 1977; Kitchener, 1986; Vuyk, 1981), it is not always appreciated that several unifying ideas have been central to Piaget's work These ideas are evident in his novel *Recherche* (1918), are developed in his early, psychological papers which were written in the 1920s, and have been elaborated throughout the subsequent three score years and ten: for example, "all real organisation is in unstable equilibrium ... but tends towards total equilibrium which is ideal organisation" (Piaget, 1918, p.98) and "modes of construction converge on general structures *qua* laws or necessary forms of organisation of all coherent construction" (Piaget et al., 1990, p.221). The general interpretation of this claim was previewed in [1]. The suggestion is that a philosophical commitment is made to the validity of nominated defining principles in a specified knowledge-domain, such as mathematics. Using the prevailing norms in this domain as the standard, an account is required to show their realisation in the human mind. Genetic (constructivist) epistemology in its restricted form simply takes these norms as given and sets out to show their formation in children's minds. In its generalised form, its concern extends to the norms themselves, which are also taken to have an origin in scientific thought (Piaget, 1950).

A brief review of some of these main ideas follows in [8]. But three substantial qualifications need to be made at the outset. First, the review is not complete. The aim is not to provide a systematic guide to the serial elaboration of all Piagetian constructs in his writings from 1918–1990. Rather, the intention is to identify a cluster of constructs that are especially relevant to the construction of necessary knowledge. Second, the review is introductory. The intention is to outline the connecting strands which link these constructs to necessary knowledge. The result is an expository survey rather than a critical assessment of their specific strengths and weaknessess. Thus, third, the review in this section sets out to elucidate rather than to evaluate Piaget's account. Issues relating to evaluation will preoccupy the chapters ahead.

According to Piaget, the aim of constructivist epistemology is to identify a constitutive feature of a normative domain so as to follow its step-by-step construction from child to adult (Piaget, 1967b, p.120) or in the course of its history in science (Piaget, 1950, p.15). In consequence, Piaget states (1950, p.13) that his constructivist epistemology views knowledge in relation to

its development in time, that is, to say, as a continuous process neither whose first beginnings nor whose end could ever be reached ... (Any knowledge) is to be considered, from a methodological point of view, as being relative to a given previous state of lesser knowledge and also as being capable of constituting just such a previous state in relation to some more advanced knowledge

In this passage, Piaget commits himself to a relational conception of intellectual progression. Schematically, the relational process of construction has two terms, each of which is a system of thinking, characterisable through a structural model. There are several points to notice about this conception: (1) construction is normative; (2) construction occurs through action; (3) action has priority over consciousness; (4) construction is a search for coherence; (5) construction occurs in the epistemic subject. Each point is now discussed in turn.

[8.1] Construction as a Normative Process

There are two respects in which intellectual construction is normative. First, the process is defined as the construction of better knowledge. Second, the process is defined in terms of progressively ordered stages.

First, intellectual construction is regarded as normative in that later knowledge is more advanced, and so better, than earlier knowledge (cf. Kohlberg, 1987; Smith, 1991; van Haften, 1990). This claim is distinctive because intellectual development is *not* regarded as an exclusively causal process. Thus intellectual development is not defined here in terms of interaction among antecedent variables. Rather, a developmental claim is seen as one in which a system of thinking is regarded bi-directionally in relation both to a weaker predecessor and to a stronger successor. The process of construction is time-related, because new constructions occur as time passes. But it does not follow from this definition that any such construction occurs at a specifiable point in time. Thus it does not follow that it is age-related (see [18]). Rather, the basis of any such normative claim in restricted versions of genetic epistemology is provisional and reliant on an argument from authority as to what counts as the defining criteria of an advance in that domain (Piaget, 1950, p.47). Any such proposal ultimately requires validation through generalised versions of genetic epistemology, which Piaget (1967/1971) takes to cover questions about both the biological basis of epistemic construction and the agreement (*accord*) of knowledge and reality. These issues are complex and will not be further pursued here. Although Bickhard (1988) has argued that Piaget's generalised position is inadequate, the issues raised by the restricted versions of Piagetian epistemology are complex enough and these versions merit prior attention.

Piaget has offered a variety of models to capture the normative difference between different levels of thinking, including axiomatised algebraic structures (Piaget, 1949; 1972), category theory (Piaget, 1980c; Piaget, Grize, Szeminska, & Vinh Bang, 1968/1977; Piaget et al., 1990), and entailment logic (Piaget & Garcia, 1987/1991). It may be objected that this selection is arbitrary, since certain models—the ones that Piaget happened to use—are assigned a privileged role whereas many other models are silently by-passed (cf. Vonèche & Vidal, 1985, p.125). This objection is well taken. It embodies the suggestion that any selection is as good, or as bad, as any other. Indeed so, on condition that the case is made good with due attention to hierarchically related systems of thinking. Now all of the systems used by Piaget have been explicitly exploited with that normative point in mind.

Second, Piaget's commitment to a stage-theory is compatible with this normative conception. Any adjacent pair of stages should always emerge both in a constant order and in the same, progressive direction (Piaget, 1923, pp.50, 74; Piaget 1967/1971, p.17). Although Piaget (1960) later identified five defining criteria of intellectual stages, it is significant that the two main criteria were formulated at an early point in his work. In consequence, it is Piaget's (1964/1968, pp.147–50) claim that any knowledge should be related both to its ancestors and to its successors. In short, intellectual development is taken to be a process the terms of which always stand in an ordered, aysmmetrical relation. This is the relation of genesis, which brings out the point that knowledge is a temporal construction, because it has a creation at specific points in human thinking. However, there is no suggestion that mental creation arises from nothing at all in accord with the maxim *ex nihilo, nihil fit* (nothing is made from nothing). Normative principles serve to demarcate hierarchically related systems of thinking, and all systems have some normative component. But the principles also identify the respects in which, and the extent to which, any lower system has a lesser normative component than a higher system. If each system corresponds to a distinct stage, higher stages are constructed from lower stages, not from nothing at all (see [25.1]).

Piaget has been inconsistent in the specification of the number of stages in the progression from infancy to adulthood, as he has variously claimed that there are three (1924/1928; 1970/1983) and four (1947/1950; 1979/1980) stages. But at least three stages are always implicated. Further, his empirical analyses reveal the same tendency. Usually three levels of response are identified (Inhelder & Piaget, 1955/1958; Piaget & Szeminska, 1941/1952), although this number rises to four levels in some studies (Piaget & Inhelder, 1941/1974, ch.3). It has been claimed that Piaget's commitment to a theory of stages is, (*pace*

Piaget, 1960; 1971), dictated by heuristic, rather than substantive, considerations (Karmiloff-Smith, 1978). But this suggestion does not square with Piaget's continued commitment to a developmental position in which primacy is accorded to the taxonomic nature of stages *qua* hierarchically and constantly ordered systems of thinking (Inhelder & Piaget, 1979/1980, p.23; Piaget, 1967/1971, p.17; Piaget & Garcia, 1987/1991, pp.128–30), that is, to the two characteristic features of stage-related progression. Piaget's research programme requires any one level of knowledge to be viewed bi-directionally at both micro- and macro-genetic levels. This position is a denial of finalism, because there are neither absolute beginnings, nor absolute ends to epistemic progression (Beilin, 1985; Chapman, 1988, pp.415–7; Piaget, 1950, p.13).

In short, two main points can be noted. One is that intellectual development is not regarded by Piaget as a process that is exclusively causal. Although this position is not binding on other developmentalists, those who set out to evaluate Piaget's position are required to heed its normative commitment. The second point is that there are many different norms, as was exemplified in [4.1]. The specific norm that is central to Piaget's account concerns necessity, rather than truth. Thus the normative restrictions that arise from this notion are central.

[8.2] Construction Through Action

Piaget presents an account of epistemic change based on action, as intellectual construction is an active, transformational process. He states (Piaget, 1964, p.176): "To know an object is to act on it. To know is to modify, to transform the object, and to understand the process of this transformation". The underlying argument is that an individual who performs an *action* thereby can perform it and so *knows* how to perform it. Further (Piaget, 1970/1983, p.104), "in order to know objects, the subject must act upon them, and therefore transform them: he must displace, connect, combine, take apart, and reassemble them". Although a living individual is always in action, not all actions are successful. Thus Piaget's definition refers to the process of *knowing* rather than to a successful outcome, which is *knowledge*.

There are several reasons behind the adoption of this position. One reason is that actions are observable. A second reason is that action precedes thought both phylogenetically and ontogenetically. Lower forms of animal life display actions, whether or not they think. Further, infants display actions, whether or not they have representational intelligence. A third reason is that actions vary in their epistemic complexity, including reflex behaviour, purposive behaviour (intentionality), purposeful (intentional) action and mental operations (Piaget 1936; 1936/1953; cf. von Wright, 1971). A fourth reason is that action is a source of change, as an individual can transform the world by acting on it. Thus an action can change externally operating causal sequences in the world, where such changes have their origin in agency as such. Whether or not determinism is true, actions are causally efficacious and yet rationally undertaken (Davidson, 1981; von Wright, 1971). A final reason is that independent actions can be coordinated. An action occurs as an irreversible process in time. Intentional activity is a sequence of actions related as means-to-end whose successive display is directed on the attainment of the goal (Piaget, 1924/1947, p.8): "the development of intelligence thus consists wholly in a progressive coordination of actions". But independent actions can be linked and so their irreversibility can be transformed into reversible systems of thinking.

Thus the key question for Piaget is to ascertain which system of thought is instantiated in any action, whether exteriorised or interiorised. This question is dependent on three asumptions. One is that an individual action can be identified. Another is the structuralist postulate that certain elements of the action can be described by reference to some system of thought. The third is that any such system will have a logical character. It is the third assumption that differentiates psychological and epistemological models of thought. The discussion of mental models research is illustrative here (see [19]).

The objection is put (Vonèche & Vidal, 1985, p.128) that Piaget "never explains the transformation of actions into operations". But Piaget can remain an official agnostic on the normative question of whether and why some actions are operations. This is because his concern is to follow the development of some fundamental notion, whether it is used in physical action or displayed in a mental operation (cf. Piaget, 1950, p.15). Thus he addresses the empirical question of the extent to which and the means by which *one-and-the-same notion* undergoes development in the transition from one expression (physical action) to any other (mental operation). This is a question in empirical epistemology and, as such, is distinct from the normative question of establishing the defining conditions that demarcate exteriorised and interiorised action.

To see the difference, consider a parallel case, concerning what must be 'added' to a physical movement for it to be an intentional action (cf. Wittgenstein, 1958b, $621; cf. von Wright, 1971). Wittgenstein's question is normative, bearing on the defining criteria by the use of which the distinction between movement and action can be grounded. But Piaget is *not* raising a normative question as to what must be 'added' to an action to yield an operation. Rather, his concern is with the respects in which a specified notion is put to differential use, whether in actions or in operations. In general, it is difficult to demarcate questions that are empirical and those that are not because (Piaget, 1950, p.8) "it can never be decided a priori whether a problem is by nature scientific or philosophical". Analogous cases are easy to find, including the question of whether the replacement of 'folk psychology' by neuro-psychology is normative or empirical (Putnam, 1988), or whether the science of physics includes in its domain putatively metaphysical questions about the initial state of the universe (Hawking, 1988, pp.10–11).

To perform a new action is to activate the process of knowing, since knowing is defined through action. Thus Piaget needs to specify the minimal conditions which have to be satisfied for any activated process of knowing to result in a successful outcome, which is knowledge. Further, these conditions will have to cover the acquisition of necessary knowledge. Piaget's (1968/1971) commitment to structuralism is a direct consequence of his relational conception of knowledge whereby structural models can describe the terms of the relational process of construction. This denial of epistemic atomism leads to the claim that any action, and so knowledge, is nested in a structure. This commitment allows Piaget to set up the defining conditions of the successful completion of an intellectual process. The process of knowing results in knowledge when the criteria embodied in a structuralist model are met. Further, these structuralist criteria are relevant to necessary knowledge because the domains of logic and mathematics can be characterised through them. This issue is pursued in [23] in relation to the construction of structures.

The main point to carry away from this section is that Piaget's account of action is wide enough to cover forms of knowledge from infancy onwards. Adapting proposals made by H.I. Brown (1988, p.156), Piaget's account can be construed as an account of ability based on the development of judgment embodied in actions. One class of abilities cover 'problem-finding', for example in recognising unusual cases, deciding how to deal with them, modifying existing rules, creating rules, or just acting rationally when clear rules of procedure are lacking. As H.I. Brown (1988, p.142) put it, "this kind of *coherent* but non-algorithmic decision-making is common and important" (my emphasis). Piaget's claim is that such actions and abilities are locatable in the actual world and yet bear on rational norms without that postulation of non-natural entities which is evident in the work of epistemologists from Plato to Popper [3.1-3.2].

[8.3] Unconscious and Conscious Processes

The reason why Piaget defines the process of knowing through action is because he needs to locate it in the actual world rather than in a Popperian 'third world' discussed in [3.2]. But because this same process results in necessary knowledge, that process cannot be confined solely to the actual world because, for reasons discussed in [25.2], an adequate epistemic system should be extensive enough to cover possibilities and necessities.

Piaget's proposal is to regard action as an instantiation of modality. To act is to do something and so to know how to do something. But any such action shows that at least *one possibility has been understood*, namely that possibility which is the goal of that action. Thus in performing an action, the individual has access (*ouverture*) to—at least one—possibility. However, if there is initial non-differentiation of what is real from what is possible and what is necessary, simple access alone is not enough (Piaget, 1981/1987, p.5). Even in infancy, the repetition, generalisation and reciprocal coordination of actions lead to the proliferation of possibilities, which have to be bound together (cf. Piaget, 1936/1953, p.354). Necessity provides such coordination through closure (*fermeture*) of the system of thought [25.2].

Epistemic search is a search for rational norms. Since the norms of reasoning with 1, 2, 3, or 4 bivalent propositions yield 4, 16, 256, or 65,536 distinct operations respectively, this search cannot be a conscious search (Piaget, 1951a, p.31). The conscious human mind cannot handle the huge number of operations that arise from even these relatively small cases. Consciousness is not sufficient for rationality, whether or not it is necessary (cf. McGinn, 1991, p.24). It is no doubt for this reason that Piaget locates intellectual processes in action, not in consciousness.

The question, then, arises as to why Piaget needs to view an account of knowing based on action as one in which consciousness is needed at all. The answer is twofold.

The first reason is because of his commitment to both conscious and unconscious intellectual processes. The second reason, which is elaborated in the next section, is that consciousness confers successive access to increasingly better sets of possibilities.

Piaget's commitment to the occurrence of intellectual processes that are unconscious is evident in his early paper on Freudian theory. Piaget (1920, p.19) states that the aim of psycho-analysis is to provide a "theory of the unconscious, a science properly called", adding that such a claim can be extended because it is applicable to the psychology of cognition and to pedagogy. Indeed, all mental life has unconscious, or implicit, elements (Piaget, 1920, p.47). However, Piaget (1921a, p.452) also notices that claims about implicit-*vs*-explicit processes are trivial, since this is to label a difference which merits explanation. This point is significant, as even recent discussions continue to include this very same reminder (Karmiloff-Smith, 1990; Moshman, 1990).

A second claim is that consciousness is not to be explained through metaphors of illumination (Piaget, 1974/1977, p.261/*332; cf. Smith, 1981). Although this is a plausible denial, it leads to a problem. On the one hand, Piaget (1961/1966, p.202) views introspection as both distorting and lacunary, and so it cannot be an unchallenged, direct source of knowledge. On the other hand, one of the specific features of introspective knowledge is its immediacy to its subject and its impenetrability by any other subject. It has widely been regarded as an incorrigible form of knowledge (Ayer, 1956; Descartes, 1637/1931). A reconciling proposal has been outlined by McGinn (1991, p.3) in terms of cognitive closure: A mind M is cognitively closed with respect to a property P "if and only if the concept-forming procedures at M's disposal cannot extend to a grasp of P". Thus an object may have the property P, whether or not any specific mind understands it, as in the case of a monkeys and electrons, or human understanding of what it is like to be a bat (McGinn, 1991, pp.4, 9). It follows that even if the deliverances of consciousness are epistemically perfect, they may bear on merely a subset of available properties. McGinn's proposal is that cognitive closure extends to introspective knowledge whose incorrigibility extends only to introspectively detected properties without the requirement that all properties have been so detected. Thus (McGinn, 1991, p.64) "there may be good theoretical reasons to postulate properties of consciousness that fall outside the reach of introspection". Such a proposal is compatible with Piaget's (1925, p.198) claim that the psychological genesis of a notion is not due merely to its manifestation in consciousness. Knowledge is not due to its simple illumination in consciousness but is instead an unconscious construction.

Thus a third claim is (Piaget, 1928, p.107) that "any act of becoming conscious presupposes a construction properly called". This claim has an underlying basis in traditional epistemology—see [3.1]—since intellectual organisation is required for the conversion of experience into knowledge. But that organisation does not arrive ready made. Rather, it is due to construction. The act of becoming conscious (*prise de conscience*) cannot be the acquisition of knowledge (*prise de connaissance*), which is epistemically prior to it (see Pinard, 1986; Smith, 1981). In short, the act of becoming conscious extends merely to a subset of the properties that form intellectual organisation (Piaget, 1931, p.149).

A fourth claim is that if successive acts of becoming conscious are partially revelatory of fundamental norms, they progressively extend to the awareness of logical necessity (Piaget, 1954a, p.136; 1967c, p.270). As noted in [1], this is, of course, the central problem (cf. Piaget, 1979/1980, p.23).

A fifth claim is a that to become conscious of intellectual organisation is to perform a mental act, namely one in which a connection is made between the intensional elements in one part of the epistemic system in use with those in other parts (Piaget, 1954a, p.142): "Consciousness is the source of connections that depend on systems of meanings. The case of 'awareness logical necessity' is a good special example". Taken literally, this is a misleading claim because, in his account of infant intelligence, Piaget (1936/1953, p.407) invokes a unitary, epistemic process which is supposed to underpin the construction of all, including primitive, knowledge. The logic of action is an intensional logic of meanings rather than an extensional logic of the contents of consciousness (Piaget & Garcia, 1987/1991, p.4). What Piaget presumably means is that the act of becoming conscious is responsible for the connection. This is because the act of making connections is a manifestation of human action in terms of which the process of knowing was defined in [8.2]. This issue is further discussed in [11].

[8.4] Sets of Possibilities

There is a second reason why some role is assigned to consciousness in Piaget's account of action. The process of construction includes the construction of necessary knowledge both through access to available sets of possibilities and through access to novel sets. Piaget states (1950, p.34, my emphasis):

> "Each new action, whilst bringing about one of the possibilities engendered by preceeding actions, itself provides access to *a set of possibilities (un ensemble des possibles)*, hitherto inconceivable. It is there, in the relation of the causally real with the possibilities opened by it but bound together by a link of virtuality that is nearer to logical implication, that is to be found the solution of the central problem of the atemporal norm and genetic becoming".

A new action can provide access to a larger set of possibilities than the set available before that action was performed. But whereas the action is performed in time, the set of possibilities that is instantiated in the action is not a causal element in the actual world. (The complex notion of a set of all possibilities is further discussed in [25.1].)

There are, then, an indefinite number of possibilities, not all of which are identical with observable reality (Piaget, 1980a, p.4). Consciousness thus plays a twofold role in Piaget's account. First, access to certain sets of possibilities, or 'possible worlds', is strictly dependent on conscious thought which serves to differentiate possibilities and so enlarges the "virtual field of possibilities" (Piaget, 1981/1987, p.186/152). Second, (Piaget, 1954a, p.139) "operations never develop separately but always in coordinated systems ... (and so) 'awareness of necessity' follows". Necessary knowledge is a criterion of closure in a system of thinking, in respect to which necessity binds together distinct possibilities.

Piaget's structural models provide a well defined description of those sets of possibilities that are stable and powerful. As such models are themselves internally coherent, so too are the systems of thinking described through them. But there is no one system that encompasses all possibilities. Construction is, then, an open-ended search for the coherence arising from the serial replacement of an available and coherent system of thinking by a better successor.

The conclusion to draw from this section is that the act of making connections is a principal feature of the intellectual process described by Piaget. It is for this reason that the justifications—and not merely their associated judgments—which individuals give are important (see [13]). The connections made between one judgment-and-other-judgments are a constitutive feature in defining *which* judgment has actually been made.

[8.5] Search for Coherence

One important, structural property is reversibility, whose two forms, namely inversion and reciprocity, are combined in some (group) structures but remain separable in other (grouping) structures (Piaget, 1961/1966). It is clear, however, that reversibility is important for Piaget because it marks the more fundamental principle of self-consistency. "The property of reversibility is to express non-contradiction" (Piaget, 1951b, p.139). There is distinguished support for the condition that any one case of knowledge should at least be consistent with any other (Kant, 1787/1933; Plato, nd/1941). The constructivist version of this condition states that new knowledge must be consistent with the system of knowledge *in either term*. The proposal is that knowledge arising from a current action must be consistent *either with possessed knowledge or with knowledge-under-construction*.

The point is that the process of acquiring knowledge is both powerful and yet inherently unstable. It is powerful both because of the infinite range of possible experience and because of the match between experience and any structure-in-use. Piaget (1967/1971, p.155) marks this point by defining a living being, or an epistemic system, as an open system. He also notes that the activation of an epistemic system is necessary but not sufficient for its success (Piaget, 1975/1985, p.6). The process is unstable because the activation of an epistemic system does not guarantee its preservation (Piaget, 1922, p.260): "There should be mutual conservation of the elements acquired by their exercise even in the incessant adaptation to new circumstances ... If acquired elements are placed neither in hierarchical order nor in a relation of mutual dependence, the adaptation will merely increase their quantity, so to speak, not their coherence". The claim is that the way a new experience is understood is not settled by its mere possession. A new experience has to be related to existing experiences with due respect to their mutual coherence. A subject of knowledge must display (Piaget, 1923, p.61) the fidelity which "consists in the conservation of self-identical premises, whatever the train of reasoning in which they are found. In this sense logical experience is a reversible psychological process ... fidelity in thinking is recognised by an awareness of a match or mismatch, of an equilibrium or disequilibrium, almost like moral fidelity itself". On this view, reversibility is a minimal characteristic of intellectual progression in which conservation is at the heart of the thinking process itself. Although Piaget (1924/1928, p.214) soon gave up the claim that there must be an awareness of the conserving features of thought, he has retained this early claim about the importance of its internal coherence (Piaget, 1921b, p.153; 1977/1986, p.310). However, this commitment can sit uneasily with those arising from the several constructivist models (see [26]).

Intellectual development is, then, not so much the search for certainty and truth (Descartes, 1637/1931, p.82) as the search for coherence (Piaget, 1928/1977, p.211; 1975/1985, p.13). There are three reasons why this search does not guarantee its own success. One is that *search* denotes a task, not an achievement, in much the way that running a race differs from winning (Ryle, 1949). A second is that even logical rules are not sufficient for their own rational use (H.I. Brown, 1988, p.71). A third is that, although the (Kantian) categories of experience are necessary, the generative mechanisms which are responsible for development in their use are not necessary in this same sense (Kitchener, 1986, pp.38, 84). Piaget (1931, pp.150-51) brings out this aspect of creative search by stating that, although the fundamental categories of thought are *functionally* present in all individuals at all levels of development, their presence is compatible with different structural exemplications. Thus, both the young child and the adult mathematician use one and the same principle of contradiction, even though there are differences in the ways in which they put this principle to use. "We know in advance that if A and B are contradictory, we have to choose between them, but we do not know straightaway if that is what they are" (Piaget, 1977a, p.211; cf. Piaget 1977/1986, p.301).

This is an important claim. Piaget does not reserve an understanding of contradiction for mature individuals at the end of their development. Rather, all individuals, at all levels of development, have some understanding of this fundamental notion. Indeed, it is fundamental for precisely the reason that it is a cognitive universal in Kant's sense [3.1]. Further, this position generalises to cover all fundamental notions, as Leibniz noted [3.1]. It is explicitly stated by Piaget (1977/1986, pp.302–3) to include the development of all forms of modal understanding. In short, there are different evaluations arising in the judgments of individuals who use the same logical principle. It is by reference to these judgments, which are normative facts (Piaget, 1961/1966, p.132), that differences in developmental levels of thinking are established.

Yet "rational necessity only ever appears at the end of development, not at its outset" (Piaget, 1948, p.40). Due to the pervasive, but merely functional, presence of organisation which is co-extensive with mental life, development in modal understanding must take place (Piaget, 1977a, p.211). The development of the notion of necessity is subtle and complex. In part, this is due to the problems of differentiating contingency and necessity (Piaget, 1922, p.252), fact and necessity (Piaget, 1977/1986, p.302), generality and necessity (Piaget, 1983/1987, p.3), pseudo-necessity and necessity (Piaget, 1922, p.257). In part, it is due to the problems of integrating these differentiated notions into coherent systems of thinking (Inhelder & Piaget, 1955/1958, p.220/*251): "Far from merely introducing some initial forms of necessity to reality, as in the case with concrete inferences, formal thought brings about from the outset a synthesis of possibility and necessity". Problems of differentiation and integration extend to other modal notions, including possibility and impossibility (Piaget, 1976b). Indeed, "the appearance of logical necessity constitutes the central problem of the psychogenesis of operational structures" (Piaget, 1967a, p.391). Its human importance resides in the capacity "to introduce new necessities into systems where they were previously implicit or undetected" (Piaget, 1980b, p.2). These issues are further discussed in [25.2].

In short, the claim is that all of the central notions and principles (conservation, identity, transitivity, number, causality, and the rest) are present in some form at every level of development. Modal notions and principles are similar in this respect. In Piaget's account, development occurs not as a transition from absence-to-presence but rather as serial differentiation and integration over time (Smith, 1991).

[8.6] Epistemic Subject

The process of construction is taken to reside not in the individual person but rather in the epistemic subject (Piaget, 1961/1966; Piaget & Inhelder, 1966/1969). Baldly stated, this is a distinction between thinkers and types of thinking (Chapman, 1988, p.33; Smith, 1986a). In part, this is a distinction between a rational person and a rational agent (H.I. Brown, 1988, p.185), "for a single person may be capable of acting as a rational agent in some circumstances, but not in others". In part, this is a distinction between the average person and the ideal subject, where the former is a composition from each-and-every personal characteristic, whether trivial, defective or abnormal, whereas the latter is composed (Kitchener, 1986, p.27) by "only certain normative defined properties". In part, the distinction is that between an actual mind and a normal mind, since (Lakatos, 1974, p.180, his emphasis) "the study of actual scientific minds belongs to *psychology*; the study of the 'normal' (or 'healthy') mind belongs to a *psychologistic philosophy of science*". Rational (mathematical, scientific) thinking is meritorious in an intellectual sense in much the same way as honesty or heroism are laudable in a moral sense. Intellectual and moral norms serve to characterise such thinking or conduct respectively, which can be investigated as "normative facts" (Piaget, 1961/1966, p.132). A normative fact is an instantiation of a norm which is manifest in the use of that norm in the individual's actions. Such use may be conscious and intentional but also unwitting and devoid of awareness. There are two points to note about the use of an intellectual norm and both can be noticed by analogy with moral norms. First, no one seriously supposes that someone who is heroic on some occasions is heroic on all occasions. Further, although not all features of actions have a moral relevance, the honest conduct of an individual is exemplary in any of its manifestations. Necessary knowledge is analogous. People do not always display such knowledge, and knowledge has characteristics other than necessity. But any manifestation of necessary knowledge is distinctive, when judged in relation to intellectual norms.

The epistemic subject is not a personal subject. As Piaget (1967c, p.279) starkly put it: "about the problem of individual differences, I have nothing to say. I haven't studied it." But an epistemic subject is an impersonal subject on three counts. Firstly, necessary knowledge is *universal*. The knowledge that an individual has acquired is not a personal possession. In principle, any one can acquire, and so possess, the knowledge that 7 + 5 = 12. Second, necessary knowledge is *self-identical* because it is the same knowledge that is acquired by all of those who do acquire it. Third, necessary knowledge is *necessary*, where this property is not due to the contingent fact that a specific person has acquired such knowledge in the actual world. Necessary knowledge is the knowlege of a necessary truth, which—by definition—is true in *all possible worlds* (Bradley & Swartz, 1979; Hughes & Cresswell, 1972; Leibniz, 1686/1973). Thus its truth could not be due to any contingent feature of the actual world nor, *a fortiori*, to particular individual in it.

In conclusion, the relevance of the distinction can be put like this. Piaget's (1953) notion of a *structure d'ensemble* is ambiguous. His position has been taken to licence predictions about the extent to which an *individual subject* can generalise *consistently* across a range of tasks that are intended to be structurally similar (Brown & Desforges, 1980; Case, 1985; Flavell, 1982). But there is a different interpretation to bear in mind. The notion of a *structure d'ensemble* can be taken to licence predictions about which standards have to be met for an *epistemic subject* to display a *coherent* level of thinking throughout any performance on the task. In essence, the difference between the two interpretations turns on whether an account is presented as a structural analysis either of a class of tasks ("which tasks can such-and-such individual perform successfully?") or of a type of thinking ("which type of thinking is needed for any individual to be successful on such-and-such task?"). In the former case, tasks are the variable and the individual is the constant; in the latter case, the task is constant and the individuals are the variable (cf. Sugarman, 1987).

[9] EMPIRICAL TESTABILITY

Empirically minded developmentalists could intervene at this point. They could say that the issues reviewed in [8.1-8.5] are, of course, important. But so too is the point made by Piaget, in [3.1], that traditional epistemology has not been sufficiently sensitive to empirical control. Their point is that, although Piaget claimed that his empirical studies were designed to provide *verifications* of his epistemological position, much available research tells against his position (cf. Braine & Rumain, 1983; Demetriou & Efklides, 1988; Gelman & Baillargeon, 1983; Halford, 1989; Harris, 1983). Moreover, this negative evaluation can be presented as the reflection of a greater sensitivity which is now shown by developmentalists to methodological norms, and notably to Popper's view that *falsification* is one essential feature of scientific progress [3.2]. In short, the suggestion is that Piaget set out to verify his account which other developmentalists have now falsified.

This tempting conclusion is too strong. First, a commitment to a falsification is better than one to verification for the reason given by

Popper (1934/1968; 1979), provided some commitment to fallibilism is also made (H.I. Brown, 1988; Haack, 1978). Since Popper's own position is itself open to interpretation (Lakatos, 1974), objection (H.I. Brown, 1988) and revision (Laudan, 1977), the status of this commitment is not clear-cut. The central feature of these differing modifications is a concern to reinstate verification in empirical work subject to control through falsification. The two are not regarded as exclusive alternatives but rather as methodological rules for use in tandem under specified conditions. Second, there is no consensus as to what are the appropriate methods and procedures to use in scientific research. Rather, preferred methods and procedures may well be different from permissible methods and procedures, where the latter are identifiable by reference to the problems to be addressed and the available theories (Laudan, 1984, pp.33–4). Third, even well-defined principles of falsifiability are ambiguous in their application to scientific theories. The logical principle that is central to falsificationism is illustrative in that (H.I. Brown, 1988, p.64) *"modus tollens* does not tell us which of the propositions we began with has been refuted, nor how many".

This point generalises nicely across Piagetian research where the unrestricted use of *modus tollens* can serve to confuse, rather than to clarify, the issues (Smith, 1992a). *Modus tollens* is the logical principle which states that the negation of a consequent of a conditional implies the negation of its antecedent or $(P \rightarrow Q)$ & $-Q$ imply $-P$ (read: if P then Q and *not-Q* imply *not-P*). The loser in a recent legal case claimed "If that is justice, I am a banana". Evidently, he was not a banana and so "I am not a banana", coupled with the initial conditional, imply "That is not justice". So much is clear, if the constituent propositions are logically simple propositions, such as "I am not a banana" or "That is not justice". Both of these propositions are simple in the technical sense that one proposition is asserted in each sentence. By contrast, a complex proposition is a combination of simple propositions that are linked by the propositional operators of conjunction (*and*) or disjunction (*or*). The point is that a scientific theory is not a simple proposition but is instead a complex proposition with conjunctive and disjunctive elements, such as $\{(P_1 \& P_2) \ v \ (P_3 \& P_4) \ ...P_n\}$, from which some consequence Q is derived. Thus even if empirical testing results in falsification, *not-Q*, the use of *modus tollens* does not identify which element—all, some, or one—in the complex antecedent must be replaced. The relevance of this general argument to Piagetian evaluation is apparent as there is a four-step procedure to follow in putting Piaget's account to empirical test (Smith, 1991):

(1) *Select an epistemological principle.* The principles that Piaget elected to study are taken to be constitutive principles of human

understanding in the Kantian sense, i.e. they are used always and necessarily as a pre-condition of objective knowledge. Piaget did not address the question of whether there are any such principles. Rather, assuming that there are such principles, his aim was to study empirically the development in their use. Central to such a study is a concern for the differentiation of the defining (necessary) from the non-defining (contingent) criteria of a specified principle. Any logical principle does have defining criteria, and so any individual who confuses these with the contingent criteria which are merely regularly associated with them does not make full use of the principle, and may indeed make no use of it at all. Further discussion of this point is made in relation to conservation [16] and the modal model of differentiation [25.2].

(2) *Design a task that requires the use of that principle.* Piaget's tasks are distinctive in two ways. First, the task is intended to exemplify the selected principle in line with his epistemological, rather than psychological, interests. Second, successful completion of the task requires the use of the principle, and success cannot arise in any other way. Piaget's designs are rarely faulted on this count. However, instances of the counter-case are given by Leiser & Gillièron (1990; Gillièron & Leiser, 1991).

(3) *Specify criteria for the identification of a successful response.* Criteria have to be stated so that a successful performance can be distinguished from one that is not. Further, procedures have to be laid down so that there is an agreed way to ascertain children's responses to the task (cf. Inhelder, Sinclair, & Bovet, 1974).

(4) *Use a method which shows that a response is durable.* Using an early taxonomy (Piaget, 1926/1929), investigators need to find out whether a child's response has been occasioned by the task and its procedures or whether it is a well-based feature of an individual's thinking.

The logic of Piaget's position is as follows. The selected principle (Step 1) refers to a fundamental capacity which is supposed to be present, and necessarily so, in all human understanding. When this capacity is present, the child will perform the task (Step 2) in accordance with the specified criteria (Step 3) as displayed by use of the method (Step 4). Thus their conjunction (Steps 1–4) can be used to make predictions about actual performance. More difficult is the conclusion to be drawn when the prediction is falsified, because its antecedent is, in this case, a complex proposition. *Modus tollens* shows that at least one of Steps 1–4 is false, if the prediction is conditionally based on them. But *modus tollens* does not indicate which. Further, the difficulty is compounded by the fact that psychological criticisms have been independently directed against Piaget's tasks (Step 2), criteria (Step 3), and methods (Step 4).

Questions can, and should, be raised about the adequacy of Piaget's tasks, criteria, and methods, but focusing on them alone leaves the main epistemological issue untouched. According to Piaget, the main question is epistemological, concerning the extent to which there is development in the use of Kantian abilities nominated in Step 1. According to other developmentalists, the main questions are psychological and methodological, as shown in Steps 2–4. So viewed, it is no surprise to find a consequential "dialogue of the deaf" (cf. Vuyk, 1981).

Two conclusions can be noted. One concerns the several, inter-dependent ways of undertaking empirical evaluations of Piaget's account. The suggestion is not that any one way is better than the others, but rather that each one is as important as the others. Empirical investigation should be such that permissible tasks, criteria, and methods are put to work in the assessment of children's use of a selected epistemological principle. In fact, many investigations are marked by their commitment to some sub-set of this quartet. The consequence is that any such evaluation of Piaget's account must be partial and provide under-determining findings. It follows that a methodological commitment to the primacy of falsification based on *modus tollens* could not settle questions about the joint epistemological-and-psychological adequacy of Piaget's account.

The second conclusion is that, in practice, many developmentalists have given exclusive attention to Steps 2–4 and have almost ignored Step 1. Moreover, this practice is now long-standing as it was noticed by Piaget (1963) three decades ago. The shift is substantive and appears in task design at Step 2. Piaget's position is to view task design in the light of the epistemological commitment at Step 1. Many development-alists view task design at Step 2 through their psychological and methodological commitments arising from Steps 3 and 4. In short, task design is viewed from different normative positions. Whatever the merits of an approach that considers psychological questions through the experimental study of children as individuals who live in a social world, that approach alone could not be used in relation to epistemological questions about the growth of necessary knowledge in the epistemic subject.

CHAPTER THREE

Methods

"But our problem was quite different: it was concerned, by contrast, with seeking to find the secrets of thinking which we did not know in advance" (Piaget & Inhelder, 1961/1968, p.xii).

[10] PROBLEMS OF METHOD

Some philosophers have regarded methodology as a specific branch of the philosophy of science which is concerned *inter alia* with the nature of scientific explanation (Nagel, 1961) or the status of scientific theories (Lakatos, 1974). On the other hand, many psychologists now use the term 'methodology' to refer to the methods that they prefer to use in undertaking empirical research. According to Laudan (1984), there is a methodological continuum, linking the former class of philosophical problems with the latter class of empirical methods. The proposal is that this unitary term covers a diverse class of methodological issues and techniques. This proposal fits Piaget's central problem concerning the construction of necessary knowledge, as this problem has both normative and empirical components for the reasons given in [7]. The methodological issue thus turns partly on the defining criteria of necessity and partly on the permissible methods to use in empirical research that is directed towards the acquisition of such knowledge.

Piaget's (1924/1947) position is that a *critical method* must be used to gain adequate evidence about children's acquisition of knowledge.

This method requires children to manipulate the task materials and then to explain their consequential beliefs. Piaget's stance is reviewed in [11]. A methodological objection to this position is reviewed in [12], namely that Piaget's method is inadequate because it results in conservative assessments of children's abilities. A counter-objection is reviewed in [13], where the argument will be that epistemological norms are implicated when questions arise about the adequacy of Piaget's method. In cases of conflict between these two types of norms, priority has to be given to epistemological, rather than methodological, norms. Thus method is the under-labourer to theory.

[11] CRITICAL METHOD

A critical method is conceived to be to be an intermediary between unguided observation and standardised testing (Piaget, 1924/1947). Its principal feature is to allow children to display the reasoning behind their actions and beliefs.

Note that the term 'reason' is ambiguous and can refer either to a task or to an achievement (Ryle, 1949), as noted in [8.5]. Taken in the first sense, to give a reason is to engage in a process of reasoning by indicating why a particular belief is accepted. Such a reason might refer to a property which is possessed by the object of that belief. Asked to explain why a figure is a triangle, someone might offer as a reason that its interior angles equal two right angles. Although this may be a true property of a specified figure, it is not the (defining) reason why that figure is a triangle. Alternatively, a proposed reason may be quite irrelevant to a belief. Asked why Geneva has two Salève mountains, one big and the other small, a reason such as that the big one is for adults and the small one for children is irrelevant (Piaget, 1923/1959, p.207). It is, therefore, entirely possible that the reasons which an individual offers for some belief are neither defining reasons nor even relevant reasons for that belief. Taken in the second sense, to reason is to reason successfully, for example by reasoning deductively. A feature of empirical epistemology is the assumption that human reasoning can be successful, even if it is not always so. Thus Piaget takes his method to be a permissible one to use in verifying the extent to which the assumption fits children's reasoning.

It was noted in [8.3] that Piaget planned to extend Freudian theory to the intellectual domain. His initial adoption of a *clinical method* is taken from psychiatry. The main features of this method are summarised in this way (Piaget, 1926/1929, p.19): "the practitioner sets himself a problem, makes hypotheses, adapts the conditions to them and finally controls each hypothesis by testing it against the reactions he stimulates in conversation". The key point to notice is that Piaget's primary purpose in using this method is to give classifying descriptions of the distinct types of thinking that mark the construction of necessary knowledge. His rational conception of scientific procedure has two steps. One is to formulate structural models of levels of thinking. The second (Piaget, 1972/1973, p.46) is "to find out whether the structures do exist and to analyse them".

It is this conception which requires the extensive questioning of children. Piaget's (1926/1929, p.21) claim is that children may respond to such questioning in at least five different ways. Their answers may be due to guessing, to romancing, to belief fabricated on the spot, to triggered belief, or to spontaneous belief. Using normative rationality as the standard, only the latter could meet the standards whereby an individual can reason productively and deductively in the absence of self-contradiction (Piaget, 1926/1929, p.35). In short, the aim is to monitor aspects of their modal understanding with respect to a coherent, and so durable, set of beliefs which can remain self-identical through challenges and transformations.

Piaget later changed from a clinical to a critical method in an attempt to demarcate psychiatric from cognitive-developmental approaches (Piaget, 1924/1947, p.7; cf. Inhelder et al., 1974, p.19; Vinh Bang, 1966, pp.73–74). There is a deeper point behind the change. Suppose an individual has only one belief and iteratively derives the same belief from it, for example "today is Sunday, so today is Sunday, so today is Sunday...". Consistency is an admirable virtue but is not in itself enough. An account of intellectual development that is concerned with the construction of new and better knowledge could not be concerned exclusively with banal consistency. Indeed, it is sometimes contended that it should not be concerned with consistency of this type at all (Cellérier, 1980, p.70; Sperber & Wilson, 1986). The key question is not whether consistency is present, but rather whether it can be maintained through irrelevant transformation. In this way conservation is a constitutive feature of rational thought because (Piaget & Szeminska, 1941/1952, p.16/*3) "all knowledge ... presupposes explicitly or implicitly principles of conservation". Any notion that is used in any belief should be used in a self-identical way through a train of reasoning, even when that belief undergoes transformation and challenge. So construed, conservation is a constitutive feature of rational thought. It is not so much that transformation and challenge to a belief allow an observer to make more accurate diagnostic assessments of children's ability, but rather that the specific character of any belief is constituted in precisely this way.

According to Piaget (1924/1947, p.7; cf. 1952/1976), a critical method is marked by "the introduction of questions and discussions only at the end, or during the course, of manipulations bearing on objects which arouse a determinate action on the part of the subject". So defined, this method is compatible with the definition of knowing through action in [8.2]. The use of this method is guided by Piaget's structuralist commitments, as the method is used to check on whether the criteria of knowledge that follow from these models have been met in children's thinking. The aim of the method is to grasp the deep logical activity of the child (Vinh Bang 1966, p.75). Viewed in this way, a distinction should be drawn between the verbal and experimental aspects of the method. Although Royon (1940, p.109) noticed that Piaget's (1926/1929) account could be interpreted as one that required the investigator to focus on children's language, priority was given by Piaget, both in practice and in attendant commentary (Piaget, 1924/1947), to an experimental—that is, critical—interpretation of their thought. Five elements in this stance are apparent, whereby children are specifically required to justify their judgments (Smith, 1992b).

First, the aim in developmental studies is to ascertain how children think and which judgments they have formed. Although children's language provides one means of access, it is not the sole way as manipulative activity is another. But because the coordination of actions is taken by Piaget to be central to intellectual construction, a substantive issue concerns the extent to which children can give reasons for the knowledge which is displayed in their practical mastery (Piaget, 1974/1978).

Second, the process of questioning was deliberately not standardised in the original studies. Standardised questioning is permissible only if two conditions are met, namely (Piaget & Inhelder, 1961/1968, p.xii) that "we know in advance what we want to get from the child and that we believe we are capable of interpreting the obtained responses". The suggestion is that neither condition can be met due to inadequacy in available accounts of intellectual development, including Piagetian accounts. In part, this is due to the poverty of the perspectives used by investigators which provide under-determining information about which variables to control and how to control them (Droz, 1972, p.37). In part, this is due to the central problems of constructivism which "presupposes both the conservation of the past and the creation of novelties" (Inhelder & de Caprona, 1985, p.8). Children are novel thinkers too. Thus it is not merely that the investigator sets out to discover types of thinking that are novel (to the child), but that such thinking could be itself novel (in relation to the investigator) due to the creative minds of children.

Third, Piaget's account states that the onset of concrete operational knowledge is one accomplishment of intellectual development. Yet any operation is a reversible, interiorised action which is defined interdependently, as a member of a set of such actions. Thus the diagnostic assessment of operational knowledge requires a child's judgment, in which any one operation appears to have been used, to be checked against that child's ability to use any other operation from the same set. As Piaget & Inhelder (1966/1969, p.96) put it, such operations "are never isolated but are always capable of being coordinated into overall systems". On this view, the child has the ability to coordinate any and all of the five general actions, which are identified through the constitutive principles of a *groupement*, namely combinativity, reversibility, identity, associativity, and tautology (Piaget, 1970/1983, pp.120–21). A judgment and its justification are taken to be displays of at least two of these general actions. The implication is that, unless the judgment is justified, there is no case for supposing that the correspond- ing judgment embodies operational knowledge. The requirement that a child should support one response (judgment) by making another (justification) follows from this definition of operational knowledge.

Fourth, good evidence is available to show that some Genevan findings, which are based on the assessment of children's justified judgments, are highly replicable for all levels of operational under- standing (Shayer, Demetriou, & Pervez, 1988).

Finally, Piaget's (1975/1985) account of equilibration identifies a generative mechanism that is responsible for developmental progression (see [23]). In an empirical exemplification of parts of this model, a causal role has been assigned to children's justifications for their judgments (Piéraut-Le Bonniec, 1990). This position requires children to display the justifications of the judgments that they express.

An individual's reasons for judgments are as important as the judgments on four counts. One is that to reason is to connect and so any such *action* is an instantiation of the intellectual process whose activation is necessary for knowledge. A second is that to reason is to link a present judgment with possessed knowledge in a *coherent* system. A third is that to reason is to forge links with a new system of coherent thinking. A fourth is that necessary knowledge is relational. This is explicit in the case of necessary relations, such as transitivity, but is equally evident in the case of necessary propositions whose truth—see Kripke [3.2]—is defined across an infinity of 'possible worlds'. In short, to give a reason is not to reason successfully (Piéraut-Le Bonniec, 1990), still less to give a proof (Piaget, 1980a, p.2). It is instead to instantiate a logical process whose successful outcome is an epistemic discovery (Piaget, 1980b).

The contrary view has also been supported, according to which it is sometimes reasonable to attribute knowledge to a child solely on the basis of that child's judgment(s) in performing a task. This contrary view is elaborated and discussed in the next section.

[12] FALSE NEGATIVES

Although some developmentalists accept that Genevan findings are reliable, their interpretation has been challenged (Gelman & Baillargeon, 1983; Halford, 1989). Piaget is sometimes credited with an account of children's understanding which is too negative. In turn, the main research aim is to design tasks that allow children to exhibit the competence which they are already presumed to have. Thus there are psychological grounds for investigating children's knowledge through their judgments quite independently of their associated justifications.

There is a methodological case for assessing children's knowledge through their judgments-alone, namely a concern to avoid incorrect attributions of ability. Following Smedslund (1969), the distinction between attributing to children knowledge which they do not possess (false positive), and not attributing to children knowledge which they do possess (false negative), should be respected. Although they are mindful of the symmetrical nature of this diagnostic snare, many developmentalists contend that the requirement that children should always justify their judgments is too restrictive in leading to 'false negative' diagnostic error. In practice, many developmentalists have tended to allow a child's display of a relevant judgment-alone to warrant the reasonable attribution of knowledge (Flavell, 1982).

Surveys of deductive reasoning are testimony to such difficulties. Some reasoning tasks are such that pre-schoolers can make appropriate deductions, whereas other versions defy the abilities of mature adults (Markovits, 1992; Moshman, 1990). Using this research as a guide, there is a case for claiming that Piaget's position is open to the charge of committing both 'false positive' and 'false negative' errors. Which charge is pressed depends on the methods, procedures, and tasks used in a study, but also on the epistemological principles at issue. The former charge has support in research on adolescents and adults using the selection task (see [19]). The latter charge is pressed by reference to research on children's development, for example in Braine's (1959) study of transitivity, and repeatedly over the subsequent 30 years (for example, Pears & Bryant, 1990). Although Piaget has been credited with a negative view of children's abilities, other developmentalist have taken their studies to be more optimistic in this respect (Donaldson, Grieve, & Pratt, 1983; Gelman, 1978; Gelman & Baillargeon, 1983).

An argument has been offered, purporting to show that the incidence of 'false positive' error is zero to low in research that uses a judgment-alone criterion, unlike the high incidence of 'false negative' error in research that uses a judgment-and-explanation criterion (Brainerd, 1973). Brainerd claims that any discussion of empirical methods should be compatible with some theoretical account of development (1973, pp.175–6). According to Brainerd (1973, p.177), Piaget's account is incompatible with his method on two counts. One is that the account contains no rationale for the claim that children should explain their beliefs. Brainerd's interpretation of Piaget's account is that a cognitive structure is an independent variable in relation to which language is a dependent variable, so that linguistically expressed explanations are sufficient, but not necessary, for the detection of the structure. A second reason is that a method in which children are required merely to display their beliefs, and not to explain them, is better suited to the account. Brainerd's argument is that 'false positive' errors are not known to be present, whether children simply display their beliefs or explain them as well, but that 'false negative' errors do surround the latter. His conclusion is that "minimally necessary evidence" can be gained by inviting children to display their beliefs without explaining them (1973, p.177). Brainerd's argument is, however, open to reply.

First, the argument is admitted to be incomplete since it does not bear on necessary knowledge (Brainerd, 1973, p.175, note 2). This is a startling admission on three counts. One is that the construction of necessary knowledge is taken in [1] to be one of the main problems that Piaget's theory addresses. A second is that although Brainerd denies that conservation embodies necessary knowledge, his denial is at variance with Piaget's (1967a, p.391) own statement of position, that the transition from pre-operational to concrete operational thought is a transition from a non-necessary to necessary knowledge. As Brainerd knows, conservation is a constitutive feature of concrete operations (Piaget, 1970/1983, p.110), a point which is elaborated in [16]. A third reason is that "nonconservation therefore indicates an effort to analyse and to dissociate variables" (Piaget, 1968, p.978). The attempt to dissociate empirical and necessary properties is a special case of this general difficulty. The upshot is that concrete operations has a necessary character, and that Piaget's theory addresses the question of how such understanding develops. By his own admission, Brainerd's views about diagnostic assessment are inapplicable to such matters.

Second, even when Brainerd's interpretation is accepted, his argument is fallacious. His interpretation is that diagnostic assessment is undertaken to detect the absence-*vs*-presence of a cognitive structure in relation to which linguistically mediated explanation is a dependent variable. That is, a structure is an independent variable whose presence is sufficient for such an explanation. Due to the inter-definability of conditionship relations, if A is sufficient for B, then B is necessary for A (Smith, 1987a; Wolfram, 1989). Thus to state that a structure is sufficient for an explanation is to state that the explanation is necessary for the structure. Yet Brainerd's (1973, p.177) claim is that an explanation is sufficient, and not necessary in this respect. This is a fallacious claim.

Third, Brainerd's argument depends on the claim that 'false positive' errors are not known to affect diagnostic procedures. This claim is suspect on two counts. One is that it is inductive. But inductive arguments are notoriously weak (H.I. Brown, 1988). The second reason is that Piagetian commentary has been in a state of turmoil over precisely this question (see Smith, 1992b for a review of the conflicting research on transitivity, class inclusion, and conservation).

Finally, Brainerd's position is open to the charge that it leads to a restricted research-programme. As Laudan (1977, p.80) noticed, a research-programme is a set of ontological and methodological "dos and don'ts". Brainerd's proposal implies that children's reasons are not directly relevant to their intellectual abilities. This is a substantive, and not a methodological, claim. It runs counter to Piaget's relational conception of knowing as reviewed in [8]. Further, research that is specifically directed on children's reasons actually requires the use of critical methods as it is only by its use that the connections can be made between an individual's current belief, the triggering reasons for that belief, and its eventual justification (Piéraut-Le Bonniec, 1990).

The purpose of this section was to review and comment on two objections to Piaget's use of a critical method. The main conclusions are twofold. One is that questions about the acceptability of this method are not exclusively methodological. Substantive issues are implicated as well. Thus objections to the use of such a method are circular, if substantive questions have been begged in advance. The second conclusion is that the specific character of the knowledge that is Piaget's main concern has been overlooked in the statement of these methodological objections. This oversight is implicit in the case of Braine's argument, and explicit in that of Brainerd's argument.

[13]   METHOD AND NECESSARY KNOWLEDGE

An empirically adequate account of the construction of necessary knowledge could not be exclusively reliant on children's judgments-alone. If this conceptual objection is accepted, research based on judgments-alone could have independent interest but could not be relevant to Piaget's main question in the absence of corroboration from studies in which children are required to justify their judgments (Smith, 1992b).

The first step is to state the objection. The discussion will centre on two dominant accounts in philosophical epistemology of the concept of knowledge. One is the foundationalist and the other is the causal account of knowledge. The objection is that both accounts lead to the same conclusion, that studies based on judgments-alone cannot be exclusively used by developmentalists who address questions about the construction of necessary knowledge.

[13.1] Foundationalist Account

The foundationalist account is the classical account of the nature of knowledge. Its sponsors include Plato (nd/1935, 201D) as well as contemporary philosophers (Ayer 1956, p. 35; Chisholm, 1977, p.102; Haack, 1990, p.199). According to this account, a person knows a proposition p if and only if three conditions are met: (i) p is true; (ii) the person believes p; and (iii) the person is justified in believing p. The explanatory value of this account can be gauged by consideration of three epistemic states which are used in the description of concrete operational knowledge (Piaget & Szeminska 1941/1952), namely false belief (level I), true belief (level II), and necessary knowledge (level III).

It was noted in [4.1] that questions about truth-value are distinct from questions about modality. To regard a correct (non-verbal) response as thereby a necessary response is both question-begging and questionable. In studies of concrete operations, Piaget & Szeminska (1941/1952) marked this distinction by invoking level II (empirically correct) responses as an intermediary between level I (incorrect) and level III (necessary) responses (Smith, 1982a; 1991). A rationale for this trichotomy is contained in Spinoza's discussion of proportionality. It is one thing to use a rule that routinely results in correct proportions; it is quite something else to use a rule that generates an answer which "had to be so, and could not happen otherwise" (Spinoza, 1660/1963, p.67; cf. Spinoza, 1670/1959, II, xl, n.2). It is widely accepted that propositions do differ as to their truth value both in normative discussions (Chisholm, 1977; Haack, 1990) as well as in Piagetian research where questions about children's correct/incorrect reasoning are central (Gelman & Baillargeon, 1983; Halford, 1989; Smith, 1992a).

The distinction between level II and level III is also accepted, as two propositions with the same truth value may differ as to their modality.

A necessarily true proposition is different from one that is possibly true. This difference is accepted both in philosophical discussions (Hughes & Cresswell, 1972; Kripke, 1980) and in Piagetian research (Murray, 1981, 1990; Piéraut-Le Bonniec, 1974/1980). Both normative distinctions are reflected in Piaget's structuralist works. However, although the former distinction has been well recognised in Piagetian commentary, the latter distinction has not been given equal attention. Such oversight is important. The key question to ask about a level III epistemic state concerns not just its truth value (is it correct?) but also its modality (is it necessary?). The importance of differentiating issues of correctness and modality is discussed again in [16].

With the distinction between truth value and modality in mind, consideration can now be given to the construal of the three epistemic states—false belief, true belief, and necessary knowledge—which the foundationalist account provides.

First, consider false belief. In studies of intellectual development, the importance of false belief is shown in the demarcation of incorrect and correct responses. Whereas the correct responses that children make can be interpreted as expressions of their true beliefs, their incorrect responses can be equally interpreted as expressions of their false beliefs. This is because belief, unlike knowledge, can take either truth value. That is, although beliefs can be either true or false, criterion (i) of the foundationalist account excludes there being cases of false knowledge. For example, if today is Thursday, then the proposition "today is Friday" is false, and so cannot describe what a person knows on any day other than a Friday. Although a person can think, or entertain the idea, or suppose that today is Friday, that person cannot know this, given that today is Thursday. Proponents of the foundationalist account would say: "Well, you might believe this but you don't know this" or "You think you know but you only believe this". In short, this account disqualifies false propositions as objects of knowledge. Since much research on intellectual development is concerned with charting the development of knowledge (Piaget, 1947/1950) or children's competence, i.e. correct understanding (Gelman & Baillargeon, 1983), this is a welcome consequence of the foundationalist account.

Second, consider the distinction between true belief and knowledge. This distinction is also a central feature of the foundationalist account and is marked by criterion (ii) which states that possession of a true belief is necessary for cases of knowledge. That is, the absence of true belief means the absence of knowledge. But a necessary condition is not a sufficient condition. Just because the absence of true belief means the absence of knowledge, it does not follow that the presence of true belief means the presence of knowledge. For example, if possession of a first degree is a necessary condition of the possession of a doctoral degree, then it follows that nongraduates do not have doctoral degrees, even though it does not follow that all graduates do have doctoral degrees. According to the foundationalist account, true belief is related to knowledge in this way, presumably because a true belief could be due to a guess, or intuition, or association of ideas, or based on an irrelevant strategy, and so on. Thus the true belief "Friday is the first day of the year 1993" is not a case of knowledge, if it is a guess. The foundationalist account captures this point by the requirement that knowledge is a true belief which is justified. Evidently, some such distinction, between true belief due to guessing and true belief that is based on justification, has been drawn by developmentalists in early (Piaget, 1926/1929) and more recent (Smedslund, 1969) discussions. The level II epistemic states of Piaget & Szeminska (1941/1952) can be classified as cases of true belief.

Third, the foundationalist account can be used in the identification of knowledge, which is defined as true, justified belief. Cases of necessary knowledge (level III) would be dependent on children's capacity to provide a relevant justification for their judgments with due attention to issues of modality. By its insistence on relevance and justification, the foundationalist account presupposes that a belief counts as knowledge only if it meets some standard of epistemic validity (Kitchener, 1987).

Two objections might arise here, one about the nature of level II responses and the other about their demarcation from level III responses. First, it might be objected that Piaget & Szeminska (1941/1952, p.13) provide cases of true belief which are taken by them to amount to knowledge. In consequence, the foundationalist account leads to inappropriate classification and so should be rejected. This objection raises an important question of exegesis, as Piagetian level II states are not homogeneous. Even so, this objection begs the question at issue. The issue here concerns the defining criteria of knowledge and, according to the foundationalist account, knowledge always requires justification. A strict consequence is that a true, unjustified belief never amounts to knowledge. Second, it might be objected that the foundationalist account provides grounds for contrasting true, unjustified belief and true, justified belief, which is knowledge. Yet the Piagetian position previously outlined was that true belief (level II) is different from necessary knowledge (level III). Thus the foundationalist account is based on one distinction (belief/knowledge), whereas the Piagetian position requires another distinction (empirical/necessary) to be drawn as well. This objection is well taken. In reply, it is suffficient to notice that the two distinctions are related in that the second presupposes the first. The second distinction concerns the subdivision of knowledge into empirical *vs* necessary knowledge. This distinction presupposes that knowledge can be distinguished from other epistemic states, of which true belief is one. Since the foundationalist objection is based on the first (belief/knowledge) distinction alone, consideration of the second (empirical/necessary) distinction can be postponed, pending its elaboration in discussion of the causal account.

If the conditions stated in the foundationalist account are jointly necessary and collectively sufficient, two consequences follow. First, all cases of knowledge are cases where these three conditions are satisfied. Second, the only cases of knowledge are cases where the three conditions are satisfied. One main problem in philosophical epistemology is to evaluate this account by checking on whether there are other conditions, whether necessary or sufficient, which have to be satisfied for a case to be a case of knowledge. This philosophical problem is difficult to resolve just because both consequences have been rejected. In turn, this means that the foundationalist account seems to merit either revision, because the three conditions are not sufficient, or replacement, because they are not necessary.

Revision: Sufficiency Conditions.   The claim that the three conditions are sufficient is the claim that all cases of knowledge are cases where a person has a true and justified belief. The counter-claim is that there are cases in which the three conditions are satisfied (the person has a true, justified belief) but which are not cases of knowledge (Gettier, 1963). The occurrence of even one counter-example is incompatible with the claim that the three conditions are sufficient, and Gettier has provided at least one counter-example where the conditions are satisfied due to accident and coincidence. Thus the philosophical question for those who wish to retain the foundationalist account in its strong version, namely that the three conditions are sufficient, is the search for an argument that shows how the 'Gettier objection' can be neutralised. Opinion is divided. One view is that the foundationalist account should be accepted as it stands, including the sceptical consequence which is the denial that there actually are cases of knowledge in ordinary life (Kirkham, 1984). A second view is that the foundationalist account can be repaired by the addition of further conditions that defeat the 'Gettier problem' (Chisholm, 1982).

This dispute can be noted and set aside for present purposes. This is because the parties to this dispute are concerned about the sufficiency but not the necessity of the three conditions. That is, the parties to this dispute agree both that the only cases of knowledge are cases where a person has a true justified belief, and that any case where a person does not have a true justified belief is not a case of knowledge. So construed, the foundationalist account of the concept of knowledge is incompatible with the view that, for assessment purposes, it is not necessary that children should justify their judgments. The argument is that the person who has knowledge would, if requested, always be able to justify a true belief, not that anyone actually does justify all true beliefs. But by failing to make such a request in research on the development of children's knowledge, there is no way of discriminating cases where a justification is present from cases where it is absent. Further, the foundationalist account requires that a justification should be valid by providing objective epistemic support for a true belief. A rationalisation or a subjective justification which the person happens to have are inadequate. Thus the view that children's judgments-alone are sufficient for the attribution of knowledge is incompatible with the foundationalist account. By contrast, the foundationalist account is compatible with the view that a child is required to provide a justification for an expressed judgment.

In short, the present argument from the foundationalist account has the consequence that no intellectual state could be assessed as a case of knowledge through exclusive reliance on children's judgments-alone.

Replacement: Necessity Conditions.   The necessity of the conditions stated in the foundationalist account has also been challenged. Such a challenge is fundamental just because foundationalists see their task as that of providing more stringent conditions, over and above those contained in the classical account. Doubting whether this task will ever be successfully completed, some philosophers have stated an alternative causal account. Effectively, a challenge to the necessity of the three conditions is the rejection of the foundationalist account.

[13.2] Causal Account

The starting point of the causal account is a commitment to provide an account that has a better descriptive adequacy than the foundationalist account, manifested in a capacity to be in accord with the psychology of human cognition. The argument is that normative questions in epistemology are concerned with idealised rationality (Cherniak, 1986) and, as such, are concerned with what human rationality ought to be like. Using the Kantian principle that 'ought implies can', the argument is that normative questions cannot be answered independently of what human rationality is in fact like (Kornblith, 1985). This argument can be adopted in either of two forms. In its restricted form, the focus of empirical study will be human knowledge. In its general form, the focus will shift to cover all forms of knowledge, including the biological origins of human knowledge at the evolutionary level and its emergence in the human mind from lower forms of animal life (Radnitzky & Bartley, 1987). Significantly, Piaget's (1967/1971) genetic epistemology makes a similar commitment. Although some developmentalists notice that Piaget's genetic epistemology provides a constructivist rather than a neo-Darwinian model of development (Gillièron, 1987), it is evident that evolutionary and genetic epistemology are similar because of the common concern with descriptive adequacy. A central assumption of naturalised (empirical, genetic) epistemology is (Maffie, 1990, p. 282) that "to construct the best possible theory of knowledge, it is incumbent upon it to make use of the best theories available". This is an important admission, because the causal account is one manifestation of naturalised epistemology. The implication is that the causal account could be preferred because of its empirical backing. Such backing would be important on condition that there is agreement among psychologists as to which methods and which theories are the appropriate ones to use in gaining an acceptable psychology of human cognition. Yet as Maffie (1990, p.290) also remarks, there are areas of potential weakness in naturalised epistemology due to the presence of disputes as to which scientific disciplines, theories, and methods may be legitimately employed.

In short, there is a *prima facie* case that an account of knowledge in terms of its causal origins could be explanatory of the procedures used in diagnostic assessment of children's knowledge on Piagetian tasks. However, a prior condition is that the causal account cannot be used to settle differences between different, empirical theories of intellectual development.

Using Goldman's account as a reference point, the aim in this part of the discussion is to characterise the conditions which show when a person's belief counts as knowledge. There is an explicit denial both that a person should be able to justify a judgment as a condition of its acquisition, possession, or display, and even that there should be such a justification at that person's disposal (Goldman, 1979, p.2). Rather, a judgment is justifiably accepted by virtue of its causal ancestry. That is, proponents of the causal account deny that justification is a necessary condition of knowledge, i.e. they deny condition (iii) of the foundationalist account. From their perspective, it is quite possible for someone to hold a belief, which is not justified by that person, provided that belief has an acceptable causal formation in that person's mind. Goldman's task, then, is to specify more exactly the commitments that are embodied in the intuition that knowledge has a causal origin.

His proposal is that at least two conditions should be met: first that the judgment should be the outcome of reliable cognitive processes and, second, that there should be no other cognitive processes which would have resulted in that person not forming that judgment (Goldman, 1979, p.20). It is clear that Goldman's proposal does have some purchase on adult (developed) cognition. Indeed, both common sense and cognitive psychology are viewed as a resource for the articulation of a more finegrained description of correct and incorrect human intellectual functioning (Goldman, 1978). In short, developmentalists could claim that the causal account is better suited to their purpose. They could concede that it may be desirable, in certain circumstances, to invite children to justify their judgments when performing Piagetian tasks. Yet they could still deny that this is necessary in the sense that justifications must be provided in all cases as a condition of the acquisition or possession of knowledge. Using the terminology of belief which Goldman prefers, the developmental sequence is stated to be a transition from false belief (level I), to true belief (level II), leading to necessary belief (level III).

The causal account is open to objection in its application to the diagnostic assessment of children's intellectual development. The causal account is stated to be congruent with the psychology of human cognition. It follows that the causal account cannot be used, without circularity, to settle disputes within the psychology of human cognition. Yet the dispute over judgments and justifications as 'response criteria' is a dispute within psychology, since the parties to this dispute do make psychological commitments. This objection will now be elaborated with reference to the differentiation of necessary belief (level III), and true belief (level II), and the latter from false belief (level I).

In the first place, the objection might be that the causal account is too weak because it is insensitive to the distinction between false (level I) and true (level II) belief. This supposition could arise from the admission, which is made by Goldman (1979), that all beliefs, including false beliefs, have a causal origin. This seems to be an embarrassing admission, one that obliterates the distinction between level I and level II beliefs. The suggestion is that the causal account treats true beliefs in the same way as false beliefs, in that each has a causal origin. The implication is that the distinction between children's incorrect and correct responses would collapse, if the causal account is retained. To see why this is not a valid objection to the causal account, consider a case where a false belief may have an acceptable origin. Suppose two flocks of birds pass overhead. In estimating their size, the judgment might be "50", when there are in fact 50 birds in the first flock. This true belief would have an acceptable causal origin, if there was insufficient time to count all the birds in the flock and a correct estimate, which reflected previous successful experience in quantifying the size of flocks of birds, was made. In estimating the size of the second flock, the judgment might be "The same—50", when there are in fact 49 birds in that flock. Even though this second belief is false, it has a similar causal origin. Further, it has the added advantage of being based on a transitive inference. According to the causal account, the formation of any belief is acceptable, provided that it arises in accordance with the conditions that the causal account sets out. Thus both judgments have an identifiable causal origin and there were no other processes that could have been used to generate a correct judgment; the conditions of the causal account seem to have been satisfied in both cases, each of which would amount to cases of knowledge. Yet in the first case the judgment was correct, whereas in the latter it was incorrect.

It is important to see what is at issue: the conceptual question as to whether both, one, or none of these two cases amounts to knowledge. This issue can be resolved either by recourse to intuition or by reference to an account that provides defining criteria of knowledge. According to the foundationalist account, the case where an incorrect judgment is made about the size is not a case of knowledge as only truths may be known. By contrast, the causal account does not seem to exclude such a possibility, as its conditions may be satisfied even in cases where false judgments are made.

This interesting epistemological question will not be pursued because such cases do not arise in research on intellectual development. In such research, the tasks are usually well-structured, closed tasks with processes and procedures whose successful use allows children to display correct responses. In a simple case, the tasks are designed so that children who use one intellectual process will make incorrect judgments, whereas children who use a different process will make correct judgments. Although the beliefs of the former children will have an identifiable origin, there are other processes that they could have used to make the latter (correct) response. In developmental tasks, there usually are alternatives because the tasks are designed precisely to differentiate false belief (level I) from true belief (level II). For example, in conservation of number tasks, a level I belief may have an origin in terms of the perceptual salience of the transformed array. But this false belief would have been different if all of the information in the array had been used. Thus Goldman's second condition would not have been met, as there were processes that could have been used to override both the formation and display of false belief.

Thus in the context of research on children's intellectual development, the causal account is sensitive to the difference between false and true belief. Moreover, Goldman's strategy of securing an account of knowledge which is congruent with the psychology of cognition is also secure. A central aim in research on intellectual development is to provide a better description of the conditions and processes leading to children's understanding and misunderstanding. Such descriptions could be added to the stock of common sense processes such as (Goldman, 1979, p.9) "confused reasoning, wishful thinking, reliance on emotional attachment, mere hunch, guesswork, and hasty generalisation" or to cognitive models of memory and reasoning (Goldman, 1978).

In the second place, the objection might be that the causal account is too weak because it is insensitive to the distinction between true (level II) and necessary (level III) belief. A level II belief is a true belief whose formation is due to the available information. A contingent process could be causally responsible for the formation of such knowledge. By contrast, a level III belief requires some understanding of necessity. But necessary knowledge could not, in principle, be the causal outcome of a solely contingent process of formation. The contingency could be false, unlike necessary knowledge which is atemporally true. Quite simply, the causal account could not be explanatory of the formation of necessity and, in that sense, is insensitive to the distinction between true (level II) and necessary, (level III) belief.

The reason why the causal account obliterates this distinction is apparent in the dispute between Hume and Kant, and was noted in [3.1]. The distinction between an empirically true belief and a necessary belief cannot be drawn solely on the basis of observable facts in the physical or social world. Whereas a level II belief can have a causal origin, owing its formation to past contingencies in the physical domain, a level III belief which is necessary is not solely based on its causal formation. From the fact that something is the case, it does not follow that it must be the case. Similarly, although the social world in which children develop may contribute to the transmission of true (level II) beliefs, necessary (level III) beliefs do not have their basis in social experience. Even if there is social agreement that something is the case, it does not follow that it must be. Further, obligation is one species of necessity (von Wright, 1951), and Piaget (1932/1932) is aware that parallel problems arise about the formation of necessity in both moral and intellectual domains. The same problem recurs (Wright, 1982), because an action charged with obligation is fundamentally different from an action that is merely in conformity with some rule of obligation. It is no doubt for this reason that Piaget (1977a, p.90) has a unitary conception of logic and logical necessity (see [25.2]) whose specific manifestations are physical, individual, and social. Thus the causal account is insensitive to the fundamental difference between empirical and necessary truth.

The distinction between truth-value and modality has a special application to mathematical truths, notably in Frege's (1888/1980, para. 78) rejection of Mill's claim that mathematical truths are completely definable in empirical terms by reference to observable facts. Frege's denial that a number can be defined in this way is supported by the rhetorical question as to which facts are asserted in the definition of the number 77864. The implication is that this question is empirically unanswerable as there is no set of facts that provides the necessary and sufficient conditions of this number. Again, Frege raised the question as to which observations have to be carried out for someone to state that $1000000 = 999999 + 1$, or which facts have to be observed in the definition of the number 0. Frege's conclusion is that mathematical truths are necessary truths, and so their definition could never be stated in physical terms, which are never necessary in this sense.

Piaget's position has its origins in Russell's (1919) re-working of Frege's theory of number. Three key notions in Russell's account are those of inclusion, transitivity, and conservation or truth-preservation in mathematical inference (Smith, 1986a). In Piaget's account, each of these is given a genetic analysis in which necessity of understanding, and not merely correctness in understanding, is asserted to be important. It is for this reason that Piaget & Szeminska (1941/1952, p.184) state that "number is the fusion of class and asymmetrical relation into a single operational whole". This is because it is not merely a brute fact that number is invariant to spatial transformation; rather, this is a necessary truth (cf. Murray, 1990). It is not merely correct that two elements which are equal to the same are equal to each other; rather, this is necessarily so (cf. Campbell & Bickhard, 1986; Smith, 1987a). It is not merely the case that the membership of a superordinate class which includes two nonempty subordinate classes is greater than that of one of its subordinate classes; rather, this has to be the case (Cormier & Dagenais, 1983; Smith, 1982a).

The distinction between truth-value and modality has been used by Piaget from his earliest studies. Thus Piaget (1924/1928, pp.26, 56) contrasted the ability to provide a valid, logical justification with the ability to provide a causal, or psychological, justification, which may be invalid. Their nondifferentiation was taken to result in contradictory thinking (Piaget, 1924/1928, p. 254), a corrective to which is reasoning based on necessity, when logical consequences are derived from relevant premises (Piaget, 1924/1928, p.1). Piaget maintained the distinction in more recent discussions, such as his contention (1967/1971, p. 269) that "general and necessary categories such as causality are never found in ready made form, especially not at initial stages". This is because any such category "goes far beyond observation or the merely inductive and experimental regularity which arises from probability or factual determinism but not from intrinsic necessity" (Piaget, 1967/1971, p.424/*306). On this view, observable knowledge arising from experience is fundamentally different from its coordination in necessary knowledge (Piaget, 1975/1985, p.8). This is because necessary knowledge transcends the limits of observable knowledge, whether physical or social (Piaget, 1970/1983).

The relevance of this argument to the dispute about whether children should be required to justify their judgments is that, following Goldman (1978) and Maffie (1990), the causal account should be congruent with the psychology of human cognition. Yet there is a family of disputes, over which developmentalists are currently divided. One is methodological, concerning the status of judgments and justifications as 'response criteria' in diagnostic assessment. A second dispute is substantive, concerning correct understanding and the understanding of necessity in operational knowledge. This dispute is reviewed in [16]. A third dispute is also substantive, concerning the extent of young children's developing understanding. It turns out that many of the developmentalists who regard judgments-alone as good 'response criteria' also claim that young children are not as intellectually incompetent as Piaget's theory is taken by them to suppose (Brainerd, 1978; Donaldson et al., 1983; Gelman, 1978). This is one position about intellectual development, but not the only one on offer. Other developmentalists, who take justifications to be constitutive features of good 'response criteria', contend that the valid justification for a judgment is itself a logical competence, one whose use is essential to the formation of certain forms of reasoning (Chapman, 1987; Chapman & Lindenberger, 1988; Piéraut-Le Bonniec, 1990). This latter position is substantively, and not merely methodologically, different from the former position. In short, there are both methodological and substantive differences within the psychology of human cognition. It would be question-begging to invoke the causal account of knowledge to settle these differences.

[13.3] Commentary

The conclusion to draw from [13.1–13.2] is that in philosophical epistemology there are two currently dominant accounts as to the nature of knowledge. Both accounts attempt to formulate conditions that can be used to classify cases of knowledge and other intellectual states. No attempt has been made to support one of these accounts to the exclusion of the other. Rather, both accounts have been examined so that their consequences for the assessment of children's intellectual development can be gauged. The specific issue concerns the implications of each account for the selection of reasonable 'response criteria' in intellectual assessment.

The view that an adequate account of the construction of *any* knowledge can be based exclusively on studies where children's judgments-alone are the 'response criteria' is incompatible with the foundationalist account. The causal account leads to a limitation on this same view which could never deal with the construction of *necessary* knowledge. In short, research that is directed on Piaget's main problem, noted in [1], could not be based on this view. By contrast, developmentalists who require children to justify their judgments are able to meet the requirements of both philosophical accounts.

Six critical responses to this conclusion are now briefly surveyed:

(i) It could be objected that the conclusion is empirically irrelevant, as it is a nice example of pointless philosophical disputation. Developmentalists should base their case on the available evidence, including evidence that has been gained, where appropriate, by reference to judgments-alone.

This objection is simply misconceived. The question at issue is not the extent of the evidence but rather the nature of that for which it is evidence. A criterial question concerns the conditions for description of cases. If evidence is gained in the documentation of a case, the question to ask is "a case of what?" Although the criteria of many notions are straightforward, philosophical accounts are needed to resolve disputes with problematic criteria. The concept of knowledge is problematic in just this sense. Significantly, explicit consideration of philosophical accounts permits rational decisions to be made about what sort of evidence is—and what sort of evidence is not—adequate in specific cases. Currently, there are two main accounts of the criteria of knowledge and both have been discussed.

(ii) The converse objection could be stated, that the conclusion is not philosophical enough, as there are other accounts of knowledge. It follows that the main conclusions of the present discussion are provisional and even inconclusive.

This objection is well taken. However, until some new (third) account has been presented, together with its implications for the selection of 'response criteria', this objection is merely noted. Its strength cannot be decided a priori, in advance of the specification of that (third) account.

(iii) It could be objected that it is in practice difficult to assess the understanding of young children, when their underdeveloped linguistic abilities mask underlying intellectual mastery.

This objection begs the question, if a prior psychological commitment is made to the position that young children do have intellectual competence which has an incomplete linguistic expression. The point to notice is that the psychological question has already been begged, unless independent support for this preferred position has been given. Crucially, there is a rival position to consider here, namely that the ability to justify a judgment is itself an intellectual, rather than a linguistic, ability. The basic intuition behind this latter position concerns the necessary connection that links a derived conclusion with its implying premises. If that conclusion embodies not merely a true proposition, but also one that is deduced from relevant premises, the individual who has made that deduction should be able to express this connection in some appropriate way. The dispute over adequate 'response criteria' is as much substantive as methodological. This dispute should not be settled in favour of one party by appeal to the merely practical difficulties arising from the position of the rival party.

(iv) It could be objected that Piaget has given different answers to his 'fundamental problem' which is the construction of necessity. In his structuralist works, the claim was made that the understanding of necessity is the hallmark of operational understanding which is manifest in middle to late childhood (Piaget & Inhelder, 1966/1969). In his constructivist works, by contrast, the claim is that very young children have some understanding of necessity, well before the onset of operational understanding (Piaget, 1977/1986; Piaget & Garcia, 1987/1991).

The first point to make in reply is that this objection raises an important issue. The objection makes the valid point that, in some recent writings, an understanding of necessity is attributed to very young children. However, the issue is not clear-cut, as in other recent studies, an understanding of necessity is confined to adolescents (Karmiloff-Smith, 1991, pp.123–124). Even though this question is important, the internal coherence of Piaget's position will have to remain unresolved at this point in the discussion, which takes a neutral stance on the timing of the initial acquisition of modal understanding. This is because, secondly, the key issue here concerns the status of justifications as 'response criteria'. On this point, there is a unity to Piaget's position. In Piaget's recent accounts, interest still centres on the justifications of very young children with attention to their understanding of aspects of necessity. In fact, in both early (Piaget, 1924/1928, p. 35) and recent (Piaget & Garcia, 1987/1991, p. 59) studies the justified judgments of children aged 3 years are given. Thus Piagetian studies are uniform in this respect, namely in requiring children to justify their judgments.

(v) It could be objected that not all knowledge requires justification. Adapting the distinction due to Ryle (1949), knowing-how is different from knowing-that. This is because (Ryle, 1949, p.30) people can "intelligently perform some sort of operations when they are not yet able to consider any propositions enjoining how they should be performed". The suggestion is that adults have knowledge which they do not, and cannot, justify, and this knowledge is shown in their activity. If this is true of adults, it would certainly hold good for children. Thus knowledge can be possessed even in the absence of its justification. Even in infancy, similar cases are easy to find, including means-end behaviour, intentional activity, and inferential search. Further, these cases embody some practical understanding of necessity, where justification is not required for practical success. In the task used by Fabricius, Sophian, and Wellman (1987; cf. Wellman, Cross, & Bartsch, 1986), young children were invited to search the doors of model houses to ascertain, on the basis of confirmatory inferences, whether a house matched a description that specified its number and type of occupant.

This objection is valid. There are, however, two reasons why its force is limited. One reason is that a distinction should be drawn between practical intelligence and its representation (Piaget, 1974/1978). This distinction turns, not on whether there are intellectual processes that underpin the mastery of skilled performances, but rather on which intellectual processes underpin their conceptualised knowledge (Piaget, 1974/1977). Although Piagetian tasks almost invariably make displays of practical knowledge possible, the tasks relevant to the construction of operational knowledge are also reliant on the formation of representational knowledge. But then the question to ask concerns the content of that representational knowledge, and the extent to which it embodies not just a correct understanding but also the specifically modal features of that understanding. The second reason is that there is a distinction to draw between the successful display of practical knowledge and an understanding of why that knowledge is the successful display that it is (Chapman, 1991; Pinard, 1986). In Piaget's (1937/1954; 1974/1977) accounts, all actions have an unconscious component with development occurring as a progressive realisation in consciousness (Smith, 1981). Indeed, a standard issue that developmentalists confront arises from the demarcation of these two distinct forms of knowledge, namely how representational knowledge develops from the practical knowledge that precedes it (Karmiloff-Smith & Inhelder, 1975).

(vi) It could be objected that justification is not necessary, provided appropriate methodological controls have been taken. Indeed, it is claimed (Karmiloff-Smith, 1986, p.86; her emphasis) that linguistic development does not require that (young) children should have "*consciously accessible, verbally statable explanations*" . In a review of metacognition, Brown, Bransford, Ferrara, & Campione (1983) contend that this polymorphous notion embodies at least two meanings, one based on the consciousness of cognition and the other on the regulation of cognition. Crucially, their suggestion is that these two meanings are independent, and so a metacognitive process could be subject to regulation but not available for conscious inspection. Again, accounts of the development of abstraction and reasoning contrast the implicit knowledge that is acquired during the earlier phases of development with explicit knowledge which is confined to later phases (Campbell & Bickhard, 1986; Moshman, 1990). Finally, developmentalists have shown an interest in the modal understanding of children during the early years of schooling (Markman, 1978; Miller, 1986; Russell, 1983; Sophian & Somerville, 1988). Provided the task has been designed appropriately, with due attention to proper experimental controls, it is permissible—so this objection runs—to use children's judgments, in the absence of justifications, as expressions of their necessary knowledge.

The short reply to this objection is that, yes, methodological norms are important in empirical research—in fact, as important as other relevant norms. But epistemic norms are also relevant norms to invoke in Piagetian research, which is directed on the construction of necessary knowledge. Norms include criteria of adequacy, with distinct norms providing distinct criteria of adequacy. It follows that evidence which is accepted as adequate by reference to methodological norms will not thereby be equally adequate in relation to epistemic norms. Further, evidence that is accepted to be adequate by reference to an epistemic norm concerning truth value will not thereby be equally adequate in relation to an epistemic norm concerning modality. Epistemic norms are especially important in relation to the adequacy of evidence about the acquisition of necessary knowledge.

There is a distinction to draw between the acquisition and possession of knowledge. One main aim in Piagetian research is to chart the successive acquisition of different forms of knowledge. It is, however, worth noticing that philosophical accounts of knowledge are primarily accounts of the possession of knowledge. This difference is important, first, because the conditions that must be satisfied for the possession of knowledge will have equal applicability to the acquisition of knowledge. This difference is also important because there may be other conditions—besides the conditions related to possession—which also have to be satisfied when questions about acquisition arise. For convenience, assume that developmental progression can be mapped on to a line such that spatial progression along the line indicates progression in the development of knowledge. The line has a numerical scale such that, for any point n on that scale, a lower point $(n\text{-}1, n\text{-}2, \ldots)$

represents less advanced, whereas a higher point ($n+1$, $n+2$, ...) represents more advanced, knowledge in the developmental sequence. A typical question that developmentalists address concerns the point on such a line which marks the initial onset of some specified knowledge. If there is independent evidence that an individual has knowledge K to level n, and if that evidence is adequate in relation to all relevant norms (both methodological and epistemic), then it is reasonable to use judgments-alone as 'response criteria' in empirical investigation that is directed on the possession of that knowledge K at that level n and beyond, including its display in relation to experimentally controlled conditions. *Ex hypothesi*, there is independent and adequate evidence that the specified knowledge is possessed. According to the foundationalist account, justification is not required as a condition of the possession of knowledge. Rather, that account requires that justification must always be available for inspection at reasonable request. Thus research that is reliant on methodological controls to elicit children's judgments-alone is compatible with a commitment to the foundationalist account, if there is prior agreement that a specified level of knowledge is possessed. The presumption is that such justifications could have been invoked by the children, even though they were in fact bypassed. Further, adoption of the causal account leads to the same conclusion. If the specified knowledge has been antecedently acquired, then, *ex hypothesi*, the conditions of the causal account must have been satisfied. It would be reasonable, on methodological grounds, to bypass children's justifications and concentrate on their judgments, for example by investigation of the causal conditions for the production of that knowledge.

Yet much developmental research is concerned with the initial acquisition of knowledge. In such cases, different theoretically based predictions may abound with dispute arising about the extent to which there is evidence that knowledge K at level n is possessed. In the presence of such theoretical disputes, it is important that there is normatively adequate evidence about the acquisition of the specified knowledge. The argument presented here is that the implications of the two philosophical accounts are clear. It follows that it is not enough that an individual can make a reliable sequence of responses under controlled conditions. Lacking independent evidence about the possession of necessary knowledge, adequate evidence about its acquisition would have to be such that the individual under investigation could distinguish truth from necessity. Failure to make this explicit is a reason for denying the validity of any claim that the epistemic acquisition by that individual was, in fact, necessary knowledge.

The distinction between reliability and validity is well known in psychometric discussions (cf. Sternberg, 1985). This distinction has equal applicability to Piagetian research. Although methodological norms have an obvious role to play in ensuring that studies are reliable, epistemic norms have an analogous role to play when questions of validity arise. Developmental tasks that are designed to be adequate may not in fact make similar demands with consequential implications for their validity. Reviews of Piagetian research are testimony to such disputes (Gelman & Baillargeon, 1983; Halford, 1989; Smith, 1992a). Even so, consideration about the epistemic adequacy of the tasks used in such studies—especially in relation to norms of modality—is quite rare [16]. This oversight is compounded by a pervasive commitment to the view that judgments-alone are adequate 'response criteria'.

In short, knowledge is knowledge, even when it is qualified as 'procedural', 'implicit', or 'self-regulated metacognitive' knowledge. The argument here is that the acceptability of such attributions is dependent on their adequacy in relation to relevant epistemic norms which lay down the defining criteria of knowledge. This argument is not a denial that some form of modal understanding may be acquired during the early phases of intellectual development. On the contrary: it was noted in reply to objection (iv) that the early acquisition of modal understanding has been investigated in the Genevan studies. Rather, the argument is that, in the absence of independent evidence, any study that states such a position will have to require children to justify their judgments. Research into children's intellectual development based on children's judgments-alone can legitimately be undertaken. Such research can address its own stock of questions and make use of methods that are acceptable to those who subscribe to its conventions. Such research should not, however, be used solely in Piagetian research when central questions are begged. Even if a genetic epistemology is an empirical epistemology, it does not follow that conceptual (non-empirical) questions are of little relevance. On the contrary, the assessment of Piaget's account is, and has to be, concerned with conceptual issues. Further, conceptual assessment does not require a commitment to Piaget's position, as a range of critical responses, including elaboration (Kitchener, 1986; Overton, 1990), reinterpretation (Chapman, 1988; Smith, 1991) and revision (Bickhard & Campbell, 1989; Campbell & Bickhard, 1986) have recently been displayed.

CHAPTER FOUR

Procedures

[Psychologists had over-generalised their] *"methods and arrived at delightful trivialities, all the more so since an army of scientists translated their results into mathematical terms. This made possible the demonstration of the most simple and natural results—and only those, mind you—through a complicated apparatus of curves and calculations"* (Piaget, 1918, p.63).

[14] PROCEDURAL CHANGES

When replications of Piagetian findings were initially reported, the studies embodied minor changes in the tasks (Elkind, 1961; Lovell, Mitchell, & Everett, 1962). But others expressed an interest in making procedural changes more systematically. Following the example set by Bruner et al. (1966), the sequel showed that Piagetian tasks could be changed in a multitude of ways. In consequence, a diverse set of altern- ative accounts is available for the interpretation of their findings. These alternatives have been reviewed in several places in relation to infancy (Harris, 1983), childhood (Gelman & Baillargeon, 1983; Halford, 1989) and adolescence (Braine & Rumain, 1983; Demetriou & Efklides, 1988).

Studies of children's thinking are illustrative of two arguments which are invoked for making procedural changes in Piagetian studies. One argument concerns evidence. It was noticed in [3] that Piaget did accord importance to the evidential basis of any account of the construction of knowledge. The first objection is that Piaget's own studies were insufficiently sensitive to the full range of variables that could be expected to influence intellectual development (Bryant, 1974; Donaldson et al., 1983; Gelman & Baillargeon, 1983). An early formulation of this objection is due to Braine (1959, p.16): "in designing his experiments, Piaget fails to eliminate important variables which are not involved in the definition of the processes he set out to investigate". Behind this objection is the assumption that Piaget's studies were designed to be experimental but that they were lacking in experimental rigour.

A second argument concerns developmental explanations. Piaget (1975/1985, p.147) did aspire to present an explanatory account of the construction of knowledge. But, so the argument runs, two sorts of study are necessary for the causal explanation of intellectual development. Intervention (experimental) studies are necessary to identify a possible mechanism of intellectual change by the exclusion of alternative variables. Longitudinal studies are also necessary to show that the hypothesised mechanism is the actual mechanism at work in real cases (Kuhn, 1974; Bryant, 1985). Developmentalists generally have undertaken few longitudinal studies (Nesselroade & Baltes, 1979; de Ribaupierre, 1989). However, Piaget's studies would have the distinguishing feature that they meet neither criterion. Thus causal explanation is precluded through the insensivity of Piaget's methodological stance.

Both arguments make the assumption that adequate evidence about intellectual development is dependent on experimental study. The requirement is methodological, namely that an adequate account of intellectual development should be based on evidence that can withstand *experimental* scrutiny. The charge is that Piaget's studies failed to meet this requirement. In consequence, many developmentalists have designed their studies with the specific aim of remedying what they take to be the omission in Piaget's work. Four features of this approach can be noticed. One is that Piagetian tasks, as originally designed, are accepted to be reliable (Gelman & Baillargeon, 1983, p.168). A second is that, even so, such tasks are designed in multiple ways which are shown in the serial changes to the procedures concerning their administration (Sugarman, 1987). A third feature is that these procedural differences typically result in variation in the demands of the tasks, which are successfully completed by children at different ages (Chapman, 1988, p.341). A fourth feature of this approach is the challenge for an interpretation of the differences. Piaget's tasks (Bryant, 1989, p.369) "were not designed to exclude alternative interpretations and it was usually the case that the plentiful mistakes that children made in his studies could be explained in more than one way".

Since Braine's seminal paper contains a concise statement of many of the key points that have been accepted in subsequent studies, it will be convenient to focus on those aspects of his paper that relate to current discussions of this issue.

[15] EXPERIMENTAL STUDIES

In this section, four issues are discussed: (i) responses and reasoning; (ii) experiments; (iii) causal explanation; and (iv) age-norms. It will be shown that although methodological questions are relevant to each issue, dispute centres principally on substantive matters.

(i) *Responses and reasoning.* In many experimental studies of transitivity, developmentalists have either followed Braine's (1959, p.7) example in trying to eliminate linguistic responses completely (cf. Chalmers & McGonigle, 1984) or have severely minimised them, for the reasons discussed in [12], by focusing instead on children's judgments (cf. Pears & Bryant, 1990). Either way, the objection discussed in [13] applies with equal force, where it was argued that children's justifications must be used in studies that seek to gain evidence for the initial acquisition of necessary knowledge. Methodological concerns are important but they do not have exclusive, still less major, importance, especially when substantive questions are unresolved.

(ii) *Experiments.* Piaget's studies are interpreted to be 'experiments' (Braine, 1959; Bryant, 1974). This is a natural interpretation of his position, because Piaget has often (Piaget & Szeminska, 1941/1952, p.123), though not always (Piaget & Szeminska, 1941/1952, p.17/*4), used this same term. Following from this interpretation is the charge that such studies are insufficiently experimental and so are incomplete. This charge is, however, ambiguous.

Piaget's approach is *not* experimental in the sense that it is directed towards causal explanation through the specification of an antecedently operating network of causal forces. Consider this statement (Piaget & Szeminska, 1941/1952, p.193/149, my emphasis):

in each task there intervenes a host of heterogeneous factors, such as the words used, the length of the instructions, the extent to which the task is concrete, its relations with the individual experience of the subject, the number of objects involved, the intervention of learned, numbering abilities, and so on ... (in such matters) *we confess to having no interest at all.*

This is a list of independent variables that are open to experimental control and, indeed, are so controlled in many studies. Such control would require the use of a standardised procedure. Piaget denies that his method is experimental in this sense. In his view, we have insufficient understanding of children's thinking whose specific identification and categorisation, and not merely its causation, are unclear. There has to be prior agreement about the identifying features of the phenomena under investigation as a pre-condition of explanation. The identification and classification of necessary knowledge is unclear in just this sense.

In a forensic sense, however, Piaget's approach *is* experimental. Questioning is undertaken in a criminal trial so as to identify the full set of facts which can then be related to an appropriate (normative) law (Smith, 1986a). A person's death may be natural, accidental, justifiable, or culpable and so questions about the guilt of a defendant can only be answered if there is prior agreement with respect to the (normative) criteria that serve in their demarcation. The role of questioning in a criminal trial is to ascertain which of these legal norms fits the facts. One issue is to establish what a specified witness takes to be the facts and, second, to test the durability of that description. In turn, the requirement is that a witness should maintain a *consistent* description of what happened through the persistent posing of rival hypotheses as to why the death took place. If a witness claims that the events were so-and-so but under cross-examination claims they were such-and-such, it is legitimate to ask whether the two claims are compatible. The obvious way to check is to find out which claims the witness retains through questioning about alternative hypotheses as to what exactly took place. It is in this sense that the critical method is experimental. The method should clarify both how an individual understands the questions that are contextualised in some task, and the extent to which that understanding remains self-consistent through the questioning.

The suggestion is, then, that Piaget did not in fact carry out experimental studies for purposes of causal explanation. As Droz & Volken (1991, p.66) put it: "what undoubtedly excited Piaget the most in his psychogenetic investigations was the discovery of 'the unexpected'. 'Hypothesis-testing' was to be a procedure whose existence he scarcely knew". This is an arresting comment. It supports the proposed interpretation that Piaget's studies were not intended to be experiments in the traditional sense. But it also implies that Piaget's practice was at variance with the standards appropriate to empirical research. That is, although in fact he did not engage in hypothesis-testing, he *should* have done so. But this is a different objection. What are the grounds on which this prescription rests?

Hypothesis-testing based on studies that control for the operation of independent variables is a standard way in which to carry out scientific research, but it is neither necessary nor sufficient for progress to be manifest in scientific theories. It is not necessary because Einstein's theory was formulated when all available evidence, and *a fortiori* evidence arising from experimental studies, was incompatible with it. It is not sufficient, because phlogiston theory does not count as a contribution to science despite the plethora of experimental studies that were undertaken to test it. The general point is that no method confers success by its mere use. Thus not all studies have to be concerned with hypothesis-testing. Such a stance is reasonable on three counts. First, hypothesis-testing could not occur in exploratory studies where there is, in advance, no way of formulating reasonable hypotheses. If exploratory studies were standardised, they would embody a design-fault for a reason which Piaget anticipated in reference to the refusal to incorporate *ne varietur* (let there be no change) procedures in his studies. Such standardisation presupposes "that we know in advance what we want to get from the child and that we believe we are capable of interpreting the obtained responses" (Piaget & Inhelder, 1961/1968, p.xii). Second, proper description is a pre-condition of causal explanation and so the primary aim is to identify and classify phenomena that may only later be explained. There is a case for maintaining that accounts of intellectual development should still focus on this primary aim. Evidently Piaget did not regard his several descriptions of intellectual construction as fully adequate despite his own taxonomic interests (Piaget, 1976a; cf. Chapman, 1988, p.181). Further, primacy continues to be given to adequate description over premature explanation (Sugarman, 1987). Third, the issue that separates developmentalists is not just the methodological value to be placed on different methods and approaches but also a substantive difference about the adequacy of available descriptions of intellectual development. Such differences are fundamental and important (Gould, 1989, p.98):

> Taxonomy (the science of classification) is often undervalued as a glorified form of filing ... but taxonomy is a fundamental and dynamic science, dedicated to exploring the causes of relationships and similarities among organisms. Classifications are theories about the basis of natural order, not dull catalogues compiled only to avoid chaos.

If this claim is valid for evolutionary theory, it has at least equal force in relation to developmental theory. Yet there are different descriptions of intellectual development which are reviewed in several places (Beilin, 1989; Demetriou & Efklides, 1988; Gelman & Baillargeon, 1983;

Halford, 1989). Many of these descriptions are substantively, and not just methodologically, different. The point of this difference often appears to be lost in the assessment of Piaget's work. Although any taxonomic proposal can be wrong, this could not be due merely to differences in methodology.

(iii) *Causal explanation*. The assumption is made that causal explanation is not merely desirable but that the causation must be of a certain type, namely explanation through efficient causality. Clearly, questions about the acceptability of a form of explanation are highly general. It will be shown , however, that such questions relate directly to very specific differences arising from experimental studies.

First, teleological explanation through final causality is a neglected but valid form of explanation (von Wright, 1971). Piaget is committed to some form of teleological, or teleonomic, explanation (Kitchener, 1986, p.57). Although the difference between efficient and final causality has a methodological dimension, there is a substantive element as well. Thus Braine (1959, pp.2–3) noticed that Piaget's concern is with the "logic of measurement". But Braine did not directly address the question of how *non-verbal* responses can be generative of *necessary* knowledge. The difference is crucial. In (mechanistic) experimental studies, children's responses are viewed as effects of hypothesised variables at work. Although this conception initially had a specifically behavioural element when applied to Piagetian studies (Braine, 1959, p.40; cf. Elkind, 1967; Gelman, 1972), this element was replaced by a methodological successor (independent–dependent variable). A quite different conception is stated by Piaget (1967/1971, p.24) in that a logic of action is expressed not as a mere response but instead as a display of reasoning that is reflective of an underlying structure. The former conception leads to the investigation of 'external' (contingent) causes of change, unlike the latter which posits 'internal' (intrinsic) processes of growth (cf. Campbell & Bickhard, 1986, p.6).

Second, a critical method is used to gain evidence for Piaget's structuralist models (cf. Vinh Bang, 1966). No structuralist model can provide an explanation through efficient or final causality, but such a model can provide a formal explanation. What a structural model can do is to index the extent of progression through a hierarchical sequence. Further, the model can do this with attention to the systemic and idealised properties of rational thought (Campbell & Bickhard, 1986, p.68; Chapman, 1991; Overton, 1991). It has been argued that 'traditional' approaches in psychology have failed to address the defining characteristics of the phenomena in its domain (Bickhard & Campbell, 1989). Such phenomena include novel capacities, intellectual productivity, and modal understanding. These phenomena cannot be known as a direct copy of the environment, and so their formation must be due to a process of intellectual growth that is intrinsic to the human mind. Causal explanation by reference to extrinsic factors could not be explanatory of that formatory process.

The result is that doubts can be raised about the acceptability of a traditional form of explanation in psychology. In turn, the resolution of these doubts turns on substantive, rather than merely methodological concerns. This same conclusion can now be related to a much more specific area of dispute.

(iv) *Age-norms*. Special attention is given to the age of onset of operational thinking. According to Braine (1959, p.15), the onset of transitive thinking is "substantially earlier" than the age of seven or eight years that Piaget suggests. The age proposed by Braine, namely five years, on the basis of his studies is supported by Halford (1989, p.342) but not by Gelman & Baillargeon (1983, p.179), who regard such thinking as an acquisition by preschoolers, in their reviews of recent studies. Evidently Braine (1959, p.39) was at one time prepared to accept Piaget's account, because he explicitly stated that his revised age-norms should not be regarded as evidence against Piaget's theoretical claims. By contrast, the position taken by Gelman & Baillargeon (1983, pp.168, 214) is that available evidence runs counter to Piagetian models. A mediating position is adopted by Halford (1989, p.347) who claims that there is no (good) evidence for the Piagetian model. Although such disputes may have psychological interest, they do not bear especially on Piaget's account for which the age of acquisition of ability has no criterial status for reasons elaborated in [18]. Accepting that empirical epistemology is a *tertium quid* [7], this is a substantive, and not merely a methodological, difference.

The point is that the postulation of *any* age as the age of onset of a specified type of thinking is dependent on some account for the interpretation of the proposed age. The only way in which these different positions can be resolved is by reference to an account of intellectual development. The question thus becomes 'Which account?'. The point is that methodological commitments alone do little to provide an adequate answer to this substantive question. This point is elaborated in the next section.

[16] EMPIRICAL STUDIES AND NECESSARY CONSERVATION

Conservation is a property of all those concepts that have defining conditions or criteria whose satisfaction is a prerequisite of that concept's successful use. Conservation is especially noticeable in scientific concepts whose importance at the turn of the century would have been familiar to Piaget in biology (Bergson, 1907/1911), mathematics (Poincaré, 1902/1905) and philosophy (Frege, 1888/1980). The central point made by Murray (1978, p.420), is that "every concept comprises a set of relevant attributes that define it. Sets of irrelevant attributes that the concept excludes are often correlated and associated with the relevant attributes. When they are, they make concept acquisition more difficult". Murray's point is that conservation poses a difficulty for children because they are liable to confuse non-defining with defining properties, for example by supposing incorrectly that the length of an array of objects is a defining feature of the number of objects in the array. Murray (1990, p.189) makes it clear that defining properties are necessary properties. Further, Murray (1978, p.420) has noted that although Piaget has investigated conservation in relation to quantitative concepts, it has a universal application to *all* concepts. This position would be well taken in philosophical discussions from Plato to Kripke where necessity is atemporally true [3.1] or true across 'possible worlds' [3.2]. Any concept should be used in a self-identical way through a train of reasoning, and necessarily so. In this way is identity a necessary feature of conservation.

Thus the logical notion of identity is central to conservation. Logicians define identity as a necessary relation: whatever x might be, it is necessarily the case that x is x (Hughes & Cresswell, 1972, p.190; Kripke, 1980, p.3). This logical principle is general in its scope. as it is presupposed in the defining criteria of any concept. The defining criteria of a concept are such that any object that satisfies them is—and has to be—the object that is described by that concept. Further, any object that does not satisfy these criteria is not—and could not be—the object, so described. Using the logical notion of identity as applied to the notion of number, a question that developmentalists need to confront concerns children's acquisition and use of its defining criteria. The point to bear in mind is that children who misuse the defining criteria of any notion are making a logical error. If it is necessary that x is x—whatever x might be—then the mistaken use of the defining criteria results not merely in error but in contradiction. In cases of nonconservation, if the defining criteria of number are necessary and yet these criteria result in different answers to the initial and second (post-transformation) questions, then the two answers must be contradictory.

A possible objection to this conclusion is the rejection of its applicability to children's development. This delimitation could occur in one of two ways. First, it could be objected that young children are not adult logicians and so they might not have used defining—and so necessary—criteria at all. In reply, this objection is question-begging to the extent that it implies that a successful response is simply a level II, rather than a level III, epistemic state, as noted in [13.1]. The criteria of number that Piaget and Szeminska (1941/1952) invoke are based on Russellian defining criteria, which are necessary (Smith, 1986a). Thus it is legitimate to raise questions about the extent to which developing children do understand such criteria. Second, the objection could be that the children might have used one set of defining criteria in their first answer but changed these criteria in giving their second answer, for example by forgetting their first answer or simply changing their minds. In reply, this objection is ineffective for reasons that were anticipated by Piaget and Szeminska (1941/1952, p.10), who point out that children can evade the contradiction by making successive use of multiple criteria. Their contention is, however, that contradictions still arise, because such children use multiple criteria in application to the same array. The outcome is that the numerosity of the array changes with these criteria and so contradictory claims are made. This is because the numerosity of one-and-the-same array is judged to change. But that array is self-identical and so instantiates the same logical principle of identity. The fundamental reason is the same, namely that the defining criteria of a concept are distinct from their non-defining counter-parts (see [25.2]).

Similar considerations apply to transitivity and class inclusion. Thus a standard definition of transitivity reads: "a relation R is transitive if, for any x, y, and z, if R holds between x and y and between y and z, then it holds between x and z" (Lemmon, 1966, p.182; cf. Lipschutz, 1964, p.85). Again, a standard definition of the relation of inclusion reads: "a class A is included in a class B if all the members of A are members of B" (Lemmon, 1966, p.207; cf. Lipschutz, 1964, p.3). The key point is that these definitions specify logical properties of relations and classes respectively. From a logical point of view, any transitive relation has the property specified by the former principle, just as any included class has the property specified by the latter principle. From a psychological point of view, questions arise as to how children use these principles in their relational and classificatory thinking. A child who displays relational thinking in this specified logical sense is in a position to make corresponding deductive inferences. Similarly, a child who displays classificatory thinking in this specified logical sense has the ability to make valid deductions. Thus the logical properties of relations and classes make possible deductive forms of reasoning in much the same way that inference-principles—such as *modus ponens* (p and, if p then q, implies q)—make possible propositional deductions. As deductive inferences are necessary inferences, the previous argument applies. Contradictory thinking is manifest in cases where these logical properties are inaccurately or incompletely understood. In short, logical inferences are truth-preserving (Haack, 1978; Quine, 1972). That is, truth is conserved through their use. This is due to their modal character, because defining properties are logically necessary. In this way conservation is an intrinsic feature of rational thought.

Identity is not, however, reducible to conservation. It has been stated by Bruner et al. (1966, p.189) that identity is a "necessary if not sufficient" condition of conservation. This claim is ambiguous. It could mean either that identity is necessary-but-not-sufficient, or that it is necessary-and-sufficient, for conservation. Developmentalists are divided because empirical research in this area is open to competing reviews in which both options have been defended (Acredolo & Acredolo, 1979; Miller, 1978). But this dispute turns on the construal of *identity*. Piaget denies that identity is both necessary and sufficient for conservation, because (Piaget & Voyat, 1968, p.2) "the principle of identity is perhaps, out of all logical 'principles', the one which remains the least identical with itself in the course of development". Qualitative identity is necessary. but not sufficient, for quantitative identity or conservation. After all, with a liquid conservation task, a five year old child can agree that it is the same liquid but deny that there is the same to drink (Piaget & Voyat, 1968, p.15).

The key question does *not* concern the absence-*vs*-presence of fundamental concepts. Bruner et al. (1966, p.186) assume that some 'primitive' understanding of necessity is innate, and Piaget (1936; 1968) makes a similar claim about conservation. Rather, the key question is how complex this 'primitive' concept is. And this question leads straight back to the distinction between the necessary properties that are constitutive of a concept and those properties that are merely correlated with it. The failure to respect this distinction results in modal errors (Murray, 1990; Smith, 1987a).

Conservation can be regarded as a cognitive universal. If knowledge arises in the application of concepts to experience, certain conditions have to be met for their use to be successful. Piaget's problem about conservation is a variant of the philosophical problem: 'is the universal knowable?' (Piaget, 1918, p.46; cf. Chapman, 1988, p.5). The point about this question is not that Piaget takes the conditions for the use of concepts to be unclear, but rather that any acceptable account of them would have to do justice to the developmental facts for the reasons given in [3] and [7]. If the conditions were too lenient, conservation would be innate; but if they were too restrictive, non-conservation would be prevalent.

Non-conservation, it has been claimed (Wesley, 1989), was first studied by Binet with whose work Piaget (1975b) was familiar. Piaget's interest in this phenomenon led him to change the philosophical question about cognitive universals into an empirical question (Piaget, 1936, p.31) concerned with how, in fact, the evolution of individual thinking progresses into the "great systems of rational collaboration which the deductive and experimental sciences constitute". Problems of conservation recur at every level of development (Piaget, 1936, p.37) and so Piaget's main question is not how an understanding of conservation emerges at any one point in development—say, childhood—but rather why the presence of conservation at any point is a successor of earlier, and an ancestor of later, forms. In short, Piaget's problem is primarily concerned with the internal constraints on epistemic transfer *within one and the same understanding*. That is, his concern is primarily with vertical rather than with horizontal, *décalage* (Piaget, 1941; cf. Chapman, 1988, p.149). Structuralists models were invoked by Piaget (1936, p.41) to identify systems of thinking that "assure necessary conservation with the invariants of experience".

There were two elements to Piaget's early account. First, intellectual organisation is always in unstable equilibrium, marked by contradictory thinking. Second, total equilibrium is an ideal limit of consistency (Piaget, 1918, p.98; cf. Chapman, 1988, pp.415–6, 434). What is required by this proposal is both a criterion to show the extent of the progress from the former to the latter and an explanatory construct for its realisation. The notion of conservation is used by Piaget to identify the degree of internal consistency in gaining knowledge (Piaget, 1918, p.163): "The tendency of *organisation to conserve itself* as such is at the very basis (*origine*) of the principle of identity". If intellectual development is, for the reasons given in [8.5], a search for coherence, conservation is one of the constitutive features of this process.

Piaget's (1936) initial studies of conservation related to matter, weight, movement, and quantity. The former trio are implicated in scientific reasoning (Inhelder, 1936) and the latter in mathematical reasoning (Szeminska, 1935). As an example, consider a child aged 10 years who is asked to add 35 + 60 + 70 and whose *verbatim* response is as follows (Szeminska, 1935, p.3):

$$
\begin{array}{ll}
35 & 0 + 5 = \text{I write } 5 \\
60 & 6 + 7 = \text{I decompose } 6 + 6 = 12 + 1 = 13 \\
+70 & \quad\quad \text{I write 3 and carry 1} \\
\hline
435 & 3 + 1 \text{ (carried)} = 4 \text{ so I write } 4
\end{array}
$$

The example is commonplace. The proposal is novel because it concerns numerical invariance where (Szeminska, 1935, p.8) "the objects of a set neither disappear nor increase arbitrarily, independently of the operations applied to them". The proposal is (Szeminska, 1935, p.14) that the child's misunderstanding is due to the non-accessibility of a "necessary logical instrument".

The proposal can be interpreted as follows. Evidently, the three addends form a set such that each addend is to be transformed through the operation of addition. Numerical invariance should be, but is not, a feature of this transformation. To see why, notice that each addend is itself a set. According to Russell (1919), any number can be defined in set-theoretical terms such that super-ordinate sets include sets that are lower in the hierarchy. Russell's analysis provides a logical model of the composition and decomposition of numbers. Thus although each addend is individuated by the child who attends to each in turn, the addends are themselves hierarchically ordered. Their internal ordering must be respected for addition to be successfully completed. But a pre-condition of hierarchical subsumption is that an element remains self-identical through operations applied to it. This condition is broken since the meaning of '3', indicated by its place-value, is '30', whereas the child treats this 'same' number as '300'. In short, one and the same number does not remain self-identical through the operations performed on it. Thus the child's thinking is non-conserving. But if this is so, the analysis of number that Russell (1919) elaborated does not fit the developmental facts (Smith, 1986a). Piaget's original studies were intended to make good a factual case relevant to a normative question, in as much as (Piaget & Szeminska, 1941/1952, p.16/*3) "all knowledge, whether of a scientific order or arising from plain common sense, presupposes an explicit or implicit system of conservation principles".

In short, the starting-point is children's difficulty with addition. This difficulty is re-cast in terms of an available philosophical model. Empirical studies are undertaken to check on whether the normative requirements of the model are, in fact, met. An interpretive account is proposed (Piaget & Inhelder, 1941/1974, p.viii) in which "conservation is both a condition and also a result of quantification".

Developmentalists have, by contrast, been preoccupied with conservation *tasks* and especially with the asynchronies that have arisen from the use of a myriad of variants within one level—say, childhood—and so with horizontal *décalage*. The expectation has been that tasks which were similar in their design would make similar, intellectual demands. The non-satisfaction of this expectation is notorious. The explanation of this discrepancy is stated to be one of the major problems facing developmentalists (Brown & Desforges, 1980; Bryant, 1985; Case, 1985; Gelman & Baillargeon, 1983; Halford, 1989).

To be sure, there are problems to confront. But Piaget's problem is *not* the problem that is taken to be outstanding in current work. Piaget's problem concerns the construction of necessary from empirical knowledge within one and the same child's mind (Pinard, 1981, p.137). The problem that is outstanding for many developmentalists concerns the variable displays of knowledge by one and the same child across a range of tasks which differ in specifiable and manipulable respects. This is a normative difference.

In elaboration of this difference, consider a task to assess the conservation of number. In the original version, the instructions are as follows. The children are shown an array of six bottles and a tray with a dozen glasses *(nota bene)*. The children are also shown that each bottle can fill exactly one glass. The child is then invited to take just enough glasses from the tray, one glass per bottle, so that the glasses and the bottles are the same. As all the world knows, young children do not do as asked. Bon, aged four years, sets the standard for such children by selecting all twelve glasses, affirming that the glasses and bottles are the same. Further, when the array of bottles is spread out, Bon even states that there are more bottles than glasses. In this way children's beliefs are revealed in a discussion about the bottles and glasses that are in front of them (Piaget & Szeminska, 1941/1952, p.43).

Thus the crucial issues are twofold. One concerns the extent to which the defining properties of number are dissociated from their non-defining counter-parts in children's beliefs. The second concerns which non-defining properties are so dissociated. In this conservation task, the non-defining properties are physical properties of line length, whereas in others they can be social properties (see [21] for an example). The general point is that differentiation should generalise to cover any-and-all types of non-defining property, of which there is an indefinite number.

According to Murray (1981; 1990), this task has six procedural steps: (i) the initial question about the number of objects in each array; (ii) transformation of a property of one array, where that property is a non-defining property of number; (iii) repetition of the initial question, leading to a correct-*vs*-incorrect judgment; (iv) questioning to establish the reasoning behind the judgment with special reference to the defining-*vs*-non-defining properties of number; (v) identification of the degree of modal (necessary-*vs*-empirical) understanding; and (vi) generalisability of understanding and extent of transfer. A survey of conservation research based on this analysis is presented elsewhere (Smith, 1992a). Three principal conclusions can be noted.

First, each of the steps is the subject of endemic disputes. Some disputes bear on the validity of experimental findings. Rose and Blank

(1974) have claimed that step (i) makes the task more difficult for younger children and that when it is simplified by omission of this step more children display conserving responses. This is a reliable finding (Samuel & Bryant, 1984). But there is a charge of oversimplification to consider here with the implication that rational understanding is not evident in such cases (Porpodas, 1987). Disputes also arise at step (ii) concerning reliability. McGarrigle & Donaldson (1974) have argued that non-intentional transformations of the array ought not to, but in fact do, affect young children's understanding. But their position has not been supported by Eames, Shorrocks, and Tomlinson (1990) who failed to replicate this finding. Step (ii) also generates disputes over validity. The assumption that underpins the study undertaken by McGarrigle and Donaldson (1974; cf. Donaldson, 1983) is that children's judgments are sufficient for the assessment of operational ability, when the experimental design includes a control for intentional and accidental transformations of the array. The counter-claim is made that although the context of the different assessment tasks has a differential effect in relation to the display of correct judgments, the interpretation of these responses is another matter. Following McGarrigle and Donaldson (1974), Light, Buckingham, and Robbins (1979) introduced a further control for intentional and incidental transformations but, once again, assumed that children's judgments alone are sufficient for the attribution of ability. This assumption has been shown to be questionable by Bovet, Parrat-Dayan, & Deshusses-Addor, 1981; Bovet, Parrat-Dayan, & Kamii, 1986) who used the design preferred by Light et al. with a further control for justifications. Their finding was that young children typically do *not* maintain their correct judgments when they are asked to support them with a relevant justification. Thus a distinction needs to be drawn between a contextually sensitive capacity and the epistemic significance of the associated responses as not all capacities amount to operational competence (Parrat-Dayan & Bovet, 1982). Similar disputes concern diagnostic assessment, at steps (iii) and (iv), and the relative priority of judgments–justifications which was discussed in [13]. Thus although it is relatively easy to make procedural changes to Piagetian tasks, it is very much harder to establish which conclusions can be clearly drawn from them.

Second, a strictly experimental approach has not been carried through. Each of the six steps has been individually subjected to serial scrutiny. But there is no study that has comprehensively subjected all of the steps to systematic control. Procedural changes have been massive and multiple, but not comprehensive. A host of interpretions has been proposed in explanation of different patterns of findings. Clearly, Piaget has no seigneural rights as to what is *the* design of a conservation task

(Gelman, 1978). Equally, studies that are based on variant designs rightly invite the interpretation of non-anticipated and interesting findings (Donaldson et al., 1983). But Piagetian critics, who scrupulously base their case on well-designed experimental studies, question whether a Piagetian interpretation of conservation is acceptable.

The *psychological* question concerns the development of correct knowledge under specificable conditions, and turns on whether any one account is explanatory of all of the miscellany of findings arising in such research. The distinct *epistemological* question concerns the development of necessary from contingent knowledge, and turns on whether any one account is explanatory of this construction. The acceptability of an account that is directed on the epistemological question is not settled by reference to the prevailing norms relevant to accounts that are directed on the psychological question.

Third, with respect to Piaget's main problem of the construction of necessary knowledge, step (v) is crucial. Yet the vast majority of studies of conservation have disregarded the modal character of children's responses. Although such studies have independent interest in relation to questions about correctness in understanding, their relevance to the main problem about the construction of necessary from contingent knowledge is indeterminate. Quite simply, psychological questions about *the* optimal set of procedures to use in the design of a conservation task are distinct from epistemological questions about the modality of understanding on any version of a conservation task.

To see why attention should be given to the modal character of children's thinking, consider the successive responses of Gol, aged 4 years, to the conservation of number task (Piaget & Szeminska, 1941/1952, p.43). In this task, the children are shown how one bottle can be used to fill one glass and are then shown an array of six bottles and a tray holding twelve glasses with an invitation to take just enough glasses for the bottles in the array. Five points can be noted. (1) Gol starts to fill each glass with one bottle in turn but at the fourth glass realises that there are insufficient bottles to fill all twelve glasses. (2) After an invitation to take merely some of the glasses, Gol attempts to match seven glasses with the six bottles by bunching the glasses together, and then states that there is the same number of each. (3) After the observer matches the bottles to these glasses, Gol realises that there is one extra glass and so asks for a further bottle. (4) Gol then matches the seven bottles with the seven glasses by linking the first bottle to the second glass, commenting that one glass in the array of glasses lacks a bottle, and that one bottle in the array of bottles lacks a glass. (5) Gol states that both another glass and another bottle are necessary, but then matches one to the other in disregard of the outstanding glass and bottle in each array.

The system of thinking that lies behind Gol's responses is contradictory. It is a contradiction, in (2), to suppose that there is the same number of elements in an array of seven glasses and an array of six bottles. It is a contradiction, in (4), to suppose that each of the equivalent arrays is lacking by reference to the other, where each array is believed to lack exactly one element. It is a contradiction, in (5), to suppose that two apparently unequal arrays are rendered equivalent by the addition of one further element to each.

By contrast, Lau, aged six years, gives the conserving response "they are always (*toujours*) the same" (Piaget & Szeminska, 1941/1952, p.67/*47; cf. similar discrepancies in the translation of the same text such as Eus' protocol p.34/*18 or Lin's protocol p.52/*33). Experimental studies that are concerned with different procedural changes have typically ignored the modal character of such responses.

In short, the studies of conservation are legion. This research has generated a commendable range of findings, so much so that the interpretive question that has dominated research concerns the across–task display of intellectual ability. There are many accounts on offer in which this latter question is addressed. The main conclusion to draw here is twofold. One is that such accounts are, of course, interesting but that, even so, they typically do not bear on Piaget's main problem. The other is that *necessity* is a complex notion. Such complexity is shown by the human tendency to conflate necessity with contingency, with empirical fact, or with regularity for the reasons discussed in [8.5] concerning the search for coherence. The systematic demarcation of necessity from pseudo-necessity has scarcely started (Pinard, 1981, p.139). It is for this reason that experimental studies of conservation, which rest on such a prior inventory, have not yet got to the heart of conservation, through neglect of the modal nature of intellectual change. It is for this reason that some commentators have accorded priority to a Piagetian account of equilibration, as it is one of the few such accounts on offer (Isaacs, 1951; Moessinger, 1978; Murray, 1990; Pinard, 1981).

CHAPTER FIVE

Tasks

"It is possible to study any reasoning and to ascertain, in the assent which sanctions the conclusion, the part due to observation and the part due to vis formae" (Piaget, 1922, p.222).

[17] ASSESSMENT TASKS

Since the process of gaining knowledge is not open to direct observation, evidence is needed from which inferences can be drawn about its nature. Assessment tasks permit observable displays of performance from which such inferences can be drawn. An empirical account of intellectual development is expected to be sensitive to performance on assessment tasks. It is widely accepted that Piagetian tasks are reliable, even "awesomely replicable" (Neimark, 1985), and on this point there is no serious dispute (Gelman & Baillargeon, 1983). Rather, disputes arise as to their validity; that is, about how to interpret the responses made on different assessment tasks. A common assumption is that the characteristic features of human thinking are revealed by specified assessment tasks which share a common structure. Thus the aim in diagnostic assessment is to use a task whose structure matches the structure of a child's understanding, to use the former in the identification of the latter. The argument will be that assessment tasks alone provide an insufficient unit of analysis in support of this commitment to matching.

The original versions of Piagetian tasks are reliable. Yet when new tasks with new procedures and new methods of assessment are used, there is a differential pattern of failure and success. In such cases, so the objection runs, children's performances are uneven and so resist interpretation through a Piagetian account. The objection is that that account is hoist with its own petard due to the pervasive presence of *décalages* or unexpected time-lags between successful displays of the same, general structure. This difficulty is summarised in the claim (Brown & Desforges, 1980, p.102) that "if *décalage* exceeds *structure* and heterogeneity is characteristic of most children's performance most of the time, Piaget's account lacks predictive validity".

To be sure, the difficulty of formulating a unitary account of children's performances across developmental tasks is formidable. There *is* currently no such account and, *a fortiori*, Piaget's account is not such an account. But this admission still leaves open the question of whether the present objection actually does pose a serious objection to Piaget's account.

First, a negative answer could be given on exegetical grounds. According to Chapman (1988, p.84), Piaget first used the term 'integrated structure'—that is, *structure d'ensemble*—in his book on infant intelligence (Piaget, 1936/1953, p.121). This notion is, however, implicit in Piaget's (1918) discussion of part–whole equilibrium and in his (1923) discussion of coherence and mental construction, as noted in [8.5]. Piaget (1928) also used the notion of *décalage* in his early papers, where the strict inter-dependence of vertical and horizontal time-lags in structural growth was stated. Logical criteria were outlined by Piaget (1941) for the demarcation of distinct types of horizontal *décalage*. But Piaget's position is not straightforward, because it is regarded as incomplete by some commentators and subject to later modification (Montangero, 1980), although there are differences about the ways in which, and even the extent to which, this should be done (Gillièron, 1980; Pascual-Leone, 1987). Other commentators have argued not only that these criteria are compatible with structuralist claims but even that developmental change should typically be marked by time-lags (Chapman, 1988, p.341). Thus the identification of testable predictions from Piaget's account is not clear-cut

Second, Piaget's account has no official concern with procedural *décalage* due to differences in the administration of assessment tasks (Chapman & Lindenberger, 1988). The point at issue is not merely the demarcation of relevant from irrelevant cases of *décalage* but rather the identification of valid from invalid predictions that can be derived from Piaget's account. Yet there is strong case for claiming that the main objection to Piaget's account arises from research based on assessment tasks, which are procedurally distinct in just this sense.

Third, the case for returning a negative answer could be made on methodological grounds due to the joint presence of both false-positive and false-negative diagnostic errors (Flavell, 1982; Smedslund, 1969). The *only* way in which both types of error can be avoided is by the design of tasks which match some agreed standard. The design of an acceptable transitivity task rests more on substantive than on purely methodological issues. The discusssion in [18.2] serves as a reminder that some transitivity tasks can be successfully completed by animals, whereas others defeat the abilities of intelligent adults. Some account of intellectual development will have to be invoked. Yet developmentalists disagree over precisely these substantive matters.

Fourth, Piaget (1970/1983) expressed a main interest in charting the logic of children's thinking by characterising the structure of their thought. But Piaget has continued to use a multiplicity of logical models of the epistemic process over and above the familiar operational models (see [8.1]). Whereas Piagetian critics have been interested in the extent to which there is a unitary account of children's performance across some class of assessment *tasks* (for example, transitivity), Piaget's interests have centred on the extent to which there is evidence from such tasks for his several *models* of thought. This is a substantive difference.

Fifth, Chapman (1988, pp.346, 363) has drawn a distinction between the formal and functional aspects of Piaget's account. The same formal structure can underpin the epistemic process in different domains without there being a unitary process of psychological functioning. There are several ways to interpret this denial. It could be denied that Piaget has an adequate account of psychological functioning and so others will have to repair this deficiency (cf. Chapman, 1988, pp.364, 432). Equally, the denial could merely be that an account directed on the construction of necessary knowledge does not have to deal with all of the factors that contribute to the acquisition and use of any-and-all types of knowledge. Thus it would not have to deal with the contribution of antecedent variables discussed in [15]. Some of the strengths and weaknesses of Piaget's strategy are reviewed in [24.3] and [25.2].

Sixth, taking a cue from Inhelder & Piaget (1979/1980), it has been argued that there is a continuity between procedural and structural knowledge of transitivity (Leiser & Gillièron, 1990). Their argument assumes the restricted version of naturalised epistemology noted in [13.2]. The comment to make is not that this one study settles the issue, but rather that it identifies one distinctive question, namely how a structural form of understanding develops from its primitive, epistemic antecedents. Even if there is no unitary account of children's performances across developmental tasks, the specific question of how the understanding of transitivity is constructed has been addressed in

Genevan studies. And it is this question which has to be addressed by those who take seriously Piaget's central question in [1].

Finally, the crucial difference is the ambiguity of *structure* as applied to thought and to tasks. Piaget's 'top-down' interests lay in the identification and description of intellectual *structures* by means of which performances on tasks are viewed. By contrast, many developmentalists have 'bottom-up' interests in assessment *tasks* which are used as the means to assess the adequacy of accounts of intellectual development, including Piaget's (structuralist) account. This difference would be minor if the connection between the structure of thought and task-structure was well defined. In fact, their inter-relation is loose, usually implicit and often ignored. So the difference takes on considerable importance.

The difference can be elaborated through the distinction between natural law and scientific theory. According to Nagel (1961, pp.79–80), a law is a singular statement linking observational terms, unlike a theory which lays down how several distinct laws can be related through its non-observational terms. This is because the theoretical terms of the theory are implicitly defined in terms of the postulates of the theory. Specifically, a theory should embody an abstract calculus, a model or interpretation, and correspondence rules. The abstract calculus is a formal skeleton, which can be mathematical or logical. The model is an inventory of the notions that give content to the abstract descriptions. Correspondence rules relate theoretical entities to observational procedures (Nagel, 1961, pp.90–105). Thus a theory is never equivalent to any finite set of laws, still less to a set of observational predictions. Rather, the relation between theory and law (predictions, observations) is indirect.

Using Piaget's theory of the operational understanding of transitivity as an example, the calculus is Piaget's (1949; cf. Chapman, 1988, pp.134–42) logical description of *groupements* V and VI. A model is given in Piaget's (1970/1983) epistemological claim about the construction of reversible thinking through the use of interdependent operations which are defined in the logical calculus. The correspondence rules are left implicit. Instead, there is a reliance on nominated assessment tasks (Piaget & Szeminska, 1941/1952). So viewed, it is fundamental mistake to draw conclusions about Piaget's *theory* on the basis of adjustments to such *tasks*. This is because the theory is not defined exclusively through those tasks. The logical calculus and model are distinct from the correspondence rules that are used to relate them to the world.

There are, of course, methodological techniques and experimental conventions, the use of which typically leads to tasks that are individually designed in a more or less appropriate manner. Thus any

Piagetian task can be used as a starting-point for serial changes to be made to its design on their basis. But there is no common theory whose use underpins those techniques and conventions and, in the last analysis, even good method never amounts to theory. Correspondence rules that explicitly link the abstract structural model with observable task performances are lacking. The analogy used in [18.3] serves to illustrate this methodological point.

Drawing inferences as to which task performances result from specified structures, or as to which structures underpin stated task performances, is a risky business on three counts. First, there is dispute as to the appropriate unit of analysis to be used in describing the process of knowing. Although some developmentalists have concurred with Piaget by regarding the key epistemic construct to be that of structure (Halford, 1982), other constructs have also been stated to be central, including stage-related attentional rule (Case, 1985), production system rule (Siegler, 1981), domain-related concept (Carey, 1985), and general skill (Fischer, 1980). Even on the assumption that performance and process stand in a one–one relationship, the same performance can be described through these different constructs. Second, with respect to any preferred unit of analysis, the assumption that there is a one–one relationship may be false. There may be a many–one relationship between observed performance and the underlying intellectual process. As Osherson (1974, p.67) has noted, two processes may generate three distinct types of performance. Each may be uniquely related to a corresponding display but, equally, the two processes may interact to generate a further, supervenient display. Third, the same assumption may be false for the converse reason that there may be a one–many relationship between performance and process. The same performance may be due to multiple processes, whether logical, cognitive, or social. Indeed, a major dispute in developmental psychology is the extent to which any preferred interpretation is better than its rivals. A standard charge is that Piaget's interpretation is neglectful of a wide range of states and processes that could be expected to contribute to intellectual development (Gelman & Baillargeon, 1983; Donaldson et al, 1983; Halford, 1989).

In short, there is a *general* problem which faces all developmental accounts where inferences about unobserved processes (structures, say) are made from observed performances on assessment tasks and conversely. There is ample scope for mismatching, in that similar tasks are used for different theoretical purposes. Pluralism is one expression, because a range of different positions is on offer. Such pluralism is inevitable in pre-paradigmatic sciences (Kuhn, 1970). The danger is that the legitimate concerns associated with any one perspective are used in the evaluation of some different perspective, which has distinct concerns. In this way is a developmental *task* an inappropriate unit of analysis with regard to the evaluation of a developmental *account*, *perspective*, or *theory*. In fact, the practice of many developmentalists is to use the former in the evaluation of the latter.

Two specific examples are now reviewed. One concerns the status of age in relation to claims about children developing abilities. The second concerns the psychological processes (mental models) that are characteristic of reasoning. The argument will be that both concerns have independent interest but that neither has any special relevance to Piaget's account of the construction of necessary knowledge. Assessment tasks provide an inadequate unit of measure of the rival principles at the heart of distinct developmental perspectives.

[18]   AGE AND ABILITY

Developmentalists are not always mindful of the fact that there are several, competing interpretations of Piagetian theory. According to one (age-of-acquisition) interpretation, that theory concerns the ages at which intellectual competence is acquired. According to a second (differentiation-over-time) interpretation, Piaget's theory concerns how new forms of intellectual competence are constructed over time. Developmentalists who accept the first interpretation often take Piaget's theory to be misleading or even incorrect. Developmentalists who accept the second interpretation often take questions about the validity and utility of Piaget's theory to be open. This is an important difference.

The age-of-acquisition interpretation has figured prominently in commentary on Piaget s work for at least 30 years. Two statements of this position are now mentioned; these have been selected because they have been influential, as other developmentalists, whether unwittingly or not, have followed suit. In his influential monograph, Braine (1959, p.1) stated that Piaget's theory has two aspects. His first point was that, for Piaget, intellectual development is the development of logical abilities. His second point was that this process is age related, such that the principal ages of transition are reported to be at 7 and ll years approximately. It is on this second point that Braine spent most of his discussion. His aim was to show that the ages given by Piaget are wrong. Subsequent commentary has tended to follow suit and the evidence has been generally regarded as running counter to Piaget's position (Gelman, 1978; Gelman & Baillargeon, 1983). A commitment to the same interpretation was given in a discussion of Braine's first point when, some 10 years later, Flavell and Wohlwill (1969, p.80) took Piaget's theory to raise unanswered questions about the transition from not-in-competence to first-in-competence. Their claim is that competence which is initially absent is later acquired, leading to the charge that Piaget's theory is conceptually suspicious because development is not an all-or-none process. Indeed, Piaget's theory has been considered problematic just because it seems to lead straight to the learning paradox—see [22]—in that knowledge is somehow made to emerge from ignorance.

The argument used by these developmentalists can be summarised as follows. According to their interpretation, Piaget's theory generates empirical or conceptual problems. Their conclusion is that these problems are so severe that it is better to replace the theory that gave rise to them. There is, however, an alternative to consider, namely that Piaget's theory is not committed to the age-of-acquisition interpretation, because it is better understood in terms of the differentiation-over-time interpretation. Conflation and attendant inconsistency can only arise if separate interpretations are not kept separate.

Thus the counter-argument is that the age-of-acquisition interpretation is neither the sole nor the safest way of interpreting Piaget's theory. The main aim is to show that the ages given in Piaget's theory are indicators, rather than criteria, of intellectual development.

The fact that Piaget attended both to empirical questions related to his theory of stages, and to the conceptual question of which criteria should be invoked when the notion of stage is used, creates a problem. Although age is not one of his criteria for developmental stages, Piaget nevertheless drew conclusions about the relation of age to developmental change in his empirical accounts. Five criteria for a coherent account of developmental stages are offered by Piaget (1960; cf. Inhelder, 1956), namely constant order, integration, consolidation, overarching structure, and equilibration. In commenting on the constant order criterion, Piaget made it clear (1967/1971, p.37/*17) that age is not a criterion, because the sequence of behaviour patterns is "constant, independently of the acceleration or delay which can modify the average chronological age due to acquired experience or social context ... In psychology, the distinction is always drawn between chronological and mental age". In this passage, Piaget was making two points. The first is that the appearance of a stage is not age-related, even though the order in which different stages appear is constant. The second point involving the distinction between chronological and mental age reinforces the first. This same denial that age is a criterion of stage is repeated elsewhere by Piaget (1970/1983). Despite these clear theoretical assertions, Piaget nevertheless frequently drew conclusions about children's age in reviewing his own empirical work. In a number of passages, he both reviewed his criteria for the identification of a stage and, in one and the same text, reported the ages at which developmental stages are attained (Piaget, 1960, 1970/1983; Piaget & Inhelder, 1966/1969). In short, Piaget's theoretical account supports the expectation that age is not a criterion of a child's stage of development, but his empirical accounts embody conclusions about the relation of children's age to developmental level. At best, this evident tension merits clarification; at worst, it marks inconsistency.

When problems are found in Piaget's theory, two general lines of response are possible. One is to devise an alternative theory. The other is to devise an alternative interpretation of Piaget's theory (Smith, 1986a; 1987b; 1987c). The approach taken here involves the second of these courses and so a reinterpretation of Piaget's empirical claims regarding age. The specific argument is that age is an indicator, not a criterion, of developmental level. This argument has a threefold rationale. First, claims about children's age are theory-laden, whereas claims about children's developmental level are value-laden. This difference renders problematic any explanation of the latter in terms of the former. Second, age is a convenient variable to invoke in the explanation of children's development, but it is not the only, and perhaps not even the main, antecedent variable. Social class, for example, is another, significant, antecedent variable, which is typically bypassed in studies of intellectual development. Third, reference to age of success frequently results in age-ranges rather than specific ages. In consequence, age is a poor criterion of developmental level. With these three summaries in mind, discussion can now turn to their more detailed elaboration.

A *criterion* of a given concept formulates the properties that must be present or absent for the criterion to be applied to particular case. A criterion is meant to be universally valid, so no exceptions to it should exist. For example, a biological criterion of maleness might specify the chromosomes that a person must possess to be male. Using this criterion, any person who has the stipulated property is and must be male, and any person who does not have this property is not and cannot be male. The biological criterion of maleness is silent about the clothes that people wear, therefore no exception to this criterion arises when a Scotsman wears a kilt or when a woman wears trousers. But the clothes that a person wears provide a convenient *indicator* of a person's gender. An indicator is more or less useful, rather than valid or invalid. Unlike a criterion, an indicator may have exceptions. The utility of an indicator is dependent not on the existence of exceptions, but on their relative frequency. The distinction between a criterion and an indicator is regularly found in philosophical discussions, ranging from Aristotle (nd/1975) on essence and accident through to Wittgenstein (1958a) on criterion and symptom. Piaget (1965/1972) is presumably familar with some version of this distinction through his explicit rejection of philosophical epistemology.

Thus exceptions to the criteria proposed by Piaget would contradict his account of intellectual stages. But if age is not one of these criteria, children may succeed on Piagetian tasks at earlier or at later ages than those stated in his empirical reports, without contradicting that account. If the ages stated by Piaget are found to be incorrect because of regular disconfirmation, their utility as an indicator is impaired. But the disconfirmation of an indicator leaves the attendant theory intact. Age is an indicator, but not a criterion of a developmental stage. The three arguments in support of this conclusion now follow.

[18.1] Facts and Norms

Piaget took his theory to be explanatory of intellectual development. Demarcating one developmental stage from another is one step towards that end. It is quite a different matter to show how the abilities associated with earlier stages generate those associated with later stages. In the latter case, there may be an implied claim that one stage is more *advanced* than its predecessor. Such a claim is value-laden and normative. A norm must be invoked in any claim that one of two abilities is more advanced than another. By contrast, observations are always theory-laden (Popper, 1979) and so observations regarding the ages at which children succeed on certain tasks presuppose some theory that can be used in their interpretation. Nevertheless, observational reports and theoretical statements are intended to be factual descriptions of what is the case. Thus, reports about the ages at which children succeed on developmental tasks, even when interpreted by reference to a theory, are always factual in character. In short, Piaget's account of the construction of necessary knowledge has a normative component, unlike merely factual reports about the age at which children succeed on developmental tasks. It is widely accepted that a normative conclusion can never be deduced from premises that are exclusively factual. This principle is known as Hume's rule, after the philosopher who is taken to have first stated it (see Smith, 1986b). The principle is general in its application, but it has a special relevance to accounts of children's development. Indeed, there are two ways in which a developmental theory, including Piaget's, is normative.

In the first place, a developmental theory is normative when it deals with the development of competences that may be possessed with varying degrees of accomplishment (Wood & Power, 1987). This distinction has a basis in common sense, marked by the difference between the mere possession of a basic competence and the possession of that competence in abundance. The distinction is revealed by contrasting the *successful* display of an ability with a display of *high* (or *expert*) ability. A successful display of an ability is such that the minimum standard for attributing that ability has been met; that a particular ability, and not some other, has been evidenced. A display of high ability requires the display to be successful, but also that some further standard has been met as well, to indicate that the ability is possessed to some exceptional degree. This distinction has a bearing on familiar discussions about receptive versus spontaneous understanding (Bryant, 1974), or about the question of transfer (Brown & Desforges, 1980). Many psychological critiques of Piaget's theory have not taken the difference between a successful display of ability versus a display of high ability fully into account. In the second place, a developmental theory is normative because it deals with children's acquisition of 'better' norms. Two mental activities differ when the (logical) principle used in one is more advanced than that used in the other. This is a normative, and not a factual, difference. In specifying the difference between concrete and formal operational thinking, Piaget (1961/1966) referred to multiplicative classification, which is one manifestation of concrete operations, whereby a child can entertain the four possible ways in which two bi-valent properties can be exemplified. Formal operations is said to be the generalisation of these four basic possibilities so as to form a combinatorial system, because there are 16 ways in which this quartet can be realised in specific cases (see [24.2]). Leaving questions about the empirical acceptability of this account aside, the account clearly addresses the crucial task of clarifying the extent to which one type of thinking might be said to be *better* than another. Again, issues relating to truth and modality turn on distinct, logical norms. A system of thinking in which both truth and modality are preserved is better than a system which is marked by the preservation of only the former alone.

Besides such valid reasons why a developmental theory is normative, it is also worth considering some *invalid* reasons why it might be thought to be normative. A developmental theory is not normative merely because the norms used by children are within its domain. It was noted in [7] that, for Piaget (1923; 1961/1966), the norms used by children can be investigated empirically as 'normative facts' in much the same way that an anthropologist can study empirically the (moral, legal, linguistic) norms used in different human cultures. Nor is a developmental theory normative merely because it embodies norm-referenced measurement, such as when a child's performance on a test is related to the performance of peers. Norm-referenced assessment generally is contrasted with a criterion-referenced assessment, in which a score is interpreted in relation to some external standard (Nitko, 1983). Psychometric tests are norm-referenced and Piagetian tasks are criterion-referenced (Gray, 1978), although some developmentalists have used norm-referenced techniques in relation to such tasks (Kingma & Koops, 1983). In such cases as these, norm has a factual and not a value-laden meaning.

Manifestly, a commitment to the general philosophical position that factual premises never have normative conclusions has a clear consequence. Purely factual reports about the ages at which children succeed or fail on Piagetian, or any other, tasks have no explanatory force when normative questions arise. Reports about the ages at which one competence follows an earlier competence cannot by themselves be used to answer the question of which competence is more *advanced*. Such reports may have independent interest, but they could not, in principle, serve as a criterion of developmental level.

[18.2] Social Class as an Alternative Antecedent Variable

Age is one of several prospective, antecedent variables that are ignored in Piaget's theory. This proposition may be explained as follows. Charting the course of cognitive growth involves establishing the sequence in which intellectual abilities develop. In this context, reports of children's ages of task mastery have pragmatic value only. Suppose, for example, a developmentalist wished to document examples of IA or IIA or IIIA operational thinking (Inhelder & Piaget, 1955/1958). Which children could be expected to display such thinking? This question has only to be formulated for the utility of age reports to be appreciated in the selection of children to participate in a study. It is plausible to argue that age reports were included by Piaget as an aid to investigators and as an approximate guide to children's abilities in their development over time. This stance is a consequence of an interest in distinctive developmental processes that are taken to be complementary to genetic, environmental, and social processes (Piaget, 1970/1983).

Without calling into question the utility of age as an indicator of cognitive development, it is also the case that the average ages given by Piaget in connection with a given developmental level can be increased or decreased by the selection of children on the basis of their social class. In fact, social class has been shown to affect the distribution of performances on developmental tasks (Demetriou & Efklides, 1979; Figurelli & Keller, 1972; Hughes, 1986; Schröder & Edelstein, 1991).

Further, these differences are often massive. The incidence of formal operational thinking has been found to be related to schooling in a national (n=10,000) study of British children by Shayer and Adey (1981). In their study, only one third of the adolescents aged 16 years were found to display formal operational thought in schools nationally, whereas this increased to three-quarters of the (middle-class) adolescents based in selective schools. Comparable differences have emerged in American studies of proportional reasoning. In a study by Karplus (1981), some two-thirds of the 12th grade children from middle-class backgrounds in the United States displayed advanced levels of thinking, in contrast to only one-sixth of the children in the same grade from poorer backgrounds. So the first conclusion to draw from these several studies is that social class can make a great difference to human performance. Consequently, the exclusive preoccupation with children's age would seem to be misplaced, insofar as the effects of class are at least as strong, and in some cases stronger than those of age. Age is one important variable but certainly not the only one, and it is perhaps not even the major antecedent variable of children's development. This conclusion is compatible with the claim made earlier that the ages given by Piaget are indicators, not criteria, of developmental level.

A second conclusion is that the studies just cited are exceptional by their inclusion of information about social class. Most studies are silent about this variable, as are most reviews of intellectual development. Social class is largely ignored by many developmentalists, including Piaget. In consequence, the criticism that the ages stated by Piaget are incorrect is premature to the extent that it is based on studies where there is confounding of age and of class. Age claims arising from studies that do not control for social class can be submerged by findings from studies that do. Curiously, experimental studies in which antecedent variables are scrupulously manipulated are remiss in failing to control for such an obvious source of variation. At best, critics who contend that age enjoys criterial status present an incomplete argument, if no counterpart control for class has been included. At worst, that argument is self-refuting, because the failure to control any one major variable, whether criterial or influential, is as damaging as the failure to control any other.

A third conclusion relates to the converse case of studies that do pay explicit attention to the social element in intellectual development. In some studies of conservation, half of the children whose backgrounds were less favourable were found to give non-conserving responses, in contrast to one quarter of the children whose backgrounds were more favourable (Doise & Mugny, 1981; 1984). Sometimes social class is invoked to explain unanticipated findings, such as the lower success rates on some conservation tasks (Light et al., 1979). Armed with such findings, some developmentalists have drawn the conclusion that the interpretive scope of Piaget's account is lacking. An account based on the social construction of knowledge is taken to have greater explanatory adequacy in this respect (Cole & Bruner, 1971; Doise, 1989; Perret-Clermont, 1979/1988b). Discussion of this position is provided in [21]. The point to notice here is that such findings do not invalidate the sequence of levels in the construction of operational knowledge, and so do not run counter to the criteria of Piaget's accounts.

The central conclusion to be drawn from this brief review is not that class should be introduced as a new criterion of developmental level, but that neither age nor social class is such a criterion. The ages given by Piaget can fluctutate, depending on the social class of the children who have been selected for study. Typically, lower class children succeed at a later age than do middle-class children. Although Piaget (1971) acknowledged that both chronological age and social class are variables that can accelerate or delay cognitive growth, neither are of criterial importance in his theory, because their presence is always necessary but never fundamental. These two variables are necessary because they always affect the actualisation of a developmental sequence. They are not fundamental, because they do not change the sequence itself. Therefore, they do not and cannot function as criteria of developmental level .

[18.3] Age Range as a Hedge against the Criteriality of Age

If it were the case that children of *specific* ages either succeed or fail on various measures of concrete or formal operational thinking, then age might have a better claim on being a criterion for, rather than an indicator of, developmental level. In fact, there are many challenges to claims about the precision of such predictions. Further, these challenges occur in two ways, because the predictions from different studies are regarded either as under-estimates, or as over-estimates, of ability.

Some developmentalists have argued that Piaget under-estimated the age at which formal operational is manifest (Kuhn, 1979; Neimark, 1975) or concrete operational (Hart, 1981; Winer 1980). Other developmentalists have argued for the contrary position, suggesting that such abilities are in place at a much earlier age than Piaget proposed (Donaldson et al., 1983; Gelman & Baillargeon, 1983). Assessment tasks for transitivity are exemplary. In his early study, Piaget (1921b) showed how a transitivity task that was designed for adolescents—see [19] for specimen reasoning—could result in erroneous reasoning. This findings led to the use of the seriation task (Piaget & Szeminska, 1941/1952). Piaget (1970/1983) stated that this concrete operational task would be successfully completed by children aged 7 to 8 years. When this task is redesigned, younger children can succeed at 4 to 5 years (Bryant & Trabasso, 1971; Pears & Bryant, 1990), or at 5 to 6 years (Braine, 1959), or at 6 to 7 years (Halford, 1982). In other studies, monkeys have been shown to be successful in dealing with transitivity tasks (Chalmers & McGonigle, 1984). In other studies again, even intelligent adults are reported not to be comprehensively successful in their understanding of transitivity (Leiser & Gillièron, 1990). In short, there is almost indefinite variability in the age at which animals, children, and adults succeed, or fail, on different assessment tasks dealing with fundamental human abilities, such as the understanding of transitivity. But if age is not even a good indicator of developmental level, it could not serve as a criterion.

As a general conclusion to the argument in [18], three claims need to be kept distinct. One claim concerns the intellectual structures that are said to underpin operational knowledge; the second the content of such knowledge; and the third the tasks to be used in investigating intellectual development. Piaget (1970/1983) could say that his theory embodied the first claim about the structural basis of development, and competing perspectives exist regarding the second claim, about how development in the content of knowledge occurs (Carey, 1985; Strauss, 1988; Glaser, 1988). In this connection, there is a case to consider for regarding operational thinking as a prerequisite for intellectual progress, including the reorganisation of the content of knowledge (Lawson, 1989; Leiser & Gillièron, 1990; Markovits, 1992; Overton, Ward, Noveck, Black, & O'Brien, 1987). Whether or not this case is accepted, undue importance is assigned to the design of assessment tasks. Yet a *theory* for the design of tasks is conspicuously absent from developmental psychology. The *practice* of developmentalists is to take one task as a paradigm by reference to which serial modifications can be judged. This practice is rational and defensible, but it neither amounts to theory nor does it provide an objective means for the resolution of theoretical disputes surrounding the first two questions. Thus Piagetians could say that answers relevant to the third claim about assessment tasks are to be judged by appeal to answers to the first claim about the structuralist basis of knowledge. Critics could say that their answers to this third question are dependent on an answer to the second question about the content of knowledge.

The temptation is to support one side of this dispute, assigning it priority over the other. In any case, there is a mediating position according to which there are multiple criteria of developmental level, and one, though only one, is age. Using the distinction between genotype and phenotype, age would function as a criterion provided three conditions are met. One is that Piaget's structural models describe the genotype and not its phenotypical realisation. The second is that good exemplars of that genotype must be found and described. The third is that confirming evidence must be to hand. Such evidence has been cited in research undertaken by Shayer and his colleagues (Shayer & Adey, 1981; Shayer et al., 1988; Shayer, Küchemann, & Wylam, 1976). One weakness of this mediating position is that discussion tends to become side-tracked onto questions about its evidential backing, leaving more important theoretical questions to one side. The mediating position is then vulnerable to a standard objection about the presence of unexplained *décalage* (Brown & Desforges, 1980; Sternberg, 1987). The basic difficulty is that notion of task is assumed to be a proper unit of analysis in the assessment of theoretical issues. Reasons for rejecting this assumption were stated in [17].

Moreover, there is a better position to adopt, which puts the objection to the mediating position firmly in its place. The point is that such disputes cannot be resolved. A resolution might be possible, if a one-to-one or one-to-many relationship existed between operational knowledge and developmental tasks. This condition has not been met. Developmental tasks vary in unlimited ways, depending on the purposes, beliefs, and values of the investigators who design them. Following Wittgenstein (1958b), their common feature is that they form a family of overlapping tasks that are *called* developmental. What they have in common is their varying degrees of similarity and difference. But it is not a condition of a task's being a *developmental* task that there should be a set of defining features that all-and-only developmental tasks share. Operational knowledge, by contrast, is well defined because there is an explicit account of its constitutive features whose presence is required in all-and-only operational knowledge (Piaget, 1949; 1972). Yet no one-to-one relation exists between operations and tasks, because by common consent there are variant tasks for each form of operational knowledge (Gelman, 1978). Nor does a one-to-many relationship exist, because the different developmental tasks that have been used in practice in developmentalists' research have not been designed by the use of a common set of principles.

An analogy may help. The *summer season* can be strictly defined by reference to universal astronomical and geographical properties, which all-and-only summers possess. A *summer vacation* is identified in terms of variable human aspirations and beliefs, bounded by specific circumstances. Although summer vacations are normally taken in the summer season, they do not have to be. Someone who did not, through pressure of work, take a vacation in the summer season might take a that holiday in the subsequent winter after taking medical advice. In this way can a summer (main) vacation be taken in the winter season. This is no more strange than the sign in motorway cafe stating that breakast is available 24 hours a day. Summer vacations may have nothing in common other than their being called just that. In terms of their defining features, Piagetian structures are like the summer season; in terms of their defining features, assessment tasks are like a summer vacation. In short, invariable predictions about ill-defined summer vacations cannot be extracted from well-defined claims about summer seasons, and conversely. Similarly, invariable predictions about the (well-defined) structure of operational knowledge cannot be based on the (ill-defined) structure of assessment tasks and conversely.

Thus there is ample scope for mismatching of intellectual and task structures due to the heterogeneity of developmentalists' practice. The point to make about this heterogeneity is that, due to its presence, confounding of theoretical and empirical issues tends to occur. To be sure, both types of issue are important. Empirical research is necessary because an empirical account of intellectual development must be subjected to, and also survive, empirical testing. And a good indicator of developmental level has obvious value in the selection of subjects. Now although there are empirical issues to confront with respect to questions about developmental sequences and transition mechanisms, such questions are primarily theoretical (Campbell & Bickhard, 1986; de Ribaupierre, 1989). The demarcation of questions about methods and evidence from questions about substance and theory is secure, when the distinction between indicator and criterion is drawn.

[19]   MENTAL MODELS

Faced with Piaget's main problem about the development of necessary knowledge, one approach is to provide an account of the respects in which human thinking has a logical, and so necessary, character. A different approach is to provide an account that is devoid of such features; one which denies that human thinking is based on an individual's use of logic. This claim would be unremarkable in application to the many types of thinking that are neither objective, such as phantasy, nor inferential, such as associations of ideas. It is a remarkable claim, however, because of its express application to deductive reasoning (Johnson-Laird, 1990, p.97): "There is no need to explain how formal rules of inference are acquired by children, because the theory (of mental models) has no recourse to them in accounting for the ability to reason". Rather, the proposal requires the individual to construct a logic-free model for use in inferential reasoning.

Several considerations make this position attractive. First, its stock of problems is evidently both logical and inferential, including problems of propositional implication (Wason & Johnson-Laird, 1972), syllogistic inference (Johnson-Laird & Bara, 1984) and multiple quantification (Johnson-Laird, Byrne, & Tabossi, 1989). Second, the stance is resolutely empirical with explicit requirements of testability and computability (Johnson-Laird, 1983). Third, the position avoids the special pleading that is characteristic of its rivals. Logic is constituted by an infinite number of logical systems. Thus it is hard to resist the objection that a privileged status has been given to one system rather than to any other as a model of thought (Johnson-Laird, 1980). Fourth, logical models are taken not to capture psychological processes in that (Johnson-Laird, 1978, p.17) "such formal models bear only a remote relation to the *mental* representation of meaning". Fifthly, even if mental logic is rejected, mental models of how deductive ability develops are to hand (Johnson-Laird, 1990, p.86). Indeed, the general availability of this approach as an instrument for the analysis of experimental findings is its primary value. This is an important feature because developmentalists who are sympathetic to a structuralist approach have noted the difficulty in gaining acceptable evidence for the use of intellectual structures such as those associated with Piaget's logical models (Markovits, 1984; Halford, 1989). Finally, research on mental models has led to the design and use of reasoning tests—notably the selection task—whose use has led to the negative evaluation of the Genevan account of formal operational thought (Johnson-Laird & Wason, 1977).

Three steps are involved in using this approach. The individual, first, forms a mental model of the formal properties of the task; then extracts a novel conclusion (if any) which is true of that model even though not stated in it; and finally attempts to construct a counter-example, which is a different model of the same premises but without the novel conclusion. Inferential reasoning, which is deductively valid, is stated to be the outcome of this psychological process which is outside logic (Johnson-Laird, 1980, p.121; 1990, p.97).

Such an approach also has defects, several of which are now reviewed. Its notable defect is an in-built *deus ex machina*. The user of the model ultimately has to take on trust that a *logical* judgment is the outcome of a *non-logical* process. The explicandum of a mental model is logical reasoning; yet the model itself is stated to be devoid of logic. It is as if an individual can successfully do arithmetical problems without knowing any arithmetic.

One objection is that model-building depends on creative search (Johnson-Laird, 1980, p.122). But this search is inductive, as is evident at step three. The individual forms a model, extracts a conclusion and tests this in another model. There are two outcomes here, and both are inductive in character. One outcome is that the creative search is successful. The other is failure in finding a counter-example.

Suppose the creative search is successful and a counter-example is found. The only conclusion that the model-building individual is entitled to draw is that one of the models *is* discrepant with the other. But this conclusion is an inadequate basis for the judgment that at least one of the models *must* be changed. What is the origin of this necessity? Notice, first, that someone who understands the premises of a deductively valid argument does not *thereby* have to draw the conclusions implied by them (Stroud, 1979). The point is that even if the model-builder's judgments are correct, this is never due to the understanding of necessity *qua* logical notion. Notice, second, that the naturalistic fallacy is committed if a normative conclusion, which is necessary, is derived from premises which are solely empirical, and not necessary (Kohlberg, 1987; Smith, 1986b, 1991; van Haften, 1990; see Hudson, 1983 for discussion of the naturalistic fallacy). If a mental model specifies the sole abilities that are used in deduction, when these abilities are psychological, then this fallacy is committed by any model-builder whose inferences embody necessity. Yet necessity is one of the normative properties that constitute deductive implication, and so should therefore be captured in the epistemic conditions of inference. Successful search is too weak because the presence of *correct* models of the premises is insufficient for the extraction of *necessary* conclusions.

Suppose now that the creative search is unsuccessful and no counter-example is found. The failure to construct a counter-example is too weak because an argument (Haack, 1978, p.22) "is valid only if it *couldn't* have, not just *doesn't* have, true premises and false conclusion". The aim in creative search is to test the validity of an argument which, in turn, requires the individual to understand that the conclusion (step 2) could not be other than it is—could not be represented by the model at step 3—given the model of the premises at step 1. The construction of any finite number of further models is sufficient to show that no counter-example *has, so far, been found*. But such a conclusion is, for the reason stated by Haack, too weak when questions about logical validity arise: it needs to be shown that no counter-example *could* be found.

Thus whatever the outcome, creative search is reliant on an inductive process as the grounds for drawing deductive conclusions. In short, this approach leads to an unwarrantable empiricism.

It could be argued that Piaget's account is open to this same objection on two counts (Markovits, 1991). First, modal errors are sometimes made, for example when a logical relationship is judged to be empirical in character. Second, formal reasoning is viewed by Piaget to have an empirical origin, including an origin in physical action. This is an interesting argument because it serves as a reminder that Piaget's account must respect the distinction between the conditions of inductive and deductive inference. But it also concedes the main point. The logic-free reasoning of the model-builder never embodies logic that is in some form always available to an epistemic subject throughout development.

A second objection is that covert use of logic is made in a mental model account. This objection has been stated by Braine (1990) who contends that truth-table analysis and inference schemata are built into model construction. This objection can be extended, because logical notions are explicitly invoked in the description of model construction. For example, *premise, conclusion, form, follows from,* and *counter-example* are all invoked by Johnson-Laird (1990, p.96), as well as *one-to-one relationships* (Wason & Johnson-Laird, 1972, p.241), *possible worlds* (Johnson-Laird, 1978, p.18), *identity* (Johnson-Laird, 1980, p.80–1) and *some-all relationships* (Johnson-Laird, 1990, p.103). These are standard logical notions. They could have a logical meaning, in which case the account does embody logic. Alternatively, a stipulative definition which assigns them a new meaning could be given, in which case model construction remains unexplained until this stipulation is carried through. Johnson-Laird rejects the former but does not carry through the latter option.

The individual who constructs a mental model faces the problem posed by Piaget (1923, p.59): "how can an individual know that the conclusions of an argument are or are not contradictory with the premises, if there are no longer any rules to govern the deduction, if the deduction is replaced by a 'construction' whose outcome cannot be foreseen in advance?". If the 'rules' that Piaget has in mind are the rules of a mental logic, the 'construction' applies to the construction of mental models. Illogical reasoning is one expression of construction which disregards logic. The evidence is to hand: the studies of self-contradiction or pathological reasoning reported by Wason & Johnson-Laird (1972) are relevant here. Other examples are not hard to find, so consider a case arising from an early study of transitivity reported by Piaget (1921b, p.146).

The subject, aged nearly fourteen years, is presented with the premises that Edith is both darker than Lily and lighter than Susan. His train of reasoning from these premises can be represented thus:

First Reading: check on coding of premises:
1) Edith is lighter than Susan (*premise*)
2) Edith is darker than Lily (*premise*)

Second Reading: check on derived conclusions:
3) Lily is the darkest (*conclusion*)
4) Susan is the lightest (*conclusion*)
5) Edith is lighter than Susan (*premise*)

Therefore
6) Edith is more blond than Susan (*derived premise*)
7) Edith is darker than Lily (*premise*)

Therefore
8) Edith is the darkest (*conclusion*)
9) Edith is average (*conclusion*)
10) Susan is light (*conclusion*)
11) Susan is darker than Edith (*conclusion*)
12) Lily is dark (*conclusion*)
13) Lily is lighter than Edith (*derived premise*)

Therefore Both
14) Lily is the darkest (*conclusion*)
And
15) Susan is the lightest (*conclusion*)

Clearly, the subject has coded the premises correctly (1, 2) and can even correctly invoke them (5, 7). But although some correct conclusions are drawn from these premises (6, 9, 11), most are not (3, 4, 8, 10, 12, 14, 15). The key question is how a subject, who is presumed not to use logical notions, can come to recognise that this train of reasoning embodies counter-examples. The natural answer at this point is to say that the subject should realise that some of the conclusions contradict others, for example (6, 8). But *contradiction* is a logical notion. A different answer would be that the subject should realise that some beliefs (8, 14) are not implications of other beliefs (7, 13 respectively) but, once again, *implication* is a logical notion. Again, the subject could notice that some conclusions are compatible (6, 11). But *consistency* is a logical notion. Finally, the subject could notice that some conclusions are not all true (4, 6). But *negation* is, of course, a logical notion. In short, the objection is that mental construction makes covert use of logical notions. A minimal use of logic is, of course, still a use of logic. (See [21] for discussion of a social exemplification of transitivity).

A third objection concerns the extent to which a mental model approach addresses *developmental* questions. An interesting declaration has been made by Wason & Johnson-Laird (1972, p.2) who are interested in "factors which governed 'performance', and made it fail to reflect logical 'competence'". What is unclear is how this commitment squares with the aim of providing an account of the *development* of reasoning ability (Johnson-Laird, 1990, p.86). The fact that different aspects of performance on assessment tasks can be interpreted through two different accounts implies neither that the accounts are mutually compatible nor how they can be combined in one inter-dependent account. The question turns, in part, on whether Piaget's position is accepted to be a *tertium quid* [7] and, in part, on the extent to which a dual use is made of positions in both cognitive science and Piagetian epistemology [28].

A fourth objection concerns the celebrated selection task (Wason & Johnson-Laird, 1972). Although it was not initially designed as a test of formal operational thinking (cf. Wason, 1966), it has subsequently been taken to pose problems for its interpretation, on the one hand (Wason, 1977) and, on the other hand, to be incompatible with the Genevan account (Johnson-Laird & Wason, 1977). Piagetian commentary is similarly marked by differing evaluations of the extent to which modification is required to the Genevan account (Brown & Desforges, 1980; Lawson, 1987; Lawson, Karplus, & Adi, 1978; Overton et al., 1987). The argument will be that the implications for the account of formal operations of research based on the selection task are indeterminate.

First, analogues of the selection task were devised in the Genevan research during the 1950s, i.e, before Wason's (1966) initial report. In one such task, children in the age-range 7-15 years were presented with a statement that all the watches made in a factory in September are faulty. The main aim was to check the interpretation of Piaget's operational account using different reasoning tasks. Notice that a universal proposition can be analysed through universal quantification in terms of implication or through class inclusion and syllogistic logic (Quine, 1972). This logical difference, with which Piaget (1972, p.352) was familar, is discussed in [24.2]. The point of the task was to ascertain whether the children based their responses on class inclusion or on implication. The children were asked what could be inferred about a watch made in that factory which was (a) made in September, (b) made in July, (c) had a fault (d) had no fault (Morf, 1957, p.175). The results of this study were similar to those reported in a companion study (Matalon, 1962/1990), namely the delayed onset of formal operational thought and conditional reasoning. It was specifically noted, however, that the design of such tasks is different from that of formal operational tasks. One difference concerns the absence of a physical instantiation of the conditional statement whereby the children can manipulate the materials in the task (Matalon, 1962/1990, p.108; Morf, 1957, p.174). See [11] for discussion of this difference.

Second, a further difference follows from this, because the main purpose of the physical instantiation is to permit the display of concrete operational thought. A requirement for the assessment of formal operations is not just that an individual has formal operational ability, but rather that the individual's concrete operational abilities have been activated in performing the task. For example, hierarchical classification and multiplicative thinking are due to a concrete operational structure but their generalisation to yield combinatorial thinking is restricted to cases where a formal successor subsumes the concrete counter-part (Smith, 1987c). This substantive point is stated by Inhelder & Piaget (1955/1958, pp. 297–99, 254) who sharply demarcate operations based on inclusion and implication such that formal operations are operations on concrete operations.

This requirement is satisfied in certain versions of the selection task, namely those taken to have familiar content, but not in others, namely those taken to have abstract content (Bond & Shayer, 1991). In elaboration of this difference, consider the conditional operation which is defined as follows (Piaget, 1972, pp.221–22):

> if $p = x_1$ is a mammal (P) and $q = x_1$ is a vertebrate (Q), then there are only three true cases: PQ (the mammals which are vertebrates), $-PQ$ (the vertebrates other than mammals) and $-P-Q$ (the ones which are not mammals and not vertebrates). But the class $P-Q$ is empty because there do not exist mammals which are not vertebrates.

Notice, first, that this definition makes explicit use of the notion of class. Indeed, Piaget follows Couturat (1914, pp.3–4) in claiming that Boolean algebra has two permissible interpretations, one styled propositional and the other conceptual. As Mays (1992, p.45) puts it, "the calculuses of classes and propositions are alternative interpretations of some basic structure or algebra of logic". Although the interpretation favoured in extensional logic assigns an ontological priority to propositions, there is the alternative to consider. Mays has presented a detailed review of Piaget's position in which classes are prior to propositions, both ontologically and psychologically. Thus, in the example, the universe is the class *animal* and so it is with respect to that class that the $P-Q$ is empty. Similarly, it is that same class which provides the universe that limits the scope of the negations in $-P-Q$: "the ones" which are neither mammals nor vertebrates are animals. The relevant point here is that an assessment task which precludes the individual's use of a concrete operational structure could not lead to the successful display of formal operational thought.

When the selection task is presented with realistic content, the requirements for the assessment of formal operational thought are satisfied. In the sealed letter version, the universe is the class *letter* which has two subordinate classes, namely *sealed letter* (*P*) and *5d stamped letter* (*Q*). By contrast, with the abstract version dealing with letters and numbers, there is no permissible superordinate class to subsume *vowels* (*P*) and *even numbers* (*Q*). This is because any superordinate such as the class *object* breaks one of the conditions of concrete operational classification which is restricted to adjacent inclusions in a hierarchical sequence (Piaget, 1961/1966). The class *object* is not adjacent to the classes *vowel* and *number* in this sense. It is for this reason that it can be denied that the selection provides a challenge to the account of formal operations. Certain versions are at concrete, and other versions at post-formal, operational levels (cf. Smith, 1986c).

Third, almost all of the research based on the selection task has failed to include any control of formal operational abilities. Although such research typically makes use of adult students, who are assumed to have such abilities, it is notorious that formal operations are not universal across adolescence (Shayer & Adey, 1981). In a recent study, adolescents, aged 15 years, were presented with formal operational tasks and the abstract version of the selection task. The results showed that success on the former was in fact a necessary, but not sufficient, condition of success on the latter (Bond & Shayer, 1991; cf. Lawson, 1989).

Fourth, it is not always realised that the inspirations behind the work reported in Inhelder & Piaget's (1955/1958) were distinct. Inhelder's (1989, p.223) interests lay in the evolution of scientific reasoning; Piaget's (1954b, p.247) independent interests lay in the evolution of "the formal operations which bear on the possible and bring about directly the synthesis of the possible and the necessary". (See also Piaget, 1977/1986, p.301.) Neither was especially concerned with the comprehension of implication defined through the extensional logic of truth-tables. Indeed, the difference between operational implication and material implication in relation to the logic of 'natural thought' was specifically noted in the Genevan discussions (Grize, 1962, pp.96–7), including Piaget's (1961/1966, p.180) reminder that extensional logic was used as a model of operational logic *only* through its convenient availability. Such qualifications are lost in the standard translation (Inhelder & Piaget, 1955/1958, p.270/*305), which reads "reasoning is nothing more than the propositional calculus", whereas a better translation would read "reasoning is nothing more than the calculus embodied in the propositional operations". The Genevans' claim is not, as the defective translation implies, that reasoning is an instantiation of the *propositional calculus*, although critics have for 20 years attributed just this claim to them (Johnson-Laird & Byrne, 1990; Wason & Johnson-Laird, 1972). Rather, their claim is that reasoning is an instantiation of the calculus of *propositional operations* (cf. Smith, 1987c, p.344). The imputed claim would be open to disconfirmation through research using the selection task because intelligent adults do not always reason in accordance with extensional logic. The actual claim is different on both logical and empirical grounds. From a logical point of view, the system of propositional operations is interpretable in two distinct, but equally valid, ways (Couturat, 1914; Mays, 1992). The interpretation adopted by the Gevenan critics is the Russellian interpretation which is specifically rejected by Piaget (1949; 1972). The empirical point at issue is whether some system of propositional thinking is already at subjects' disposal. This assumption underpins the design of the selection task (Johnson-Laird & Wason, 1977). But what needs to be shown is how any such system has been acquired with special attention to its modal characteristics. The Genevan account does at least address this question, claiming that operational implication is a construction from concrete operational thinking based on class inclusion. This is a possible answer to the question and, as such, is better than no answer at all.

In short, there are doubts as to whether the inductive character of a mental models approach ever could present an acceptable account of deductive reasoning; doubts as to whether such an approach could address the construction of necessary knowledge; and doubts as to whether the selection task can be put to valid use in the assessment of formal operational thinking. The key issue was noted in [3] in the Bruner-Piaget exchange, as an analogous challenge applies to mental models research. Is the *case* for a mental models approach logical or not? If it has no logical basis, it can be dismissed out of hand because its rationality must be suspect. So if that case is worthy of rational scrutiny, for example in its empirical evaluation, the same question arises about any psychologist who accepts that case. Is the *thinking* of any such psychologist logical or not? If the psychologist's own thinking is not logical, that thinking can on rational grounds be dismissed out of hand. But if it is logical, questions arise as to how that logic was acquired.

In fact, the three questions outlined in [1] recur. First, if human thinking has a logical element, which systems of logic can be used in its description? Second, what are the psychological conditions to be met for the formation of primitive manifestations of that thinking? Third, how does the process of epistemic construction occur such that the primitive analogues can develop into instantiations of the formal systems? These substantive questions could not be adressed using a mental models approach. Yet they have to be addressed by any minimally adequate theory of intellectual development.

Leaving developmental questions on one side, it is, of course, reasonable to investigate how any available system of logical thinking is actually used. With such a question in mind, a mental models approach is welcome and is compatible with Piaget's (1923) argument which was noted in [7] about a developmental theory being a *tertium quid*. Attaining mastery of an available system of logic is different from the development in thought of that system of logic. In short, there is nothing intrinsically objectionable in a mental models approach. To the contrary, the argument has been merely that interpretations and findings associated with assessment tasks should not be too hastily generalised beyond their own domain in the provision of under-determining evidence for developmental theory which is beyond their scope.

CHAPTER SIX

Alternatives to Constructivism

"We note, on the one hand, that at all levels of mental evolution the mind searches for some form of coherence (coherence between actions, feelings, elementary beliefs, judgments, reasoning, etc): by virtue of its unifying function, the principle of contradiction is therefore present everywhere and thus contributes to the functional invariants of all intelligence. But, on the other hand, what appears contradictory to some is not so to others; primitive people and children assess coherence quite differently from us, mathematicians quite differently from the man in the street"
(Piaget, 1931, pp.150–51).

[20] PLATONISM REVISITED

The argument in Chapters 3–5 has been that although there are psychological challenges to consider in relation to the acceptability of Piaget's account of the construction of necessary knowledge, those challenges do not require substantial change to that account. Piaget's main problem has been variously by-passed or subjected to inappropriate operationalisation in much psychological research. This research may have contributed substantially to the psychology of childhood without significantly addressing a central issue in empirical epistemology.

The aim in this chapter is consider two challenges to constructivism. One concerns the commitment to individualism, shown in the importance assigned to the epistemic subject in [8.6]. The other concerns the normative aspect of developmental change, which was stated in [8.1] to be the acquisition of better knowledge.

The former challenge arises because in Piaget's account the epistemic subject is an impersonal subject of knowledge. Yet knowledge has a social nature because it is never the unique possession of one person. Today is Tuesday and John knows that today is Tuesday. But Mary can have the same knowledge and may even have acquired that knowledge from John. Knowledge is also open to inter-personal test. If John also claims today that tomorrow is Monday, his claim does not amount to knowledge, whatever he might think. Indeed Mary can show that the two epistemic claims are incompatible. The challenge is whether Piaget's commitment to there being an epistemic subject embodies an excessive commitment to individualism. A rival position states that individual construction is always due to prior, social construction. This challenge is discussed in [21].

The second challenge concerns the normative aspects of development. In Piaget's account, progression occurs as the acquisition and use of increasingly better logical structures. A commitment to structuralism ensures that the demarcation of lower from better level structures is well defined, for example in the differentiation of grouping and group structures (Piaget, 1970/1983). Yet the commitment to constructivism requires that the better structure is a later construction from the earlier but weaker structure. Thus the joint commitment, at best, embodies tension and, at worst, amounts to a contradiction. A rival view states that the obvious way to overcome this challenge is to regard all knowledge structures as innate, and so to deny that development is a normative process of growth. This challenge is discussed in [22].

The common feature of these two challenges is an apparent commitment to platonism, that is, to the view that objects of knowledge already exists in some form prior to their acquisition by individuals. If knowledge structures have a social construction in advance of their individual construction, then such structures are pre-existent. Again, if all structures are innate, then they are available in some form in advance of their individual use. Yet it was noted in [3.1] that platonism poses a direct challenge to constructivism. First, Piaget (1970/1972, p.88) claims that his account states constitutive conditions of the formation of knowledge, and not merely conditions of access to pre-existing knowledge. Second, Piaget takes his account to be explanatory of the production of novel thought, whether in children (Piaget, 1975/1985, p.67) or in the history of science where the growth of mathematics is taken to be both rigorous and creative (Piaget, 1950, p.286). Third, these two arguments combine, as the constitutive conditions of knowledge are conditions of epistemic construction by the adult genius and not merely by the apprentice child. In short, if platonism and constructivism are contraries, an exclusive choice must be made between them. It is for this reason that platonist challenges are serious.

[21] SOCIAL CONSTRUCTION

There are two versions of the challenge based on the social construction of knowledge, which are characterised hence as social constructivism and social constructionism.

The former position is stated to be compatible with Piagetian constructivism. "Cognitive constructivism in the Piagetian sense is to be completed by a more general theory of socioconstructivism" (Doise, 1989, p.398; cf Doise & Hanselmann, 1991, p.126). Provided prerequisite abilities are in place, intellectual development is the "fruit of anterior, social interactions" (Perret-Clermont, 1979/1988a, p.3). This challenge implies that one position (Piagetian constructivism) can be improved by a richer successor (social constructivism), which expands its interpretive scope. So construed, the weak challenge amounts to the identification of a gap in an otherwise acceptable position.

Quite different is the strong challenge that arises from a non-Cartesian and anti-Piagetian framework for developmental theory which is styled social constructionism (Harré, 1986b). The claim is that development is not a linear progression from low-to-high levels of competence but rather (Harré, 1986b, p.289) that "development usually occurs by the appropriation of structure and content from quadrants I through quadrants II, III, and IV, and finally by conventionalisation, to quadrant I, the realm of social being". The quadrants are formed by orthogonal axes, which form public–private and individual–collective 'space', where quadrant I is public–collective, and quadrant III private–individual, 'space'. This version of the challenge requires the elimination of Piaget's position, which is taken to be radically defective.

The difference between the weak and strong challenges is important. Developmentalists who press the weak challenge claim that Piaget's position merits clarification and elaboration. Piaget's claim is taken to be that all cognitive functioning is both psychological and social in being the exemplification of a unitary logical structure (Doise & Mugny, 1981/1984, p.6). But this general claim, so the weak objection runs, is compatible with several different empirical claims. These dual exemplications could be concurrent or consecutive and, if the latter, the social could precede the psychological, or conversely. Experimental studies can be used to examine critically these variants. However, in the final analysis, construction is required at both psychological and social levels because certain levels of individual construction are prerequisites for benefits to arise from social construction (Doise & Mugny, 1981/1984, pp.30, 35, 173). By contrast, the strong challenge requires that construction should start from public-collective 'space' and that development would occur as eventual transition to the private-individual (quadrant III) 'space' which must feed back to public-collective 'space' (quadrant I). The transition could not require the presence of prerequisite construction within the individual just because the transition is defined as one that must start from and terminate in quadrant I, which is stated to have a natural priority over the other quadrants (Harré, 1986a, p.122). Thus, in the final analysis, construction is intrinsically social, not psychological.

Socio-cognitive-developmental perspectives are influential. As they are well reviewed in several places, it is sufficient here to make three points in their favour. First, they can command theoretical support, both in theorising by Vygotsky (1934/1962; 1934/1978), which is taken to be worthy of respect and elaboration (Bornstein & Bruner, 1989; Wertsch, 1985), or in the philosophy of Wittgenstein (1958b), which is taken to be directly relevant to developmental theory (Hamlyn, 1982; Harré, 1987; Russell, 1987). Second, they have provided both a new stock of problems in developmental psychology and have contributed answers to them (Doise, 1989; Light & Perret-Clermont, 1989; Valsiner, 1987; Wood, 1980, 1988). Third, they have been given an applied use in education, notably in the interpretation of school learning and development (Donaldson, 1978; Edwards & Mercer, 1987; Newman, Griffin, & Cole, 1989), and in the design and use of intervention programmes (Feuerstein, 1980; Lysynchuk, Pressley, & Vye, 1990; Palincsar & Brown, 1984). Even so, a constant theme pervades many of these discussions, namely their negative implications for Piagetian theory as expressed in the weak and strong challenges.

The question to ask, then, is not whether such perspectives are worthy of continued attention, because of course they are, but rather the extent to which their acceptance requires modification to Piaget's account of the construction of necessary knowledge. Several issues merit closer scrutiny (Smith, 1989).

A first issue is whether Piaget's account has unacceptable social and educational consequences. Rather than accept these consequences, so the objection runs, it is better to modify, or even replace, the account that generates them. The reply will be that this objection rests on a false premise, shown by the difference between Piaget's own position and that attributed to him, between Piaget, the giant of developmental psychology (Hunt, 1969), and those of the straw-man who is facetiously styled PRJ (Wheldall, 1985), the phantom of the secondary literature. This phantom has as much reality as Macbeth's dagger—vivid to the beholder but transparent under the spotlight.

We are told: (i) Piaget states a maturational theory, emphasising states of readiness (Hughes, 1986, p.17)—in fact, Piaget (1964, p.178) denied that his theory is maturational and denied that teaching should be moulded to the stage-theory (in Smith, 1985); (ii) Piaget takes young children to be illogical and devoid of intellectual ability (Tizard & Hughes, 1984, p.128)—in fact, Piaget (1968, p.978) argued that logical abilities are present throughout childhood, error arising when there is a failure to differentiate variables, whether physical or social or moral (Piaget, 1962/1985; 1983/1987, pp.4–5); (iii) Piaget takes physical interaction to be the basis of development (Edwards & Mercer, 1987, p.18)—in fact Piaget (1970/1983; 1979) resisted the temptation to conflate action and physical or material activity; (iv) Piaget portrays development as a long and essentially solitary struggle undertaken by the lone child (Light, 1986, p.172)—in fact, Piaget (1969/1970, p.180) maintained that "social life, introduced in the classroom through the agency of effective collaboration among the students and the autonomous discipline of the group, implies the very ideal of the activity we have described as being characteristic of the new school".

Such attribution is, frankly, incredible. This objection should be ignored, though whether exorcism can be performed to put the phantom of the secondary literature to rest is a matter of faith. Piaget's (1969/1970, p.137) definition of education as a two-termed relation, linking "on the one hand the growing individual; on the other, the social, intellectual, and moral values into which the educator is charged with initiating that individual" is compatible with social perspectives. The systematic application of Piaget's position to educational practice— which could effectively be undertaken only with teachers' cooperation (Piaget, 1932/1932, p.414)—is not even addressed in this objection.

A related objection is also based on the false premise, that Piaget's account is limiting because it ignores the social dimension of knowledge (Edwards & Mercer, 1987; Harré, 1986b; Light, 1986). Not so according to Piaget (1947/1950, p.156): "The human being is placed from birth onwards in a social environment which operates in the same way as the physical environment". Further, (Piaget & Inhelder, 1966/1969, p.95) intellectual operations apply both to the physical as well as to "an interpersonal or social universe ... (since they) always involve a possibility of exchange, of interpersonal as well as personal coordination". In short, Piaget's account is fully compatible with the claim made by social constructionists, that development must start in a fully social—that is, public-collective—world.

It will be replied that these statements do not go far enough. They are too general to count as effective social theory. Nor have they been empirically elaborated in Piaget's studies (cf. Doise & Mugny, 1981/1984). Indeed, such claims are sometimes taken to show Piaget's failure to dissociate distinctively social from non-social aspects of development (Perret-Clermont, 1979/1988a, p.2). Further, recent experimental studies are taken to show that social factors are influential in the promotion of intellectual development at the individual level (Doise, 1989), leading to the conclusion (Light & Perret-Clermont, 1989, p.110) that "pragmatic, intersubjective agreements-in-meaning are seen as lying at the heart of the developmental process...as both the source and the substance of conservation".

But this conclusion rests on a conflation of the weak and strong challenges. Quite simply, the same social factors cannot simultaneously have causal and constitutive relations with the epistemic process in individuals. Accepting the weak challenge, social factors that promote intellectual advance can be identified, and so such factors can be regarded as prior to, and so the *source* of, operational knowledge. This implies that some modification is needed to Piaget's account, but that it is permissible to make identifying reference to the individual's knowledge, which is separable from—since causally produced by—nominated social factors. But the strong challenge is implied by that same conclusion, as social factors are stated to be the *substance* of operational knowledge, that is, to provide its constitutive or defining features. Yet the strong challenge requires the elimination of Piaget's account, as it is not permissible to make identifying reference—one that is devoid of social reference—to an individual's knowledge. This is clear from the comment made by Doise (1989, p.397), who quotes with approval the claim that "there are no independently identifiable, real world referents to which the language of social description is cemented", adding that "such a conclusion is certainly not incompatible with the social constructivist approach". At issue here is not so much whether Piaget's account requires change, but rather the respects in which there is a social dimension in epistemic construction. Both Piaget and his social critics state that there is a social dimension, but they differ as to the implications of this commitment. The key issue turns on two points. One is whether socioconstructivism is correct in maintaining that prerequisite abilities must also be reckoned with. The other is the extent to which the instantiation of a universal, logical principle has a social element.

Consider again the reasoning task reviewed in [19]. Transitivity is instantiated in the premises which state the ordering of the hair colour (physical property) of Edith, Lily and Susan. But this same relation is also instantiated in premises about the beliefs (psycho-social property) of these girls as to who is the darkest. Suppose that the three girls have never been in their joint presence, but that Susan and Lily have each met Edith on separate occasions. If Susan's belief is given by (1)—Edith is lighter than Susan—and Lily's belief by (2)—Edith is darker than Lily—then Edith should draw from these premises the conclusion that Susan is the darkest (cf. Smith, 1982b, p.175). Thus logical principles do have a social instantiation and such principles are part of a common culture. What does it profit a person to have a rich cultural heritage which is completely lacking in this respect?

A third objection leads to the same conclusion. Piaget's (1923/1959) account of cognitive egocentrism has been criticised on the grounds that it fails to do justice to the social nature of communicative competence (Donaldson, 1978; Harré, 1986b; Vygotsky, 1934/1962). Once again, this objection has varying force because it can be used in support of both the weak and strong challenges.

To see why, note that Piaget denied neither that children are social beings nor that they are sometimes effective communicators (Piaget, 1962/1985, p.4): "Cognitive egocentrism, as I have tried to make clear, stems from a lack of differentiation between one's own point of view and the other possible ones, and not at all from an individualism that precedes relations with others". In this reply to Vygotsky, Piaget acknowledges the presence of social experience, identifies non-differentiation as a constraint on thinking, and points out that its removal requires children to relate any one judgment to other possibilities in the system. His claim is that, with the best of intentions, children do not always realise that there are other points of view—that is, possibilities—to take into account besides their own. His point is not that cognitive egocentrism exhausts social communication but rather that a communicative exchange will be unsuccessful, if cognitive egocentrism is present. That is, the latter is a necessary but not sufficient condition of the former. This claim is relevant to studies of social interaction. In some studies, social interaction has been shown to have a facilitating effect on intellectual progress in certain contexts (Doise & Mugny, 1981/1984; Murray, 1972; Perret-Clermont, 1979/1980). But there is counter-evidence as well, where no evidence of these facilitating effects has been reported (Russell, Mills, & Reiff-Musgrove, 1990; Tudge, 1989). It is for this reason that a principled distinction is needed to show the conditions under which social interaction amounts to social exchange.

The fourth objection serves to expand this conclusion. Some experimental studies have successfully shown that operational knowledge is contextually sensitive. The suggestion is that Piaget's studies have disregarded this social feature. Thus Cole & Bruner (1971) have argued that social variables such as class and race influence displays of ability; a finding that is reported in other developmental studies in [18]. Doise and Mugny (1981/1984) and Doise and Hanselmann (1991) have identified social marking as an influential factor in intellectual progression, in that social regulations correspond to the individual regulation of knowledge. Perret-Clermont (1979/1988b, p.8; cf. Schubauer-Leoni, Bell, Grossen, & Perret-Clermont, 1989) has argued that contextual factors are operative and identifiable in the "*hic et nunc* at the very heart of the testing situation".

In reply, a distinction drawn by Cole & Bruner (1971, p.874) is apposite. Their argument is that empirical studies are concerned with displays of competence, but that whereas competence is blind with respect to both situation and culture, its displays are definitely not. The trouble is that this distinction can lead to either of two contrary conclusions. One states that there are underlying competences within the individual and that these can be assessed, albeit on the basis of their variable social display. The suggestion is that the assessment of competence is more difficult than Piaget's account implies, although it is not intrinsically impossible. Such a conclusion is presupposed in Vygotsky's (1934/1978) claim that any intellectual function appears twice, first inter-personally and then intra-personally. The other conclusion states that the detection of 'pure' competence within the individual is a futile endeavour because its displays are always socially mediated. If such competence exists, it does so in the culture, not the child. This conclusion is presupposed in discussions where social relationships are constitutive, and so not causally independent, of intellectual development (Harré 1987; Walkerdine, 1988). Socioconstructivism is committed to the former, unlike social constructionism which implies the latter, conclusion. However, these two conclusions are contraries and so a choice has to be made between them. Thus the key issue is whether ideal competence is a cultural construction which is never located in its display by individuals and to which access never requires prerequisite levels of individual competence.

The resolution of this issue turns on the ambiguity of *success*. With respect to any interaction, one question to ask is whether it is social; another is whether it is effective. An interaction, which has been successfully identified as social, must meet other conditions for it to be identified as successful, that is, effective. Such accounts are not in abundant supply. Yet Piaget's (1977a) model of social equilibration, which does specifically note this ambiguity, is almost invariably by-passed. One feature of Piaget's model is the explicit distinction drawn between exposure and exchange. A social interaction is necessary for intellectual development, but not sufficient as the interaction may amount to exposure alone. According to Piaget (1977a, p.144), it is a mistake to regard the mere presence of another person or of a social collective as an effective socialising agency. Thus other conditions have to be met, including shared values which are conserved throughout the interaction on a reciprocal basis (Chapman, 1986; Kitchener, 1981; Mays, 1982; Smith, 1982b). What counts, then, is social exchange. Piaget's account embodies two claims that are essential to any acceptable model of successful interaction. One concerns the use of a shared system of thought, meaning, and modes of reference. The other concerns the triadic nature of communication which is never reducible to a dyadic relation between two people but always, and in addition, includes a shared object of reference. Communication cannot, in principle, succeed, if the communicants do not use a common, referential domain. The latter is epistemic and intellectual and, as such is addressed in Piaget's account of social equilibration (Chapman, 1991, p.215).

Consider a study of social marking and conservation (Doise, 1989; Doise & Mugny, 1981/1984). Non-conserving children are invited to share two drinks between two children who had done equally well (social marking) or simply to share two drinks equally (control). The results show that there were fewer conserving responses in the control condition. But this is exactly the point of conservation studies! Conservation—see [16]—is the continued use of defining properties of a concept through their dissociation from those properties that happen to be co-instantiated with them. In the original studies, the dissociation concerned physical properties, such as the height or width of the container. In studies of social marking, social properties, which are not defining properties of quantity, must be equally differentiated from the same defining properties. Thus the findings are compatible with individual constructivism on two counts. First, the profusion of non-defining properties, based both on social marking and on physical properties such as height, provides further opportunity for cognitive conflict within the mind of the non-conserving child. Second, conservation requires the dissociation of *any-and-all* non-defining property from the defining properties of the concept under investigation. Non-defining properties may be physical, but they may also be social.

In short, social theory includes many problems in its domain. But one of them concerns the social instantiation of logical principles. Displays of logical competence are contextually sensitive, and so are subject to variation and control in social interaction. The latter will be effective only in cases of social exchange. And social exchange requires the dissociation of the distinctively social aspects of the interaction from the defining properties that are constitutive of specified logical principles. It is in this sense that Piaget's (1977a) model of social equilibration is important because it sets out further conditions to show when social experience, which is always present in some form in all actions, counts as an a successful experience making possible a valid exchange of views.

A fifth objection concerns the platonism that is implied by social constructionism. Central to a culture are its stock of artefacts (novels, paintings), symbols (crucifix, national flag), rules (dress, professional conduct), and values (justice, equality). Such cultural objects also include logical objects (Russell's paradox; 4, IV; transitivity; truth). The culture in which an individual is placed is influential in two ways because (Piaget, 1950, p.17) it "not only plays the role of accelerator but even transmits a host of notions which have themselves a cultural history". The same point is made by Newman et al., (1989, p.63), that children "cannot and need not reinvent the artifacts that have taken millenia to evolve in order to appropriate such objects into their own system of activity". And Harré (1987, p.4) raises the question of "what belief systems are available in a culture?" So there is agreement that there are cultural objects to which children have access. There is latent disagreement, however, about how this claim is to be interpreted in the three positions.

Piaget (1977a, p.170) is committed to the presence of "a general logic that is both collective and individual". The suggestion is that the conditions applicable to the construction of knowledge within the individual's own mind are equally applicable to shared construction between individuals. It is not that the conditions of individual construction are exhaustive of social construction, but rather that any further conditions applicable to social construction will have to include those applicable to individual construction. Socioconstructivists appear to be similarly committed, with the substantial qualification that there actually are further conditions applicable to social construction. For example, a social display of a logical structure may precede that in the individual. Thus Newman et al., (1989, p.1) state that "cognitive change is as much a social as an individual process", whereas Doise and Mugny (1981/1984, p.12) stress that "intelligence is not just an individual property but also a relational process between individuals". But the unity of this second position breaks down. Whereas Doise and Hanselmann (1991, p.126) continue to stress individual construction as a condition of intellectual progress, others take a different stance. Newman et al. (1989, p.59) argue that the individual is not always the best unit of analysis for examining intellectual change because (p.72) the location of "the representation in the functional system cannot be decided a priori". By this is meant that a representation of an intellectual task may be located within an individual, but it may instead enjoy a social location in the culture. Thus there is no requirement that all representations are individually locatable. In short, there is tension in this position. The reason is clear when consideration is given to social constructionism, which specifically delimits individual construction and excludes it altogether when initial appropriation occurs from a public-collective 'space' (Harré, 1986a).

What, then, is that social 'space'? It is evidently not physical space. Nor is it a construction from the minds of individuals. It is analogically similar to a Popperian 'third world'—see [3.2]—which is neither a physical world nor a mind-dependent world. In this sense, a social 'space' and a Popperian 'third world' are both exemplifications of platonism. A social 'space' is an abstract object which is mind-independent and so meets the platonist criteria outlined by Hale (1987) in [3.1]. Note that platonism does not imply a commitment to the occurrence of static, unchanging objects. Dynamic relations can hold between social objects that may be the subject of serial evolution. However, platonism and constructivism are incompatible. Of course, in experimental studies, the adult knows how to do the task, unlike the child who may not. Indeed, educational applications of socio-constructivism trade on this very point, since new concepts are introduced by the experimenter or teacher (Newman et al., 1989, p.66). Models of reciprocal teaching are defined through the appropriation by the learner of the expertise antecedently possessed by the teacher (Palincsar & Brown, 1984). But the issue is not whether this sometimes happens but whether it always does. The point is that social constructionism returns a positive answer here. It must always happen because appropriation always starts from the antecedently existing social 'space'.

The objection is not that a position which is committed to platonism must thereby be rejected. Rather, the objection is that social constructionism is a position that has platonist commitments and, as such, is incompatible with constructivism. In short, socioconstructivists must make an exclusive choice. Two specific claims are now considered with this choice in mind.

First, Cole & Bruner (1971) distinguish contextually sensitive displays and 'pure' competence, which is insensitive in this respect. The suggestion is that developmentalists should pay more attention to the former than to the latter. But this suggestion leads to three questions. Considering any display, the question always arises "a display of what?" One way to answer can be given by specifying a competence that is described through some logical structure. But any such structure is a 'pure' structure. Second, the question then arises "what is the ontological status of any such 'pure' competence?" At issue here is whether that competence has a mind-independent existence in a social 'space' or whether its existence is mind-dependent. Third, the epistemological question arises "how is an individual's access to 'pure' competence made possible?". At issue here is whether prerequisite competence— within the individual—is also required. Social constructionism is committed to a negative response of the third question, unlike Piagetian constructivism which is committed to an affirmative response. Socioconstructivism requires a choice to be made between these alternatives.

Second, socioconstructivists claim that certain social interactions are characterised by necessity (Doise, 1989, p.395). The suggestion is that the necessity which is so instantiated is the source of the individual's understanding of necessity. Certainly, the modal relationships holding between possibility and necessity are analogous to those between permission and obligation (Piaget, 1932/1932, p.322; Piéraut-Le Bonniec, 1974/1980, p.26; von Wright, 1951). This point is further discussed in [25.2]. But this suggestion leads straight to the problem that has been manifest in Piagetian research on individual construction. Any instantiation, whether physical or social, is such that the defining properties of a concept or structure can be conflated with the properties which are associated with them in that instantiation. In a conservation task, the individual who believes that the length of a line is a defining property of number will exhibit nonconservation in much the same way as the individual who uses social marking criteria. Thus the same three questions arise. With respect to any display, the first question is "a display of what?". Necessity instantiated at the social level may in fact be understood as a contingent relationship for all that. The second question also arises as to the ontological status of necessity *qua* characteristic feature of a social 'world' independently of human understanding. The third, epistemological question also arises, concerning the conditions that have to be met for an individual to acquire a specified form of modal understanding.

In short, the status of socioconstructivism as a reconciling project is in doubt. Certain early studies of social interaction are taken not merely to be compatible with, but even to imply, Piaget's account of equilibration (Murray, 1972; 1990). Other studies have led to the elaboration of the distinctively social aspects of human displays of knowledge in social settings (Light & Perret-Clermont, 1989). It is one thing to enlarge the paradigm for psychology by the inclusion of specifically social elements (Doise, 1989) and quite something else to do this by exclusion of specifically individual elements (Harré, 1987). The social construction of logically necessary structures of knowledge is a case in point. *Social construction*, under one of its interpretations, is implied by Piaget's constructivism but, under the other interpretation, implies platonism. Since constructivism and platonism are contraries, this exclusive difference is important.

[22] THE LEARNING PARADOX

An argument, which is styled the *learning paradox*, has the consequence that constructivism in any of its several forms is impossible (Bereiter, 1985). This argument has its basis in the conditions that would have to be met for the learning of a new predicate in a natural language (Fodor, 1976). This is a strong challenge, amounting to the claim that intellectual development could not—in principle—take place in the way suggested in constructivist accounts. The counter-argument to be considered here is that Fodor's challenge itself has an unacceptable consequence, namely its commitment to platonism, which leaves completely unresolved the problems that constructivist accounts address, including the construction of necessary knowlege.

The argument formulated by Fodor is taken by him to require the assumption that learning a predicate occurs through the formation and confirmation of hypotheses, that is, through hypothesis-testing (Fodor, 1976, p.95). This is an important admission; indeed, Fodor admits that the main point of his argument is to show how disreputable this assumption is (1976, p.82). The learning paradox is, then, the reminder that if hypothesis-testing is the only way in which a new predicate could be learned, then such learning is impossible. The implication is that this consequence is unacceptable and so the assumption on which it depends should be rejected, and replaced with a better successor. The difficulty, states Fodor, is that there is currently no better successor to hypothesis-testing.

But Bereiter (1991) has noted that the learning paradox is general, claiming that the assumption identified by Fodor covers a family of learning theories. This is evident in Bereiter's response to the argument offered by Boom (1991) who claims that Piaget's account embodies an alternative model of learning through reflective abstraction from action, and the construction of complete compensations between affirmations and negations (cf. Piaget, 1974/1980; 1977b). Boom's claim is that Piaget has offered an intelligible alternative to hypothesis-testing, and so the learning paradox is resolved. Bereiter disagrees, supporting his denial through the distinction between (a) covert forms of hypothesis-testing and (b) alternative processes which do not operate in this way. His claim is that the processes in reflective abstraction are covert forms, and not alternatives (Bereiter, 1991, p.295). Thus the challenge posed by the learning paradox is applicable to a range of learning theories, whether or not such theories nominate hypothesis-testing explicitly.

Several formulations of the learning paradox have been given. In its most general form, Bereiter (1985, p.204) takes this problem to concern the generation by a structure of a structure more complex than itself. In Juckes' (1991, p. 264) formulation, structures are learned through a developmental process, which Piaget has named equilibration, as it is through this process that novel understanding is made possible. Both formulations have many analogues in Piaget's writings (cf.1950, p.13; 1969/1970, p.27). But the formulation due to Fodor identifies perspicaciously the central point at issue. According to Fodor (1976, p.80), there is a minimal condition which a theory of novel learning must meet, namely the extensional equivalence of the novel concept and an available concept. This condition states that the learning of a novel concept is possible only if some connection is made with a concept already at the learner's disposal. The connection is extensional equivalence in that the available and novel concepts should subsume all-and-only the same individual instances. The reason for the requirement of extensional equivalence is because the learner of a putatively novel concept must formulate some hypothesis such that its criterial attributes pick out the very same instances as those picked out by an already available concept. The suggestion is that 'something is an instance of (novel) concept C_1 if and only if it is an instance of (available) concept C_2'. There is no suggestion that this is the sole condition, otherwise no concept could be different from any other. Rather, the suggestion is that if the condition about extensional equivalence is not met, the learning of a novel concept is not possible.

The key condition is stated in terms of the truth-conditions of predicates corresponding to such concepts. Consider any predicate P which is novel for the learner. The learner must relate P to some existing predicate, say G, where G is already at the learner's disposal and where G is extensionally equivalent to P. That is, the learner must formulate a hypothesis about the conditions under which P is true in terms of some other predicate G, whose truth-conditions are related systematically to those of P. But the existing predicate must already be at the learner's disposal because it could not itself be a novel predicate for that learner on pain of a regress. So if the predicate G is not novel, then the learner must already have learned it. Thus the learning of an apparently novel predicate is possible only if a co-extensive predicate has already been learned. Thus learning amounts to the fixation of belief, and not to the acquisition of a new concept or intellectual structure (Fodor, 1976, p.87).

Fodor's argument is a dilemma. Either any predicate of a novel concept is co-extensive with those of an available concept or it is not. If the former, the concept cannot be novel; if the latter, it is unlearnable.

This conclusion is stated explicitly by Fodor to be applicable to Piaget's stage theory, although Fodor is candid enough to admit that his interpretation of Piagetian theory may be idiosyncratic (Fodor, 1976, p.92; Fodor, 1980, p. 147). Interpreting adjacent stages as instantiations of progressively stronger logical systems, Fodor argues that structural growth could not, in principle, occur. This is because an inventory of the truth-conditions of the novel predicate, P, would require use of the stronger system, whereas the truth-conditions of the available predicate, G, would be restricted to the weaker system. Yet the stronger system differs from the weaker system precisely because the former has notions that cannot be embodied in the latter (Fodor, 1976, p.93). Fodor's conclusion is that intellectual development could be described in much the way that Piaget suggests but its explanation is another matter. Lacking an intelligible account of how a new, and better, structure can be constructed from an available, and weaker, structure, the implication is that nativism is the only alternative (Fodor, 1980, p.147).

The obvious comment to make about Fodor's argument is that it cannot be novel. It cannot be novel since the argument is dependent on the concepts used in its formulation and there can be, so that argument runs, no novel concepts. The argument is, in effect, the statement of a tautology. And this tautology has a general application, because it excludes there being any genuine cases of novelty, not just in the minds of developing children but also in the advancement of science. Yet Piaget (1979/1980, p.150) observed that he had some difficulty in accepting the suggestion that Cantor's theories had a genetic basis. To see the problem here, consider Newton's remark that he had achieved so much because he had stood on the shoulders of giants. This remark is normally understood to be an expression of modesty to the effect that his theory was only a modest advance over those of his predecessors such as Galileo. But if Fodor's argument is accepted, Newton's theory could not be an advance over that of Galileo at all, still less that of Aristotle. From Fodor's argument it follows that, in some sense, Aristotle had the concepts of Newtonian physics. But in what sense? Taken literally, this implication does not square with the historical facts. Thus Fodor would have to claim that even though Aristotle and Newton possessed a common set of physical concepts, their respective beliefs attached to their use of these concepts were —no doubt modestly—different. In reply, one point to make is that this is an odd way to regard the difference between Aristotelian and Newtonian physics, which are contradictories (Kuhn, 1977; McCloskey, 1983). The more important point is that it raises the question of what it is to have a concept attached to which are discrepant, and even contradictory, beliefs. Indeed, it was noted in [5] that the history of science is littered with such cases. It is Piaget's claim that children's development is similar in this respect. Examples are given in [25.2].

Second, Fodor's argument is not entirely novel in a different sense. His argument has its origin in Plato's (nd/1956, §87A) contention that all knowledge is recollection, as the slave-boy knew all along the length of the side of a square whose area is double that of a square two units long. Socratic questioning merely allowed the slave to make conscious use of the relevant concepts which were already at his disposal. Paradoxically, claimed Plato, new knowledge is possible only by virtue of its prior possession through which it—the new knowledge—can be recognised as the knowledge it is. But Aristotle (nd/1975, §I.1) turned Plato's conclusion on its head. He pointed out that "all intellectual learning comes about from already existing knowledge". There would be a genuine paradox only if a person already knew something in exactly the same way as it is currently being learned. Aristotle's point is that what is known in one way can be learned in some other. Someone may well know the defining properties of triangularity but may still have to learn that the figure in a semi-circle is a triangle. According to this conception, learning is the forging of novel connections by means of the knowledge that is already at the person's disposal. What counts is not prior knowledge but rather the use to which it is put.

A third point follows from this, namely that the notion of learning is complex, so distinctions must be drawn. Central to constructivism is a family of contrasts between learning and development. Thus Piaget (1959, p.38) identified learning in the wide sense with (a) all intellectual acquisitions, which are both (b) mediated, and (c) due to experience or not. By contrast, learning in the narrow sense is a sub-set of the mediated, intellectual acquisitions due to experience.

One consequence of this definition is that some knowledge is due neither to heredity, nor to perception, nor to experience. Novel learning provides instances of this epistemic class. Inhelder & Sinclair contrast learning—construed as the incremental addition of observable information—and development—construed as re-discovery and re-invention through the use made of that information (Inhelder & Sinclair, 1969, p.21). In this definition, developmental change is novel epistemic construction. An analogous contrast has been stated (Lawson & Staver, 1989, p.170; their emphasis) about emergent properties that "do *not* rise from novel parts. Rather, they arise from a novel arrangement of the *same* parts". However, Carey (1985, p.5) has specifically contrasted weak re-structuring, in which new relations are formed between concepts, and and strong re-structuring, in which changes are made to the concepts themselves. This family of distinctions is relevant to Fodor's position as follows.

Fodor's position that all concepts are innate can be refuted by the identification of just one concept that is not innate. Putnam (1988) has pointed out that *carburettor* is just such a concept, which was presumably unknown in the Stone Age. But Fodor (1976, p.96) has anticipated such a response by speculating that complex concepts—his example is *airplane*—can be decomposed into simpler constituents. Yet Fodor's response is idle, as too his related claim that a stock of concepts, all of which are innate, may be possessed even if not literally present at birth (1976, p.96). Very well; but the question to ask is: "How does the formation of complex-from-simple concepts differ from the fixation of beliefs to available concepts?".

Suppose that there is a stock of concepts present at birth in much the way that Leibniz suggested in [3.1]. These concepts would be the fundamental categories of thought in the Rationalist sense. But this admission is fully compatible with Piaget's (1931) claim—see [8.5]—that the categories of thought are functionally present at the outset of experience; functionally, but not structurally, present. The point is that the same categories are put to differential use by children during their development and by adult thinkers in the history of science. The distinction between learning and development serves to demarcate two types of epistemic construction. Applying this claim to Fodor's argument, Piaget is explicitly committed to some analogue of the nativist claim that there is a common stock of concepts which are innate. Even so, there is an important difference in the epistemic use to which this common stock of concepts is put. The real problem is less concerned with the absence-*vs*-presence of concepts than with the manner of their use. That is, the real problem lies in specifying distinct types of epistemic use of commonly possessed concepts. In particular, a substantive question is whether conceptual re-formation can result in novel forms of understanding. But there can be no answer to this problem in Fodor's nativism. Piaget may have proposed an incomplete, even a bad, explanation in response to this problem, but a bad explanation is better than none at all—and the nativist position is no explanation at all (Cellérier, 1980, p.80).

Why is the nativist position no explanation at all? One reason is elaborated in detail by Campbell & Bickhard (1987; Bickhard & Campbell, 1989). Their objection is that Fodor's position carries an implied commitment to some version of a correspondence theory of truth, because mental representation is conceived to be a copy, or encoding, of what is represented. This conception has unacceptable consequences. Some forms of knowledge, such as knowing-how, are not representational, and so could not be a copy of anything. The supposition that the stock of innate concepts are foundational is incoherent, as there could be no independent knowledge of what is so represented. And novel copies would be impossible.

A second reason is that Fodor's position simply pushes the problem one step back. If the stock of concepts in the human mind has a genetic basis, to what is their origin in the genome due? In particular, how are logically necessary conceptual relationships caused by biological factors that are not necessary? This is, of course, Piaget's main question stated in [1]. Unlike Fodor, who declines to answer, Inhelder & Piaget (1959/1964, p.15) have specifically argued that development in the use of a concept occurs as the reciprocal interplay between its intension and extension, for example in hierarchical classification. As concepts are presumably hierarchically related, late development in their use can be expected, if hierarchical classification is a guide. This is because hierarchical classification is late in onset, perhaps manifest during middle childhood but certainly not present in early infancy. This claim is elaborated in [24.3]. The point to make here is that a proposed solution is better than none.

A third reason is that Fodor's nativist position is a form of platonism. Platonism is assumed in the claim that concepts are, in some sense, present in the human mind from the outset, and that learning is a matter of fixation of beliefs to these innately possessed concepts. But in what sense? A range of questions arise at this point; one about which concepts are simple, another about the attachment of beliefs to concepts, and a final question about the replacement of true beliefs by necessary beliefs.

First, some criterion is required for the identification of simple concepts in the common stock. Exactly which concepts are these? As the concepts cited by Putnam and Fodor are not well defined, well defined logical concepts provide an ideal case for answering this question. This proves, however, not to be so, because normative disputes, as noted in [4.1] abound. For example, although Russell (1919) and Quine (1972) have regarded the propositional calculus as more fundamental than class logic, the independence of these two logical systems has been shown by Couturat (1914) and Mays (1992). As logical systems are defined through an explicit set of primitive notions, they provide ideal candidates for making the requisite inventory of the stock of innate concepts. Yet such an inventory cannot be carried through because there is nothing in a concept *qua* concept to show that *proposition*, unlike *class*, is a simple concept, or conversely. Following Wittgenstein (1958b, $47) and Piaget (1950, p.13), it can be claimed that there is no absolute answer, but rather an indefinite number of answers that are relative to some system of knowledge. Although there has to be some prior system, there need not be any specific system. In short, Fodor's nativist position leads straight to an unanswerable question.

Second, how is a belief initially attached to an innate concept? Fodor contends that a concept can be possessed but not used. An account is owing as to how a belief is initially attached to an innately possessed concept, to which no beliefs have been hitherto attached. Assuming the independence of any pair of innate concepts, Fodor is committed to the view that beliefs attached to one concept can be re-assigned to another. This is because of his co-extensionality requirement in stating the learning paradox. But then Fodor's nativism provides no escape from the learning paradox. Consider concept P, which is possessed but not used, and concept G, which has already been used by the learner. According to Fodor, hypothesis-testing is the only way in which learning occurs. So the learning of P must occur in this way. But this is impossible because *ex hypothesi* these two concepts are independent and so the resources of the concept-already-available will be insufficient to formulate the the hypothesis to be tested about the concept-to-be-learned. Using a logical analogy to which Fodor (1976, p.93) is partial, if *conjunction* is an innate concept which has been used, unlike *universal quantifier* which is innate but has not hitherto been used, the learner could not re-assign beliefs from the former to the latter. At least, not by hypothesis-testing.

Third, how is one belief, attached to one concept, replaced by another belief, attached to the same concept; for example a false by a true belief or a true by a necessarily true belief? The point is that these are intelligible questions, that constructivism attempts to provide answers to them, but that Fodor's nativism has no answer to them. Suppose concept G is part of the stock of innate concepts but its possessor fails to differentiate the defining, and so necessary, properties of those concepts from those properties that happen to be correlated with them. Conservation reviewed in [16] provides examples. According to Piaget, there is development in the use of concept G whose possession is dependent on successful differentiation, whereby radically discrepant beliefs are replaced by a coherent system of understanding. That is, bare possession of concept G counts for very little when there is non-differentiation of its defining and non-defining properties. In consequence, the distinction between learning and development is central. Learning is the use of a concept, whose defining properties are understood, in the acquisition of further beliefs and knowledge. Development, by contrast, is that epistemic process during which the defining properties of concept G are initially acquired through differentiation. According to Fodor, because concept G is innate, its defining criteria must be understood, whatever the nature of the beliefs that are subsequently assigned to it. Thus there is no need for a distinction between learning and development. But there is a double price to pay for this apparent parsimony. First, an explanation is owed as to how the defining properties of a concept are innately fixed in the first place. Second, an explanation is owing as to how a concept, whose defining properties are innately fixed, can be used with so little regard to them. Conservation, marked by due regard to its modal features (Murray, 1981, 1990; Smith, 1987a), is alien to the mind of the two year old child. Fodor's platonism provides no explanation of non-conservation, unlike Piaget's constructivism, which does.

It could be replied that a commitment to nativism is compatible with a mental models approach. But for reasons given in [19], this reply is not enough. The search for mental coherence cannot be comprehensively carried through by use of an approach which is, in the last analysis, inductive. Nativism fails to address such questions; constructivism does at least present answers to them. The understanding that Socrates was trying to elicit depends on transitivity and some form of hypothetical reasoning (Smith, 1987a, p.206). There are evident differences in the *development* of these forms of understanding both in the case of transitivity (Leiser & Gillièron, 1990; Pears & Bryant, 1990) and in hypothetical reasoning (Markovits, 1991; Moshman, 1990). Manifestly, Piaget's account addresses such questions and is taken to have contributed to their resolution. So construed, constructivism provides a *better* explanation than nativism whose implied platonism precludes there being answers to substantive questions.

There is an objection to this construal of constructivism, namely that it simply begs the question. After all, a purported answer is not an answer. To be sure, constructivist accounts set out to show how new structures are constructed. But the point is that their accounts are explanatory failures. Recall that the whole point about the learning paradox is not to set out a positive case for nativism but rather to serve as a reminder that nativism will have to be accepted by default, because constructivist accounts have not *successfully* shown what they set out to show. As Bereiter (1985, p.205) put it, there is a dearth of plausible mechanisms by reference to which intellectual competence could be explained.

This reply is well taken. In fact, it is easy to find versions of this same retort even in commentary that is otherwise sympathetic to a Piagetian position. Piaget's account of conservation is taken by Pinard (1981, p.23) to be such that its descriptive success is no guarantee of its explanatory adequacy. A similar claim is made by Campbell & Bickhard (1986, pp.12,

131) who reject Piaget's structuralist descriptions just because these are taken to be explanatory failures of the process of construction. Boden (1979, p.17) has claimed that Piagetian constructs serve to name, rather than to explain, cognitive change. The same claim is made by Vonèche (1982; Vonèche & Vidal, 1985) who has noted that the pervasive reference to internalisation in Piaget's account, for example in the transition from practical to representational intelligence, is merely to name a process that requires detailed specification. The absence of the latter means that Piaget's account could not provide a full, and perhaps not even any, explanation of intellectual development. Byrnes & Beilin (1991) have claimed that the process of differentiation, which Beilin (1989, p.116) noted to be central to Piaget's account, ultimately has only a descriptive, but not an explanatory, value. Although both Overton (1991) and Chapman (1991) assign some explanatory value to Piaget's account, because the structural models are explanatory as formal, though as neither efficient nor final, causes, this concession is limited. A formal explanation identifies the pattern of growth but does not identify the means by which growth occurs.

However, Piaget (1975/1985, pp.147–48) denied that his account of equilibration was merely descriptive, maintaining that it did constitute some explanation of intellectual growth. In fact, similar claims are evident throughout his work (1936/1953; 1960; 1970/1983). Consideration must then be given to Piaget's account of equilibration. This is the topic of the next chapter.

But the issue is clear enough; it is not whether Piaget's account provides a fully adequate explanation of the development of necessary knowledge, but rather whether that account has any explanatory potential at all. It is common ground that the former can be rejected out of hand. But the latter option is another matter, as any explanatory advance over nativism is welcome.

CHAPTER SEVEN

Epistemic Construction

"The role of reason is thus to introduce new necessities in systems where they were only implicit or remained unnoticed" (Piaget, 1980b, p.2)

[23] STRUCTURES AND CONSTRUCTION

Structural models provide well defined criteria which can be used in the identification of necessary knowledge across an indefinite range of epistemic domains. This same commitment generates two problems, which Piaget has long noticed. One problem is about developmental sequences. This problem concerns the individuation of the elements in a sequence with due regard to the demarcation of earlier from later elements. The second problem is about the mechanism responsible for progression through the sequence. This problem is concerned with the means by which the replacement of any element by its better successor occurs. Adapting a cartographical analogy due to Toulmin (1953), the first problem is to chart the stations on the multiple lines of a railway system, and the second is to show how travel occurs through the system. This analogy breaks down, of course, at two crucial points. With respect to intellectual development, how are the 'lines' and 'stations' to be fixed? Further, how does 'travel' along any 'line' occur in such a way through the system that it always terminates at a better 'destination'?

Piaget has returned typical answers to both questions in his early and more recent work. To the first question, Piaget (1923; 1971) has proposed that a developmental sequence is marked by a hierarchically ordered series of structurally defined levels or stages. In response to the second question, Piaget (1918; 1957a; 1960) has proposed an explanation through equilibration, which is the construction of better structures from existing structures. But the strength of his answer to the first question could be regarded as the reason for the weakness of his answer to the second. There are two issues of special difficulty.

The first difficulty is: how can structural change occur at all as a process of internal change? Of course, there is no problem in making a structural change, for example in changing syllogistic for predicate logic (see [4.1]). If there are two logical systems available, the main issue is whether one can be preferred over the other. But, according to Piaget, the source of the availability of the later system lies within the initial system. However, a well-defined structure is a structure, and so there are no internal reasons for it to change. For example, Piaget states that the structure of children's thinking is that of a grouping. Any grouping has a concise specification and is defined through five common properties: closure, reversibility, associativity, identity, and tautology (Piaget, 1939, p.291). Doubts have been expressed about the power and elegance of such a structure (Osherson, 1975; Parsons, 1960) but other logicians have noted its internal consistency (Papert, 1963; Wermus, 1971). Thus such a structure could serve as a model of thought. The difficulty is that any such model can, at most, provide a static description of thought and, as such, is incapable of representing its dynamic features. A well defined structure shows what are the main characteristics of a fragment of human thinking, but thereby does not show why and how that thinking can be changed through the adoption of some other structure. The conclusion has been drawn that there can be no structural reasons as to how structural changes take place (Campbell & Bickhard, 1986, pp.4, 52).

The second difficulty is: why is structural change the construction of a better structure? In some cases, structural change can result in a weaker structure. For example, system S5 of modal logic can be changed by the dropping of one axiom to yield system T, where the latter is a weaker modal system than the former (Hughes & Cresswell, 1972, p.49). Further, some structural changes can result in problematic structures. Accepting the intelligibility of both quantificational logic and modal, propositional logic, Quine (1961) has argued that systems of quantified, modal logic are incoherent. Although there are rival evaluations of the merits of quantified modal logic, the point to note here is that the issue continues to be problematic (Haack, 1978; Sainsbury, 1991). However, if Piaget's position is accepted, any such structural change could be expected to yield a better logical system, period. To repeat: the issue is not whether Piaget's operational logic is acceptable, as its intelligibility can be shown (Apostel, 1982; Grize, 1987; Mays, 1992). Rather, the issue is how a well defined structure is itself generative of a better successor, in the way in which the more powerful and consistent group structure of adolescent thought is stated by Piaget to be the outcome of the less powerful, but equally consistent, grouping structure. The conclusion is frequently drawn that Piaget's position is incomplete and even inadequate in relation to this issue (Boden, 1982; Hamlyn, 1978; Moessinger, 1978).

One reply is to note that a structural model is a model of a term of a relational process of construction. Because the process links its terms, it is (conceptually) independent of them. A full account of intellectual progression must do justice both to those terms and to the process that links them. But an account of the terms does not also have to be an account of the process. A structural model is a description of one term of a relational process, not a description of the process itself. Further, there is common agreement that descriptive taxonomies are an indispensable prerequisite of scientific advance (Chapman, 1988; Gould, 1989; Sugarman, 1987). In short, the difficulties concern the process of structural change and not the terms described through the structural models.

A second reply is the reminder that the acceptability of an account is a relative, not an absolute, matter. The twin difficulties are general difficulties and so apply to any developmental account based on the construction of new structures (e.g. Carey, 1985; Case, 1985; Halford, 1982). So the difficulties are not peculiar to Piaget's account. Further, there is currently no acceptable way to resolve the twin difficulties and, *a fortiori*, Piaget's constructivism provides no adequate resolution. This admission is not as startling as it may seem. An account may not be completely successful and yet can still have some interpretive force by comparison with other accounts. It is in just this sense that Piaget's account can be preferred when the question of the development of necessary knowledge is addressed. That question is one of the main questions addressed in Piaget's account. Further, Piaget has provided a wealth of considerations, both theoretical and empirical, relevant to its adequate answer.

According to Piaget (1970/1983), there are external factors in nature and nurture in whose absence intellectual growth does not occur. But a necessary condition is not thereby a sufficient condition. It is for this fundamental reason that equilibration is taken by Piaget (1918; 1960; 1975/1985) to be a distinct but necessary factor that contributes to developmental change. Piaget's position underpins the argument, in [9], which set out to limit the strength of purely psychological challenges to

Piaget's account. It also underpins the argument in [20] and the incompatibility of platonism and constructivism. In short, the general form of Piaget's position is clear, as it can be identified negatively as a rejection of the sufficiency, though not the necessity, of rival positions.

One allied interpretation of Piaget's position is that his account states necessary conditions of the understanding of deductive necessity, which occurs as the outcome of a necessary process of construction (Smith, 1987a; 1992a). Equilibration is one necessary condition of the development of modal understanding. The proposal is the denial that equilibration can be disregarded because this internal process of construction is taken to have equal importance with these other factors.

This proposal can be supported in two ways. The weak case is the identification of the respects in which equilibration is a distinct process. The strong case is the elaboration of the respects in which equilibration operates inter-dependently with other plausible factors. It can be argued that more attention was given by Piaget to the former than to the latter, if only because the claim about inter-dependence presupposes the claim about the distinctness of equilibration.

In effect, the strong case has suffered by neglect. In consequence, the weak claim is incomplete, since equilibration could not operate independently of the other factors.

A symptom of this incompleteness is shown by the pervasive use of the expression *sooner or later* (*tôt ou tard*). This expression litters the structuralist texts (e.g. Inhelder & Piaget, 1955/1958, p.283; Piaget & Szeminska, 1941/1952, p.166). Its comprehensive presence is evident in the constructivist texts, including the review of equlibratory sub-processes (Piaget, 1975/1985): the use of a scheme *sooner or later* leads to a disturbance (p.82) so that an individual will *sooner or later* make a modal error (p.26), leading *sooner or later* to reflective abstraction (p.193) which culminates in optimising equilibration *sooner or later* (p.40). The question to ask is obvious: does knowledge grow sooner (and if so, under what conditions) or later (and if so, under what conditions)? By its concern with the weak case, Piaget's account could not provide full answers to these questions (Smith, 1987a).

To be sure, claims about inter-dependence have not been made good in Piaget's account. But this admission leaves untouched the weaker claim that equlibration is a distinct and necessary process. It is, of course, a fallacy to infer that Piaget's claims about the distinctness of equilibration are suspect just because his claims about inter-dependency are not carried through. Yet many developmentalists may well have committed just this fallacy.

In short, there are grounds for considering Piaget's account of the construction of necessary knowledge, even if that account does not completely eliminate the twin difficulties. Crucially, the structuralist aspects are not exhaustive of Piaget's account. That account stands in need of interpretation, which should identify the further respects in which the strength of the difficulties could be reduced, culminating in their eventual elimination. The discussion here will have three aims. One is to review, in [24], similarities and differences in Piaget's several approaches to the construction of knowledge using classificatory thinking as a case study. A second is to outline, in [25], a modal model of the construction of knowledge. The discussion in both sections is selective, with the central aim of identifying general aspects of Piaget's account that should be open to further elaboration. A third is to survey, in [26], some strengths and weaknesses of Piaget's account.

[24] CONSTRUCTION AND CLASSIFICATION

The first point to make in an interpretation of Piaget's position is that his work embodies multiple models of epistemic construction. These models include the use of individual logical principles relevant to deductive reasoning in his early studies (Piaget 1921a, 1921b); axiomatised operational structures (Piaget, 1949; 1972); category theory (Piaget, 1980c; Piaget et al., 1968/1977; Piaget et al., 1990); and entailment logic (Piaget & Garcia, 1987/1991). But different models may be expected to make a difference. The global claims about Piaget's 'theory' may well be premature for reasons stated by its chief revisionist (Piaget, 1970/1983, p.103). An exhaustive survey of Piaget's position would have to do justice to these different statements of position. The present survey is, by contrast, selective because its concern is with Piaget's several discussions of the development of classification based on class inclusion. The discussion is in three parts, dealing with the understanding of class inclusion logic, the development operational thinking through classification, and the necessary character of class inclusion reasoning.

There is, however, a preparatory comment to make about some key elements of systems of classification in human thinking. Consider again Russell's (1919) paradox about the classes that are not members of themselves, which was reviewed in [5.2]. Some classes are, and some are not, members of themselves: the class of teaspoons is not a teaspoon, but the class of things which are not teaspoons is one of the things that are not teaspoons (Russell, 1959, p.58). The specific point at issue is identified by Lemmon (1966, pp.202, 210). It concerns the admissibility of the assumption that, with respect to a class defined through a property F (the class of things with property F), an object is a member of that class if and only if it has property F (all-and-only objects with property F are members of that class). Now it might seem that the relevance of this assumption to issues surrounding children's intellectual development is non-existent, because the specific point at issue turns on complex notions relevant to the philosophy of mathematics. But this is not so, because the specific point exemplifies a general point as well. And the general point concerns the relation between the intension of a class and the level of the objects in its extension. According to Russell (1919, p.137), a key requirement relevant to all forms of classification is the level of an object in a logical hierarchy. In turn, this requirement embodies the implication that an adequate classification system should be able to cope with hierarchies. If this requirement is not met, the inadequacy of the system of classification will generate contradictions. Russell (1959, p.53) provides examples of such contradictions in the writings of philosophers of mathematics prior to Frege who "thought of numbers as resulting from counting, and got into hopeless puzzles because things that are counted as one can equally be counted as many". As an example, Russell cites a football club which is one club with many individuals in it. The point is that a question about how many objects there are in a class can be intelligibly answered only in relation to the question "Of which class is this object an instance?". And the point of this latter question is that not all classes are at the same level in a logical space.

The relevance of the general issue to issues in the development of classification in children's thinking is threefold. One concerns counting. It has been argued that mathematical understanding has its basis in pre-schoolers' counting abilities rather than in systems of classification (Gelman & Gallistel, 1978). Accepting the evidence cited in support of this claim, the issue to confront is not whether mathematical understanding owes its initial formation to counting. Rather, it is whether such an origin alone could ever be enough for the reasons given by Russell in his rejection of pre-Fregean philosophy of mathematics (cf. Smith, 1986a). A second link concerns hierarchical classification. Some developmentalists have contended that children do have primitive numerical abilities and can cope with hierarchical classification, although the display of these abilities is contextually constrained (Donaldson, 1978; Hughes, 1986). But even if such claims have a sound evidential basis, they conflict with Russell's requirement that an adequate system of classification, and so of number, must be robust enough to handle simultaneously both non-hierarchical and hierarchical relations, such as the relations of membership and inclusion respectively. It is not clear that this requirement has been met

(Smith, 1982a). A third issue concerns contradictions in classificatory thinking. Although the development of classification during childhood has attracted the attention of many developmentalists, the key issue is taken to concern the distribution of correct classificatory thinking in relation to specified independent variables (Winer, 1980). But this leaves untouched the modal character of children's classification and the extent to which such thinking is contradictory (Smith, 1987a).

In short, there are rational considerations to bear in mind in the empirical investigation of the development of children's ability to classify. In fact, classification is a test-case, because it is a fundamental ability of human understanding. According to Russell (1919), an adequate system of classification requires the use of a logical space that is hierarchical in structure: the failure to use such a system results in contradiction. According to Piaget, the logical space of children's classification is not always hierarchical: the failure to classify hierarchically results in contradictions. The development of thinking based on class inclusion, which is both hierarchical and necessary in character, provides a test case. Indeed, Piaget (1951b, p.139) takes reversibility to mark the absence of contradiciton in human thought.

[24.1] Class Inclusion as a Logical Principle

In his early study, Piaget (1921a) assumed a conventional definition of the relation of inclusion, such that "a class A is included in a class B if all members of A are members of B" (Lemmon, 1966, p.207; cf. Lipschutz, 1964, p.3). Two features of this definition can be noted. First, this definition presupposes that the notion of *class* is already intelligible in that the relation of class inclusion is defined through the distinct relation of class membership. Second, deductive inferences can be drawn from this definition. In any pair of non-empty included classes, the extension of the including class must be greater than that of either included class.

In the early study, Piaget's aim was to find out whether adolescents, aged ten to fourteen years, can understand class inclusion, so defined. They were presented with a statement made by John to his sisters, namely that "a portion of my flowers are yellow". The task was to identify the colour of his bunch of flowers. Three choices are offered, corresponding to his three sisters. Marie's claim is "all of your flowers are yellow"; Simone's claim is "some of your flowers are yellow"; Rose's claim is "none of your flowers are yellow". The adolescents typically responded erroneously by claiming that Marie is correct. The assumption is that the adolescents have some understanding of collections, which in this case is a bunch of flowers. The issue centres on the extent to which this prior (psychological) understanding of collections is in accord with the logical definition. Piaget's proposal is that the adolescents conflate "some of my flowers" with "some flowers, which are all … " and so make the wrong inference. In consequence, not all psychological notions do meet the standard set in logical definitions. The psychological notion *bunch* and the logical notion *class* are exemplary in this respect. Although Piaget noted that cognitive and linguistic factors made a contribution to the adolescents' responses, Piaget proposed that logical factors were also responsible (1921a, pp.478–50). In this study, the claim is that a specific form of classification, based on the logical relation of class inclusion, is not always understood even in adolescence.

In a related study of multiplicative classification, similar claims were made (Piaget, 1922). But in this study, the modal character of deductive reasoning based on logical principles was explicitly noted (quoted in [2]). Piaget's proposal is that, due to logical incapacity, developing individuals are only able to represent what is real, what is possible, and what is necessary on *different* mental levels. Thus any "mental model" (*modèle interne*) runs the risk of confusing the representations at these three levels (Piaget, 1922, p.257). One coherent, multi-level representation is lacking. Reasoning aspires to be deductively necessary and yet is manifest as pseudo-necessary reasoning.

This early position is interesting on several counts. First, it is concerned with the development of necessary knowledge. Second, there are clear similarities between this position and that outlined in later studies, notably where the non-differentiation of reality, possibility, and necessity is stated to be the key aspect in intellectual growth (Piaget. 1922, p.256; Piaget 1983/1987, p.4). Third, development is stated to occur from contingent (Piaget, 1922, p.252), or from factual (Piaget 1983/1987, p.4), to necessary knowledge. Fourth, there are internal constraints arising from the confusion of the intension and extension of a class (Piaget, 1922, pp.237-8; Inhelder & Piaget, 1959/1964, p.7). The intension of *bunch* has some meaning for the adolescents but this is evidently not the (full) logical meaning, as its extension is incorrectly quantified. Finally, the evolving character of thinking through successive stages is noted (Piaget, 1921a, p.461; Piaget, 1970/1983).

Note that in this early study, Piaget explicitly raised the question of whether a (psychological) collection amounts to a (logical) class, returning a negative answer. The argument in [24.2] will be that Piaget's early answer is compatible with recent studies of collections, where it is specifically noted that hierarchical thinking through collections precedes that through classes just because a collection is not a class

(Markman, 1989). A related issue, which is addressed in [24.3], is the modal character of such thinking, concerning whether necessity is understood.

Yet two issues are neglected in the early studies over and above the methodological concerns expressed by Piaget (1924/1947) about an over-reliance on linguistic understanding (see [11]). One is a fuller characterisation of the developmental sequence, which culminates in a psychological understanding that matches an agreed logical standard. The other is an account of intellectual progress, showing how necessary knowledge is constructed from previous intellectual states which are neither epistemic nor necessary. These are, of course, the twin difficulties that were reviewed in [23] and which face any developmental account.

[24.2] Class Inclusion and Operational Logic

Piaget attended to the former deficiency through the use of operational logic (Piaget, 1939; 1949; 1972) whose formal features were stated in advance of its empirical use (Inhelder & Piaget, 1959/1964; Piaget & Szeminska, 1941/1952). Operational logic was formulated by Piaget as an alternative to the logicist programme in mathematics. This programme required numbers to be reduced to sets, which in turn were characterised through extensional logic (Russell, 1919). Evidently, Piaget (1950) viewed the necessity and fecundity of mathematical thinking as constitutive features in the domain of any minimally adequate theory of intellectual development. In the empirical studies, the aim was to ascertain whether children had developed the requisite abilities that would enable them to display necessary and novel mathematical thinking (Smith, 1986a). His position is not a denial of numerical competence in early childhood but rather a statement of conditions that have to be met for necessary and novel thinking to be possible. Early numerical competence counts for little if class inclusion is not understood. But the logicist programme embodies the clear implication that lower numbers are related to higher numbers through the relation of inclusion.

This aspect of Piaget's position has suffered by neglect, especially in relation to the modal aspects of class inclusion reasoning (Smith, 1982a). A typical task requires children to explain which is the bigger of two classes, where one is included in the other. For example, in an array of flowers (B) the majority of which are daisies (A) with the remainder roses (A'), the question concerns the quantification of the membership of class A in relation to that of an including class B. Psychological issues arising from these studies are reviewed in several places (Gelman & Baillargeon, 1983; Smith, 1992a; Winer, 1980). Five points are worth noting about Piaget's position: it concerns the construction of necessary knowledge; construction occurs as differentiation; differentiation occurs through a sequence of levels; successive levels provide access to a more coherent logical space; progress occurs through tranformation of an available logical space.

First, in studies of class inclusion the construction of necessary knowledge is one main concern. This is clear from the statement (Piaget & Szeminska, 1941/1952, p.206/161, my emphasis; cf. Inhelder & Piaget, 1959/1964, p.282) about arithmetical operations, which embody logical operations such as inclusion: "the real problem, if the roots of these operations are to be attained, is therefore to know *how the child becomes aware of their necessity* through their discovery at the very heart of numerical compositions". It is sometimes claimed that Piaget's class inclusion question 'are there more daisies or more flowers?' is an odd question, devoid of human meaning (Hughes, 1986). Yet the question has a perfectly clear logical meaning, one which bears on a paradigm example of necessary knowledge. Murray (1990) has noted that the modal character of human thinking has been insufficiently addressed in Piagetian research, even though it is central to Piagetian discussions.

Second, Piaget & Szeminska (1941/1952, p.163) presuppose a standard definition of class inclusion, such that there are at least two respects in which children may experience difficulty. One is the failure to relate the intensions of two classes systematically to their extensions, when one class includes the other. A second is the use of non-necessary strategies to gain a correct understanding. Both difficulties had already been noticed in Piaget's early studies. The two points are related in that logically necessary deductions relevant to the relative size of two classes depend on the inter-relation of their intensions and extensions. In support of this position, Inhelder & Piaget (1959/1964, p.119) point out that the initial understanding of class inclusion—though not, of course, thinking based on the more primtive relation of class membership—requires an understanding of partial complementation or negation under the including class. When a class B includes two non-empty classes A and A', it is not enough to dichotomise the including class by reference to the two included classes (Inhelder & Piaget, 1959/1964, p.134). Either included class must also be identifiable as the complement of the other under the including class (Piaget, 1977b; Smith, 1982a). In short, the symbol A' has a dual use: it refers both to the observable knowledge which permits the identification of one of the included classes and to the inferential knowledge based on logical subtraction under the including class. Thus the operation of identity alone is not enough, as the capacity to make reversible operations must be present as well.

Third, different levels of classificatory thinking are proposed, notably classification based on class membership, on the inclusion of classes, and on the inclusion of complements.

The point behind this proposal is that it secures a linkage between concrete and formal operations based on the generalisation of negation when a formal operation bears on an already activated concrete operation (see [19]). The restrictions on complementation need to be lifted, for example in propositional thinking which is not restricted to adjacent elements in a hierarchy. Notice that Piaget (1953; cf. Mays, 1992) is well aware that Boolean algebra has instantiations in both class logic and predicate logic. Thus it is possible to use the latter as a model of classificatory thinking bearing on the quantification of 'some' and 'all' (Piaget, 1978, p.222; cf. Johnson-Laird, 1990, p.103). But there are epistemological grounds for resisting such an approach due to the restrictions on negation. It is one thing to understand negation in terms of the subtraction of a class under an including class which is adjacent in the hierarchy; it is quite something else to understand negation in its general form without this restriction (cf. Inhelder & Piaget, 1959/1964, p.142). Two intriguing empirical studies are relevant to this theoretical claim. Both studies focus on the transition from class inclusion thinking to reasoning through propositional implication.

One study bears on the claim made in [19], that propositional implication is understood only in cases where concrete operational classification through inclusion is also undertaken. Progression from inclusion to implication is stated to be due to reflective abstraction (Piaget, 1977b, p.110). The reason is as follows. Both inclusion and implication generate four cases, which are shown in Table 7.1. The comprehension of inclusion is compatible with an indeterminate fourth

TABLE 7.1
Truth-tables for Inclusion and Implication

Case	Inclusion $A \subset B$			Implication $p \to q$		
1	1	1	1	1	1	1
2	1	0	1	1	0	1
3	0	1	1	0	1	1
4	0	?	0	0	1	0

Note: With two classes (A, B) or with two propositions (p, q), there are four cases to consider. The logic of concrete operations covers the first three cases of the truth-table of inclusion, leaving the fourth case indeterminate. The logic of formal operations covers all four cases of the truth-table of implication (Piaget, 1977b, p.82; Piaget, 1978, p.222).

case. Implication, by contrast, requires all four cases to be coherently related. Consider concrete operations with restrictions on the negation of a class A under its including class B. The array for the inclusion task provides confirming instances of A and B as well as A' and B. There is of course no confirming case of A and B'. Thus concrete operations permit an understanding of these three cases, including that of A' and B. This is quite an achievement, as it is counter-intuitive to regard as true an implication with a false antecedent (Piéraut-Le Bonniec, 1974/1980, p.20; von Wright, 1957). With respect to an array of roses, the implication 'if there is a daisy, it is a flower' is true, corresponding to A' and B. In Piaget's (1977b, p.88; cf. Smith, 1982a) study, the conditions for the understanding of inclusion based on the operational logic of concrete operations are re-stated. But concrete operations leave indeterminate the fourth possibility, A' and B' which is the relation between the complements of these classes, due to restrictions on negation (Piaget & Inhelder, 1966/1969, p.132). However, the full truth-table for implication requires all four possibilities to be coherently related, including cases where both antecedent and consequent are false. It follows that formal operations are more advanced than concrete operations just because they subsume all four cases. What is required, then, is access to this fourth possibility. In turn, this requires the restriction on negation to be lifted.

A second study addresses a different aspect of the transition from inclusion to implication, relating to negation and contradiction (Piaget, 1974/1980, Chap.8). In the latter, children were presented with eleven cubes such that seven contained a bell. The children were shown that the five red cubes contained a bell whose presence was detected by shaking. The children were not permitted to shake the three yellow and three blue cubes. Instead they were told that any of these cubes may, or may not, also contain a bell. All the cubes were then hidden behind a screen and the child was invited to shake each, in turn and out of sight. The task was to find the red cubes using the auditory cue. The task could be regarded as a reasoning task ('if the cube is red, it contains a bell') or as a task based on inclusion logic (the class of red cubes is included in the class of cubes with bells). One finding was the committal of false symmetries whereby 'all red cubes contain bells' was conflated with 'all the bells are contained in red cubes'. A second finding was that the children who realised that a cube with a bell could be any one of the three colours did also succeed on a class inclusion task. A third claim is the interpretation of these findings through operational logic. The children who committed the fallacy did not see the contradiction. Their misunderstanding was taken to be due to the incorrect quantification of the extensions of the classes instantiated in the array. Irreversible thinking is due to incomplete compensations between the observed properties of the cubes (red, yellow, blue) and their inferred properties (the non-red cubes are yellow and blue). A fourth claim was that the distinction drawn by Inhelder & Piaget (1955/1958) between material and structural possibilities was compatible with the findings. However, this distinction is tied to operational logic and so does not advance the argument.

These two studies are illustrative of a general tendency in Piaget's constructivist studies. These studies are usually persuasive because they show how Piaget's operational logic can be extended in the explanation of new findings through the use new constructs (in these two studies, reflective abstraction and contradiction respectively). But they are not conclusive, because an independent description of the new constructs is not systematically provided. The new constructs should clarify the process of intellectual change other than by reference to its terms. However, they are themselves ultimately given an interpretation by reference to the reversibility of operational structures. That is, the structural descriptions are invoked in elaboration of the constructs intended to describe the process. It was stated in [23] that the structuralist commitments made by Piaget did not suffice in the elaboration of a developmental mechanism. But the new constructs that are supposed to provide that elaboration, turn out to be partially dependent on the structuralist models.

Fourth, the advance to formal operations increases access to a better, logical space (see [8.5]). This extension is elaborated by Piaget (1949; 1972) and reviewed by Smith (1987b). Consider two classes, A and B, and their negations (cf. Inhelder & Piaget, 1955/1958, p.275). Multiplicative classification based on concrete operations leads to a quartet of classes, corresponding to the four possibilities (i)–(iv) of Table 7.2. From the 'horizontal' vantage-point of concrete operations, there are four distinct possibilities. So viewed, there is non-differentiation of a further set of 16 possibilities, corresponding to the 16 operations of Table 7.2. This can be seen from the 'vertical' vantage-point of formal operations. Although the case for rejecting the account of formal operations has been stated (Braine & Rumain, 1983; Keating, 1990), the counter-case is also to hand (Bond & Jackson, 1991; Byrnes, 1988; Gray, 1990; Smith, 1987b).

The difference between the levels is well defined through Piaget's logical models, so their empirical use requires the recognition of the cases subsumed by the cells in the available logical space. That is, the issue is not whether an individual can entertain a proposition, think of imaginary and so logically possible cases or have some understanding of negation (cf. Markovits, 1992; Moshman, 1990). Rather, it concerns *which* possibilities are available for making *which* necessary inferences on the basis of *which* actual observations.

TABLE 7.2

System of 16 Binary Operations

Binary Operation	Possibilities			
	(i)	(ii)	(iii)	(iv)
	$p \& q$	$p \& -q$	$-p \& q$	$-p \& -q$
1 Complete affirmation	1	1	1	1
2 Complete negation	0	0	0	0
3 Disjunction	1	1	1	0
4 Conjoint negation	0	0	0	1
5 Incompatibility	0	1	1	1
6 Conjunction	1	0	0	0
7 Implication	1	0	1	1
8 Nonimplication	0	1	0	0
9 Converse implication	1	1	0	1
10 Converse nonimplication	0	0	1	0
11 Equivalence	1	0	0	1
12 Exclusion	0	1	1	0
13 Affirmatiion p	1	1	0	0
14 Negation p	0	0	1	1
15 Affirmation q	1	0	1	0
16 Negation q	0	1	0	1

Note: Each operation corresponds to one of the 16 unique combinations linking any pair of bi-valent (true-false) propositions. There are four base possibilities (i)–(iv) whose comprehension is secured during concrete operations. Each member of this quartet is an observed case such that 1 indicates the presence of a confirming instance and 0 the corresponding absence. The system is adapted from Piaget (1972, pp. 213, 254) and reviewed by Smith (1987c). Bond and Jackson (1991) offer examples and evidence corresponding to each operation.

Fifth, transitions both within a level and between adjacent levels occur as an internal process of epistemic change. The force of this claim is reliant on the specific character of the inter-dependency of equilibration and other plausible factors. But this fuller characterisation has not been systematically carried through. In the structuralist models, logical operations are regarded as transformations that are defined as internal changes *within* a system of thought. The transformational character of operations was noted in [8.2], as an operation is a universal mode of coordination that is effective both intra-individually and inter-personally. Concrete operational thought is based on the successive use of two types of reversibility; inversion for classificatory thinking, and reciprocity for relational thought (Piaget, 1961/1966). Reversibility both secures the coherence of a chain of reasoning and permits transitions between any one element in the chain and any other. Similarly, formal operational thought combines simultaneously the two types of reversibility in unitary acts of thought

(Piaget & Inhelder, 1966/1969). But Piaget (1972, p.253) regards reversibility, rather than identity, as the basis of logical thought. Thus the transformational character of reversibility in formal operations makes possible the systematic, and coherent, interchange of different operations within the system of 16 formal operations of Table 7.2. An inventory of the interchanges, based on the law of duality (Inhelder & Piaget, 1959/1964, p.143; Piaget, 1972, p.234; Piaget, 1977b, p.89), is shown in Table 7.3.

The logical intelligibility of the system shown in Table 7.3 is not in doubt. It is defined as a system of transformations, because each operation is itself a source of change permitting changes within the system. In this sense, an operational structure is mobile. Once this system is activated, no further explanation is required as to why the transitions occur as they do. An inverse operation *is* the complement of the corresponding direct operation under complete affirmation.

The purpose of the system in Table 7.3 is to explicate the transformational character of the formal operational system of thought in Table 7.2. The binary operations of conjunction and disjunction are related (operations 6 and 3 respectively) but recognition of their inter-dependence requires a further mental act. Piaget's claim is that *ad hoc* and partial recognition of some of the inter-relations in the system shown in Table 7.3 is less advanced than their full and coherent recognition. The system has three important features. First, it is a progression from the system shown in Table 7.2, which in turn was an evolution from less developed systems of thought. Second, it permits deductively necessary understanding as an outcome of previous understanding, which is not always necessary in this sense. Third, it characterises some respects in which intellectual transitions occur rationally—that is, coherently and deductively—in a logical space within a developing system of thought (Braine & Rumain, 1983, p.318).

Although this system was never rejected by Piaget (Piaget & Garcia, 1987/1991, p.7), doubts have been expressed about its epistemological suitability by others (Apostel, 1982; cf. Grize, 1987). The psychological credibility of the system has been doubted on the grounds that humans do not, in fact, reason in accordance with this system (Piéraut-Le Bonniec, 1974/1980, pp.54–9; cf. Braine & Rumain, 1983). Evidently, the system of INRC operations is under-determined by the available evidence. For example, in the balance task (Inhelder & Piaget, 1955/1958), translational deficiences are endemic in the standard translation, which renders illogical several symbolic claims. Crucially, some of the evidence is subject to massive over-interpretation, as in discussion of propositions (8)–(17), where formal relationships stand in for the evidence that is supposed to underpin them. So the evidence and

TABLE 7.3
System of INRC Operations

Binary Operation	INRC Operations			
	(I)	(II)	(III)	(IV)
1 Complete affirmation	*p * q* 1111	*(o)* 0000	*p * q* 1111	*(o)* 0000
2 Complete negation	*(o)* 0000	*p * q* 1111	*(o)* 0000	*p * q* 1111
3 Disjunction	*p v q* 1110	*–p & –q* 0001	*p / q* 0111	*p & q* 1000
4 Conjoint negation	*–p & –q* 0001	*p v q* 1110	*p & q* 1000	*p / q* 0111
5 Incompatibility	*p / q* 0111	*p & q* 1000	*p v q* 1110	*–p & –q* 0001
6 Conjunction	*p & q* 1000	*p / q* 0111	*–p & –q* 0001	*p v q* 1110
7 Implication	*p → q* 1011	*p & q* 0100	*q → p* 1101	*–p & q* 0010
8 Nonimplication	*p & –q* 0100	*p → q* 1011	*–p & q* 0010	*q → p* 1101
9 Converse implication	*q → p* 1101	*–p & q* 0010	*p → q* 1011	*p & –q* 0100
10 Converse nonimplication	*–p & q* 0010	*q → p* 1101	*p & –q* 0100	*p → q* 1011
11 Equivalence	*p ≡ q* 1001	*p w q* 0110	*p ≡ q* 1001	*p w q* 0110
12 Exclusion	*p w q* 0110	*p ≡ q* 1001	*p w q* 0110	*p ≡ q* 1001
13 Affirmation [*p*]	*p [q]* 1100	*–p [q]* 0011	*–p [q]* 0011	*p [q]* 1100
14 Negation [*p*]	*–p [q]* 0011	*p [q]* 1100	*p [q]* 1100	*–p [q]* 0011
15 Affirmation [*q*]	*q [p]* 1010	*–q [p]* 0101	*–q [p]* 0101	*q [p]* 1010
16 Negation [*q*]	*–q [p]* 0101	*q [p]* 1010	*q [p]* 1010	*–q [p]* 0101

KEY

I Direct operation, corresponding to each binary operation (see Table 7.1)
II Inverse operation, corresponding to the negation of I
III Reciprocal operation, corresponding to the inversion (negation) of the elements in I
IV Correlative operation, corresponding to the negation of III

Note: Each binary operation in Table 7.2 permits three further operations which form the system of INRC operations. For example, the direct operation corresponding to (6) is conjunction (*p & q*) which has an inverse (negation) in (*p / q*). The reciprocal of operation of (6) is formed by negating its elements, or constituent propositions, to form (*–p & –q*) whose inverse (negation) is the correlative operation which is (*p v q*). The system is truth-conserving under the transformations due to the four INRC operations and is adapted from Piaget (1972, p. 258).

interpretation are circularly related. Similar features mark more recent discussions. Piaget (1977b, p.89) states that progression from the restricted to the unrestricted use of negation, and so from inclusion to implication, occurs through the construction of de Morgan's law of duality. A logical derivation is thus presented as an empirical explanation.

Even so, the premature dismissal of Piaget's account should be avoided. Despite early doubts about the intelligibility of the system of 16 formal operations (Bynum, Thomas, & Weitz, 1972; Ennis, 1976; Parsons, 1960), that system continues to have a theoretical and applied value (Bond & Jackson, 1991; Mays, 1992; Smith & Knight, 1992). The point to notice is that the INRC system is not intended as a description of how humans do typically reason, but rather how their reasoning could in fact be rational. It provides a structural description of a term in the process of epistemic change. What is also required is a further account of aspects of the process itself. This issue is pursued further in [25.2] because Piaget's account of class inclusion has been subjected to psychological scrutiny.

[24.3] Class Inclusion Reasoning

The essence of the psychological criticism of the operational account is evident in an early study (Kohnstamm, 1963), which set out to show that children aged five years could be taught to reason hierarchically. Kohnstamm concluded that his results did show that training could be effective under certain conditions but that his finding did not impair Piaget's theoretical position. His conclusion was challenged by Pascual-Leone & Bovet (1967) on two counts. They contended that Kohnstamm did use different methods and procedures, and that his position leads to the neglect of the main theoretical problem about intellectual construction (see [9]). In the sequel, psychological research took a familiar course. Interest centred on the identification and characterisation of perceptual, cognitive, and training issues relevant to class inclusion thinking (cf. Winer, 1980). But although such research is psychologically interesting, it leaves the epistemological question untouched. This claim is now discussed in relation to two issues, one concerning inductive categorisation and the other concerning logical elements in class inclusion reasoning.

Inductive categorisation has been shown to be present in early childhood. Thus Rosch, Mervis, Gray, Johnson, & Boyes-Braem (1976) have shown that categorisation is correctly undertaken on oddity-selection tasks by three-year old children, and on sorting tasks by five year-old children. Categorisation in relation to natural kinds has been shown to depend on inductive procedures (Gelman & Markman (1987). Gelman and O'Reilly (1988) have argued that such inferences, based on an object's appearance, can be extended to the membership of a superordinate category.

With Piaget's question in mind, this research is limited in three respects. First, induction is not deduction, so this research could never address Piaget's epistemological question about human reasoning based on the principle of class inclusion, which is deductively necessary. Second, some types of categorisation are based on superordination relations. But the conditions of the latter will be similar to those appropriate to class inclusion reasoning, and so require some analogue of Piaget's inclusion task. These conditions have not been satisfied in available research. An inductive inference about membership of a superordinate category is not a deductive inference about the relation of the intensions and extensions of that category. Third, categorisation is paradigmatically displayed in relation to thinking about natural kinds. But although Gelman and Markman (1987; Markman, 1989) refer to Kripke's (1980) discussion of natural kinds, they fail to exploit his central claim, namely that a natural kind, such as gold, has a necessary identity across 'possible worlds' (see [3.2]). But if a natural kind such as gold has a trans-world identity, epistemological questions arise. One is how children gain access to relevant sets of possibilities that constitute 'possible worlds'. Another is how these possibilities are coordinated in deductively necessary systems of thought. Again, Gelman and Wellman (1991) provide evidence to show that pre-school children understand that objects have essential, or intrinsic, properties which are distinct from their externally observable counterparts. But a non-external and non-observable property is not thereby a necessary property, still less is a non-observable property one of the defining and logically necessary properties constitutive of its identity. Despite the fact that such distinctions are explicitly drawn by Piaget (see [8.5]), Gelman and Wellman suppose that their work invalidates central claims in Piaget's account. But not all knowledge is necessary knowledge, including knowledge whose identification is due to methodological ingenuity. In short, there are both inductive and deductive elements in categorisation, but the latter have not been fully examined in research on inductive categorisation of natural kinds.

This same conclusion applies to the research on the second issue concerning the logical aspects of inclusion reasoning. One of the few studies dealing with the necessary character of inclusion reasoning was undertaken by Markman (1978). In this study, children were invited to justify their judgments in relation to tasks using novel criteria for the recognition of necessary understanding. Markman's conclusion was that such reasoning is late in onset and due to formal operations. This conclusion is, of course, incompatible with Piaget & Szeminska's (1941/1952, p.161) claim that the modal character of class inclusion is understood in concrete operations. It is also incompatible with Piaget's (1977/1986) claim that some understanding of necessity is manifest in early childhood. But Markman's conclusion can be disputed.

First, it is not clear that the pre-test was adequate. The sample was formed by children who succeeded on three out of five pre-test questions dealing with class inclusion. But the size of the arrays (6 cards) was small, unlike the larger arrays (40 cards and 20 cards) used by Piaget & Szeminska (1941/1952, pp.176, 169; cf. Inhelder & Piaget, 1959/1964, p.101). The difference is non-trivial because children could have based their responses on empirical based counting, which is not necessary in character (for examples, see Piaget & Szeminska, 1941/1952, pp.43, 175–6). Large numbers were used in the Genevan studies precisely to ensure that children's responses were due to the logical properties of the array, and not to their size. Second, Markman did not list all of the admissible justifications, and empirical procedures may not have been discounted (Cormier & Dagenais, 1983). Third, admissible justifications rested on identity ('because all the flowers are daisies'), when the Genevan studies specifically excluded this justification because reversibility was required as well. Finally, Markman's sample included children aged seven to eleven years. The older children could be presumed to have concrete operational abilities, but age is not a criterion of developmental level (see [18]). Further, inclusion thinking is reported to be late in onset (Winer, 1980). Thus the sample could have included stage II rather than stage III children (Piaget & Szeminska, 1941/1952). This difference corresponds to the use of empirical and necessary strategies respectively (see [13.1]).

Second, Markman's assessment tasks used novel criteria for the recognition of necessity. Two of her criteria can be challenged. The 'hidden' criterion required children to close their eyes while members of the including class were removed. But a correct response due to non-observation is not thereby a necessary response, and Piaget (see [8.5]) has specifically contrasted (factual) generalisation and (normative) necessity.

Further, concrete operations require the co-presence of both an observable property and logical property, such that the latter is differentiated from the former. This is explicit in reviews of Piaget's conservation task (Donaldson, 1978; Murray, 1981). It has equal force in relation to all other concrete operational tasks. The 'novel' criterion is open to similar challenge, because children were given information about a secret language with novel codings of members of the major included class. But Moshman (1990) has noted that the distinction between a new fact and a deductive consequence may be confounded due to this criterion. Further, this criterion was used with a distinctive question dealing with the extent of the child's certainty ("can you tell for sure ...?") rather than with the modal (alethic) character ("necessarily, there are more ... ") of the inclusion relationships. So this difference provides another reasoning for taking Markman's classification of the responses to be indeterminate.

By contrast, Markman's 'modification' criterion required children to explain whether the array could be modified to produce more members of the included than the including class. This criterion required the children to consider, and then discount, a possibility by deduction of the relevant conclusion. But this criterion has its origin in work undertaken by Inhelder et al. (1974, p.174) for use in training, and not merely assessment, studies of inclusion reasoning. Further, the success rates associated with Markman's study are comparable with those reported in the Genevan studies. Inhelder & Piaget (1959/1964, p.109) stated that two-thirds of the responses of children aged eight years were at level III, whereas Markman (1978, p.171) claimed that three-quarters of her fourth graders (aged nine years) met the 'modification' criterion. In short, if only one criterion used in Markman's study is acceptable, her study is broadly compatible with Piaget's account.

Notice that the reversibility criterion, based on Piaget's operational logic, is central. Consider again an array, where class B includes two classes A and A'. Piaget's identity criterion states that $B = A + A'$: the flowers are daisies and roses. The reversibility criterion states that $A = B - A'$: the daisies are flowers other than roses. What is the purpose of such criteria? Answer: these criteria are criteria that bear on the unit of analysis used by a child in classifying the world. The issue is not whether very young children can classify—they can—but rather how they do so. Classification by categories, collections, and classes are three possibilities as to the appropriate unit of analysis. By common consent, classification through logical classes is more difficult than inductive categorisation. So independent evidence is required to show that children do use the former, and not just the latter, as their unit of analysis. The null hypothesis states that young children do not use classes. The alternative hypothesis is that they do use class B as the superordinate class to classes A and A' when their thinking is reversible. This is because one included class is identified through subtraction of the other included class from the including class. Further, the same criterion (reversibility) is evidence of modality. As there are only three classes, one included class is identified as the complement of the other under the including class. But a complement is a logical object with necessary properties: a complement must be smaller than the including class, provided both included classes are non-empty. Evidently this proviso is met in the design of the standard task, because there are members of each of the three classes. Thus the children who can inter-relate in one train of thought the positive and negative characteristics of the classes are in a position to have understood a logical relationship that is necessarily true.

Third, Campbell & Bickhard (1986, p.100) have argued that Markman's position is open to objection because it ignores relevant distinctions which are well stated in Piaget's account. If her position is accepted, children who succeed on the standard class inclusion task do so using empirical strategies, and the modal character of inclusion is a later acquisition. Their counter-claim is that logical strategies underpin success on the standard task. This conclusion is supported by reference to their knowing-levels analysis in which a distinction is drawn between the making of a logical (necessary) inference and the realisation of its necessity.

A related claim is that the higher knowing-level is a development from the lower level through the processes of reflective abstraction (Piaget, 1977b). By contrast, Cormier & Dagenais (1983) have argued that correctness in inclusion reasoning precedes the understanding of its necessity. Their suggestion is that the latter is a higher level response for which constructive generalisation is responsible (Piaget, 1978). The lurking difficulty here is that different constructive processes, both of which are invoked in Piaget's work, are taken to lead to different empirical claims about the onset of deductive reasoning.

The underlying problem arises from the twin difficulties noted in [23]. Piaget has not made out the strong case about the inter-dependence of equilibration and other plausible factors responsible for developmental change. But the attention given to the weak case about the distinctness of equilibration leaves open questions about how contingent and necessary factors in epistemic construction operate together. The trouble is that Piaget's concern with the weak case has led to a preoccupation with the demarcation of necessary processes in developmental sequences, without equal consideration to their joint operation with empirical processes. However, some intelligible version of the strong case is required to secure the credibility of the weak case. This general comment is now illustrated.

Consider, for example, Campbell's (1991) study of inclusion reasoning. His conclusion is that such reasoning is necessary, and due to abstractive processes which Piaget (1977b) has left unexplored in relation to modal understanding. His related argument is that such reasoning does not occur through logical compensation. In fact, the root difficulty is the same. The Kantian distinction between intuitive, intensive, extensive, and metric quantification is invoked to mark the developmental sequence in operational understanding (Piaget & Szeminska, 1941/1952, pp.37–42/*20–24; note well: the standard translation is marked by major omission). This distinction has also been invoked in later studies (Inhelder, Blanchet, Sinclair, & Piaget, 1975). Logical compensation is central to this sequence, as it is taken to underpin all forms of quantification, where developmental differences arise due to incomplete compensation (Piaget 1975/1985, p.22). With Piaget's inclusion question in mind, intuitive thinking is based on non-relevant properties (see Bon's response on the conservation of number task cited in [16]). Intensive quantification is shown in claims as to whether the including class has 'more or less' members than the included class. Thus Gon, aged seven years, has counted correctly the 40 brown beads and the two white beads. Even so, Gon initially declared that there are as many beads as brown beads, later reversing this judgment (Piaget & Szeminska, 1941/1952, p.175–6). Extensive quantification is dependent on a grasp of ratios which are not precisely calculated. Plat declared that there were "two white beads more" (p.176), where this correct judgment is not a precise calculation of the relative sizes of the extensions. Metric quantification requires numerical reasoning as such, and so an exact understanding of proportionality.

The trouble is that in making out the weak case, Piaget needed to show that there are situations where non-logical strategies alone are insufficient. Thus counting that is based on a non-operational structure is insufficient. A clear case is provided in the study of class intersection (Piaget, 1980c). Children were presented with arrays of objects formed by two intersecting classes. The simplest array had three objects, one blue duck, one white duck, and one white hen. The children were asked both to count all the objects, and then to count together the number of white objects and the number of ducks. Their task was to explain the apparent paradox whereby the result of the former (3) is different from the sum of the latter (4). A typical response is given by Ald, aged seven years, who claims that there are "three animals" and "four animals" in this simple array. To the reply that there are only three animals, Ald retorts that there are two ducks and the two whites, and hence four altogether. Lacking an understanding of the intersection of classes, the counting skills of the children prove to be insufficient to allow them to resolve the 'paradox'. The study is successful in relation to Piaget's weak case, as it shows that young children do not realise that the extension of the union of two classes is smaller than the sum of their individual extensions. But the strong case is not elaborated because no systematic attempt is made to show how empirically based counting connects with, and operates together with, logical compensation as such. Yet some version of the strong case needs to be made out, for the credibility of the weak case to be made good.

In short, Piaget's multiple discussions are marked by this same tendency. His epistemological question concerns the construction of necessary knowledge. But in an attempt to identify the necessary features of this process, the demarcation of the non-necessary features is so sharply undertaken that necessary-and-empirical features are regarded as an exclusive opposites, when they are more properly regarded as inclusive.

[25] CONSTRUCTING NECESSARY KNOWLEDGE

There is an interesting reason why Piaget's stance is defensible, despite his preoccupation with questions about the distinctness of equilibration. The reason is apparent in a contention that bears on the foundations of modal logic (Hintikka & Hintikka, 1989, p.73): "We consider it as self-evident as anything in philosophy that one cannot do justice to actual human experience without a conceptual system that includes *possibilia*".

The philosophical problem centres on the intelligibility of claims about possibility and necessity. The relevance of this point to the construction of necessary knowledge is that epistemic logic is analogous to modal logic (Hintikka, 1962; Piéraut-Le Bonniec, 1974/1980). Any suspicions about the intelligibility of the latter apply with equal force to the former as well. What an individual knows may be true not only of the actual world, in which the knower lives, but also of an indefinite number of alternatives. The number of such alternatives is a variable that is dependent on the "S-O circuit" (Piaget, 1947/1950), linking an individual's knowledge with the 'worlds' accessible to that individual. The anticipation of the movements of invisible objects by infants is at one end of a continuum, and the comprehension of the 16 binary, propositional relationships is at another. Doubtless, there are more advanced sets of possibilities as well, but there is no suggestion that any individual can inventory all of them. The philosophical problem is not merely that doubts have been raised as to whether quantified modal logic is coherent at all (see [23]) but questions of coherence still arise under the commonly accepted interpretation due to Kripke (see [3.2]). The accessibility relation from the actual world to any other 'possible world' must at least be reflexive, in which case it is too weak. Reflexivity suffices to make accessible to the knower what is true merely in some range of 'possible worlds', of which the actual world is one. But it does not guarantee that what is true of all other possible worlds is also known. Even if it is argued that accessibility is an equivalence relation, which is reflexive, symmetrical, and transitive (Hughes & Cresswell, 1972, pp.59–80), the requirement is both too strong and too weak. It is too strong, because it confers ideal rationality on the knower who is presumed to know all of the logical consequences of possessed knowledge. This makes little sense on epistemological grounds (Cherniak, 1986). It is too weak, on logical grounds, because it does not follow that the set of accessible 'worlds' is the set of all 'possible worlds' (Hintikka & Hintikka, 1989, p.2).

In Piaget's account, there is a realisation that the construction of modal (possibility, necessity) understanding is central to intellectual development, and that the construction of possibilities and necessities is not straightforward. This is, of course, the initial claim in [1]. The discussion in this section is in two parts. One concerns two different interpretations of Piaget's account with an argument for the rejection of one (absence-to-presence) and retention of the other (differentiation) interpretation in [25.1]. The other is an outline of a modal model of differentiation in [25.2].

[25.1] Intellectual Construction as Differentiation

Piaget offers a general argument to show that construction has to be open-ended. The argument turns on whether there is a set which is *the set of all possibilities*. If there is a such a set, intellectual development would terminate in its comprehension. It was noted, in [8.5], that Piaget had implicitly committed himself to this notion. An explicit commitment appears in his claim (1957b, p.96) that operational structures "bear upon the set of possibilities (*l'ensemble des possibles*)". But he later changed his position by regarding this same notion as antinomic (Piaget, 1968/1971). His argument is compressed and can be interpreted in two ways.

One interpretation is that there can be no set of all (*tous*) possibilities, because the whole set (*tout*) is itself merely a possibility (Piaget, 1975/1985, p.142). So viewed, the argument can be taken to depend on Russell's paradox in [5.2]. Suppose that there is such a set and that it is non-empty. Then each and every possibility is included in it. Because the set is itself a possible set, it is a member of itself. But in that case, the set is merely *one* of the possibilities that are elements of the set. From this it follows that the set cannot be the set of *all* possibilites. Thus if there is such a set, there could not be such a set (cf. Lemmon, 1966, p.210).

A different interpretation is that there can be no set of all (*tous*) possibilities because the 'all' is mobile, comprising an extension that is relative to the structural powers of the epistemic subject (Piaget, 1981/1987, p.4). So viewed, the argument can be taken to depend on a thesis of minimal rationality (cf. Cherniak, 1986). Suppose that there is such a set, which is non-empty. Then the set comprises all of the available possibilities. But the available possibilities are not co-extensive with the total possibilities because some possibilities can be noumenal for a subject who has no access to them due to cognitive closure (cf. McGinn, 1991, p.3).

Using the distinction between the two versions of Piagetian epistemology in [7], the latter interpretation is compatible with a restricted epistemology. The possibilities that are noumenal for one subject can be phenomanally present for a more advanced subject. But the former interpretation is compatible with generalised epistemology, as there can be no comprenhensive set of all possibilities. Thus the former interpretation would seem to be the better of the two.

One consequence of Piaget's argument is that any mechanism responsible for intellectual development will have to be similarly open. The mechanism will have to be compatible with any outcome, including the production of novel, routine, and regressive thought. Intellectual search is not by its occurrence successful, even though creative advance is a desirable outcome (see [8.5]). The empirical question thus centres on how intellectual search can be progressive. In consequence of the argument, Piaget's concern in his constructivist works has been with the elaboration of respects in which equilibration is a distinct factor in development (weak case), rather than with its inter-dependent operation with other plausible factors (strong case). Summaries of these studies abound (Beilin, 1989; Chapman, 1988; Gallagher & Reid, 1981; Inhelder, 1982; Vuyk, 1981).

Some developmentalists have interpreted Piaget's account as one in which intellectual development occurs from absence-to-presence of ability (Donaldson et al., 1983; Gelman, 1978). So construed, an ability is either absent or present and must be one or the other, and no ability can be both at once. As Flavell and Wohlwill (1969, p.80) put it, development occurs when there is a transition from "not-in-competence to first-in-competence". Although these developmentalists have been quick to point out its inadequacy, the question of whether it is a permissible interpretation of Piaget's position does not seem to have arisen. A contrary interpretation states that intellectual development occurs as the differentiation and integration of abilities which are initially non-differentiated (Beilin, 1989; Smith, 1987a; Uzgiris & Hunt, 1975). This position has been formulated by Piaget (1923) for 60 years and is evident in the full range of his writings from infancy (Smith, 1987b) to adolescence (Smith, 1987c). A typical expression of this view is in a discussion of conservation (Piaget & Inhelder, 1941/1974, p.8), in which young children's understanding is marked by "relative non-differentiation between the quantity of matter, weight and volume and this is why the child's justifications are circular". Another is in the discussion of formal operations (Inhelder & Piaget, 1955/1958, p.345), requiring both the multiplication of possibilities in a closed system of thinking that presupposes "differentiation and coordination of the points of view". Differentiation of abilities starts from their initial nondifferentiation and leads to their later integration or coordination (Piaget, 1983/1987, p.4).

There are four reasons for rejecting the absence-to-presence interpretation. The implied conclusion will be that the differentiation interpretation offers a preferable interpretation of Piaget's account.

First, an absence-to-presence interpretation has been explicitly rejected by Piaget, for example in his early account of equilibration as the source of operational thought (Piaget, 1957b, p.95): "operations do not ... arise *ex nihilo*". A similar rejection is stated by Inhelder & Piaget (1959/1964, p.285) in the claim that changes in classification do not arise as "simple emergence or creation *ex nihilo* but (rather) in terms of differentiation and coordination". This rejection was noted in [8.1].

Second, an absence-to-presence interpretation conflates the lack of a specified ability with the lack of ability as such. To see this, consider the transition from concrete to formal operations. When Piaget and Inhelder (1941/1974) referred to the "absence of conservation" they had in mind young children's lack of one logical ability (conservation), not the lack of all logical ability. In general, if all thinking is structured and all structures are logical (Piaget, 1977b, p.321), then all thinking has some logical basis. The question raised by Piaget is not whether thinking is logical, because it always is, but rather what sort of logical thinking is acquired at different points in intellectual development. It is no doubt for this reason that multiple models have been used in Piaget's constructivist studies specifically to find and describe precursors of operational thought.

Third, the absence-to-presence interpretation cannot handle intermediate abilities, of which stage II responses are paradigm cases. With a formal operational task, a stage II response exemplifies concrete operational thinking. Thus any such response is intermediate in a relative sense by virtue of its role as a precursor of some more advanced successor. Further stage II responses on concrete operational tasks are intermediate responses for reasons given in [13.1]. Empirical conservation (stage II) represents an advance over nonconservation (stage I), because correct judgments can sometimes be given, although it is not as advanced as necessary conservation (stage III). Finally, constructivist commitments are evident in Piaget's (1960) stage criteria, according to which earlier stages are precursors of later stages. They are evident in the denial that there is an absolute beginning (Piaget, 1964/1968) and an absolute end (Piaget, 1977/1986) to intellectual development.

The fourth reason for rejecting an absence-to-presence interpretation is that it is self-refuting. According to that interpretation, all intellectual change occurs as a process of "not-in-competence to first-in-competence" (Flavell & Wohlwill, 1969). Thus the development of modal understanding must occur in this way. It follows that, at the outset of development, the human understanding lacks these notions altogether. But any such claim is self-refuting on two counts. First, the actual is an instantiation of the possible and so any actual understanding already embodies some minimal understanding of possibility. Second, necessity is defined through the absence of negation, and so any actual understanding for which there is no possible alternative is, to that extent, necessary. It is no doubt for these reasons that Piaget (1981/1987, p.5) stated that intellectual construction is the removal of constraints due to "an initial lack of differentiation between reality, possibility and necessity".

[25.2] A Modal Model of Differentiation

The differentiation interpretation states that intellectual development occurs as the demarcation in the use of one notion from another, and their coherent connection in a unified system of thought. It is worth noting that the claim made by Hintikka & Hintikka at the outset of this section is compatible with this interpretation. Differentiation operates through the use of modal notions (Piaget, 1977/1986, pp.302–3):

> A new necessity emerges only after its having been made possible by earlier states and it generates, in turn, new possibilities. Conversely, access to new possibilities takes place in a framework of previous necessities, leading to the constitution of later necessities ... These turn-takings, which are in fact those of a ceaseless succession of access and closure (*ouvertures et fermetures*), are due to the general law of equilibration.

One aspect of differentiation is the reduction in modal error which is an invariant aspect of intellectual growth (Smith, 1986c, 1987a). On this interpretation, modal notions are viewed as Kantian epistemological principles that are used in some form at all intellectual levels in the search for coherence. Thus both necessity and possibility are used in some form throughout intellectual development for reasons given about the search for coherence in [8.5]. Development in their use takes place, and this is shown by the reduction in modal errors, which are of two types.

A false-positive modal error about necessity occurs when an individual judges to be necessary that which is not necessary. Such cases are styled "pseudo-necessity" by Piaget (1983/1987). A false-negative modal error about necessity occurs when an individual judges to be not necessary that which is necessary. Such cases could be styled "necessity-blindspots" (cf. Piaget, 1974/1977; McGinn, 1991). Modal errors about possibility are analogous.

The parallel structure of some-all and possibility-necessity under negation was first noticed by von Wright (1951). This structure is shown in Table 7.4. There is a long-standing interest in the former whose importance in empirical epistemology continues to be attested (Johnson-Laird, 1990). Analogous interest in modal operators is probably still overdue (Braine & Rumain, 1983).

Because modal notions are inter-definable (Hughes & Cresswell, 1972), modal errors are inter-related. Thus modal errors about necessity may be manifest as erroneous judgments as to what is and is not possible. Conversely, modal errors about possibility may be manifest as erroneous judgments about what is and is not necessary (see Table 7.5).

As an example, a false positive modal error about necessity was made by children who were invited to make inferences about the unobserved sides of a box whose visible sides were white (Piaget, 1981/1987, chap. 3). Inferential errors were evident as when Phi, aged five years, committed an inductive fallacy by inferring that all the sides of the box were white. This response was compounded by modal error because in justifying this faulty inference, Phi argued that the colour of the other sides of the box could not be otherwise (p.31). This is effectively the

TABLE 7.4
Parallel Structure of Quantifiers and Modal Operators

	Modal Operator	
Quantifier	Necessity	Possibility
E some	L necessary	M possible
−E none	−L not necessary	−M not possible
−E− all	−L− possible	−M− necessary

NOTE: The parallel structure of quantifiers and modal operators with respect to their transformation through negation (von Wright, 1951).

TABLE 7.5
False Positive and False Negative Modal Errors

| | Necessity Judgment | | Possibility Judgment | |
Line	False Positive	True	False Positive	True
1	L	–L	M	–M
2	–M–	– –M–	–L–	– –L–
3	–M–	M–	–L–	L–

| | Necessity Judgment | | Possibility Judgment | |
	False Negative	True	False Negative	True
4	–L	L	–M	M
5	– –M–	–M–	– –L–	–L–
6	M–	–M–	L–	–L–

NOTE: The modal operator L stands for Lögisch (necessary) and M for Möglich (possible). Using standard modal equivalences (Hughes & Cresswell, 1972, p. 26), the necessity operator (L) governs a transformation where a negation is not possible (hence –M–), whereas the possibility operator (M) governs a transformation where a negation is not necessary (hence –L–). These equivalences are used in the transformation from LINE 1 to LINE 2 with simplication of double negations in LINE 3. Corresponding transformations and simplifications apply to LINES 4, 5, and 6. By virtue of such transformations, necessities yield possibilities, and conversely. Modal errors occur as either false-positive or false-negative judgments, which are contradictories of true judgments, with conflation of necessity and possibility.

definition of necessity used in modal logic. It is unsurprising that Phi has sufficient linguistic ability to use some notion of necessity, since Byrnes & Duff (1989) have shown that modal expressions are used by pre-school children. But there is a cognitive element in Phi's error, as the notion of necessity is put to incorrect use. Thus there are two options, either that Phi has the linguistic terms associated with necessity but not the corresponding concept, or that Phi has an incomplete grasp of that concept. Quite different is the response of the children, such as Bir aged nine years or Lai aged ten years, who claim that the unobserved sides could be "any colour at all" (p.34). As whiteness is not a necessary property of boxes in general, nor of this particular box, it is possible for the unobserved sides not to be white and so to be any other colour.

Examples of false negative modal errors about necessity occur in concrete operational tasks. Two lines do not have to have an equal number of counters. But the initial judgment of their equality does have the consequence that they are necessarily equal. It is this necessary property of the array that is ignored in nonconservation judgments (see [16].) Analogous claims apply to class inclusion reasoning in [24.3].

Five features of the modal model can be noted:

First, modal notions are not given through observation of reality. Possibilities are instantiated in, but not exhausted by, the actual world.

Necessities transcend the contingencies of the actual world by virtue of their atemporality. Thus an account of the construction of knowledge defined through such notions must be independent of factors in nature and nurture, even though equilibratory processes always occur inter-dependently with other plausible factors. This feature is noted by Piaget (1981/1987, p.3) and was noted in [23].

Second, modal notions are used in some form throughout intellectual development as noted in [8.5] and [25.1]. Differentiation occurs as a gradual process of relative improvement in their use. Modal errors are multiple and polymorphous. This claim can be illustrated in the study of tree structures, where children were invited to infer the route of a car as it passed through a series of tubes containing three (A, B, C), successive, dichotomous crossings. The unitary initial route could terminate in eight garages (G). A record of the actual route was obtained by lifting a series of shutters on different portions of the tube to reveal a ribbon trailing from the car (Piaget & Garcia, 1987/1991, chap. 3). Sab, aged four years, denied (false negative necessity) that a check at A or B would serve to locate the final destination of the car (p.21). By contrast Rac, aged six years, made a partial advance in the realisation that a car in A1 can pass to B2 (modal success). But Rac then inferred (false positive possibility) that from B2 the car could pass to G8 (p.23). Lau, aged six years, specifically stated (false positive necessity) that it is necessary to examine B first to ascertain the route (p.24). More advanced is the response of Did, aged eight years, who realised (modal success) that three observations suffice to trace the route of the car. But Did also claimed (false positive necessity) that it is necessary to make a full observational check (p.25). Finally Cri, aged eleven years, displayed modal success by the realisation that three observations alone suffice, because the non-observation of the ribbon means that the car has taken the complementary track (p.26).

Intellectual development occurs as the reduction in the errors arising from the pervasive use of modal notions. This proposal fits the argument, which was presented in [13] and [16], that progress occurs when the defining properties of a concept are dissociated from their non-defining counterparts. There is a further point to note, namely that, with respect to the actual world, a defining property of some concept is always co-instantiated with some set of non-defining properties that happen to be associated with that concept. It is for this reason that intellectual development is an open process, in that the complete removal of modal error is unattainable due to the co-instantiation of properties in the actual world.

The differentiation of these two types of property is necessary for an intellectual advance to occur. But such an advance can occur only by virtue of the modal knowledge as to which properties can be, and which could not be, transformed in other 'possible worlds'. This modal knowledge corresponds to knowledge of possibilities and necessities respectively. That is, some form of modal knowledge is necessary for knowledge of the actual world. A developmental change is a change in modal knowledge. But because, in the actual world, the two types of property are always co-instantiated, their dissociation can never be complete. Thus the complete removal of modal errors is the unattainable limit on epistemic change (Chapman, 1988, pp.415–16; Piaget, 1918, p.135). There is empirical evidence compatible with this claim relevant to necessary knowledge, including studies of adults' misunderstanding of the analytic–synthetic distinction (Apostel, Mays, Morf, & Piaget, 1957) and of the necessity of conservation (Hall & Kaye, 1978). There is also evidence to show that even adults persist in using a misconceived notion of object permanence despite its initial acquisition in infancy (Subbotskii, 1991a, b). Yet a paradigm example of necessity occurs as identity: necessarily, any object is self-identical (Kripke, 1980). In short, modal errors are shown to be present throughout the life span of developing individuals.

Third, the initial and non-differentiated use of modal notions is marked by circular reasoning and inconsistency. Circular reasoning arises when children fail to *maintain* the difference between distinct notions. This failure is manifest as nonconservation, for reasons given in [16], namely that the defining properties of a notion have to be respected for *that* notion, rather than any other, to be put to use. Consider the serial conservation of quantity, weight, and volume. The suggestion is not that young children lack these notions altogether. Rather, these separate notions are merged in a gross notion of size. Thus Chev, aged six years, claimed that one ball of clay is bigger than another because it is heavier, and that it is heavier because it is bigger. Chev also claimed that one ball of clay is bigger because it has more clay, and that it has more clay because it is bigger (Piaget & Inhelder, 1941/1974, p.6). Two separate notions (quantity, weight) are merged in one notion (size) and this is shown by Chev's circular reasoning about each. Such reasoning is due to the non-realisation of the possibility that other properties are implicated in the use of distinct notions. Inconsistency arises in the use of distinct criteria whose implications are incompatible. Conservation is once again illustrative. Blas, aged four years, claimed both that the higher level of one of two equivalent quantities of liquid resulted in there being *more liquid*, and also that there was *less liquid* in that container by comparison with an equivalent amount distributed in three separate containers (Piaget & Szeminska, 1941/1952, p.6). The inconsistency does not arise because the criteria invoked by Blas are formally incompatible. Indeed, these criteria (height of liquid level/ number of containers) are distinct. Rather, the implications arising from the use of two separate criteria are contradictory. One and the same quantity of liquid increases or decreases relative to the criterion used.

Fourth, intellectual advance typically does not occur through the comparison of a false judgment with a true one along the lines set out in Table 7.5. Piaget (1953, p.40) has long denied that mental logic is available to conscious inspection for reasons given in [8.3]. Intellectual advance does not occur as the deliberate and conscious identification and appraisal in advance of alternatives and their consequences.

So much is clear from genuinely problematic encounters. An example was given in [4.2] concerning extensional and intensional logics. Extensional logic includes an explicit proof that a contradiction strictly implies any proposition. Intensional logic embodies the counter-argument that this proof is invalid. This rational dispute centres on which premises of the proof can be retained and which consequences follow from the rejection of specified premises. Thus extensional logic embodies standard principles of reasoning, such as *modus ponens* and the disjunctive syllogism, but also leads to the paradoxes of implication. Such paradoxes can be removed by appeal to intensional logics but only if severe restrictions are placed on these standard logical principles. It is no surprise to find that circular reasoning and inconsistency are endemic in discussions of whether intensional logic *is* better than extensional logic.

The developing minds of children are faced with analogous problems, where the use of an available system of thought requires the gradual creation of a more differentiated successor. New possibilities arise as new ideas, whose rationality is dependent on the connections imposed by the epistemic subject. These connections are expressed in the individual's judgments whose coherence may be retrospective, related to a previously used system of thought, or prospective, related to a successor under formation and thematisation (Henriques, 1977).

Fifth, the differentiated successor emerges from within the current system of thinking. According to Piaget (1978, p.228), with respect to any property, "differentiations or 'intrinsic' variations can be determined by necessary deductions starting from the meaning of that property and the differentiations or 'extrinsic' variations produced from without by factual considerations". As an example, Piaget cites the property of length, which is an intrinsic property of a triangle, the sides of which must be of some length, although not any specific length, which is an extrinsic variation. Thus the understanding of *any* property requires modal understanding, because the defining or intrinsic properties are necessary. Such properties have logical consequences whose non-recognition leads to contradiction. Thus one problem is to identify which properties are, and which are not, these defining properties. A related problem is to identify which are, and which are not, their logical consequences. Contradictions in thinking provide a sure test that the necessary properties of some notion have not been fully identified. In this way is the notion of necessity central to intellectual growth. Further, the notion of possibility is equally central. The only way to escape from circular or contradictory reasoning is by appeal to new possibilities. But any new possibility bears on some property and so the same problems arise. It is no doubt for this reason that Piaget (1918; 1950) envisages the construction of knowledge, both within the individual and in scientific growth, to occur as a spiral process which is always open.

[26] PIAGETIAN CONSTRUCTIVISM AND CONSISTENCY

A striking feature of Piaget's constructivist account is the retention of the structuralist claims about the importance of reversibility in operational thought (Piaget, 1975/1985, p.22). Multiple models are used to complement the structuralist models. Thus use is made of category theory in an attempt to identify show how comparison is a precursor, not a replacement, of transformation (Piaget, 1980c, p.5; Piaget et al., 1990, pp.15–16; cf. Davidson, 1988). Again, use is made of logical principles, such as contradiction, to show the development of logical thinking (Piaget, 1974/1980, p.167). Or use is made of intensional logic to show that there can be primitive versions of the formal operations in the thought of the young child (Piaget & Garcia, 1987/1991, pp.40–41). Such prodigality is welcome, since Piaget (1976a; 1987) specifically noted that his work was incomplete. The presumption is that the structuralist claims are insufficient for Piaget's theoretical purposes, and that the constructivist models could remedy this insufficiency. Although many developmentalists would accept the former assumption (see [22]), the latter assumption generates questions about the internal consistency of Piaget's position.

Not all of the constructivist commitments are consistent with the structuralist models. A notable example arises from the use of entailment logic (Piaget & Garcia, 1987/1991; cf. Ricco, 1990). Sympathy with this logic can be traced to a comment by Grize (1962, p.97) who, at a Genevan symposium, noted that "$p \rightarrow q$ only if p and q have something in common and, in normal case, something more than truth-value". The suggestion is that common variables are required for operational thinking to be manifest. It is short step from this claim to the replacement of extensional by intensional logical systems, in which

(Piaget, 1980a, p.5) "*p* implies *q* if, and only if, a meaning of *q* is incorporated in that of *p* and if this meaning is transitive". The proposal made by Anderson & Belnap (1975) is that a set of premises (*A*) entails (→) a conclusion (*B*) just in case the relation $A \to B$, where *A* is relevant to *B*, is, if true, necessarily true. Entailment is a necessary relation between premises that are relevant to the entailed conclusion. The difficulty is that both the relevance and necessity criteria of entailment logic engender problems for Piaget's account (Smith, in press).

The relevance criterion poses problems due to the restrictions placed by entailment logic on the validity of the disjunctive syllogism. The disjunctive syllogism $(p \text{ v } q) \& \text{-}p \to q$ is a standard argument: from a disjunction of propositions and the falsity of one disjunct, the remaining disjunct can be inferred. In extensional logic, this argument form is valid (Haack, 1978) and is accorded a key place in empirical studies of reasoning (Braine & O'Brien, 1991). Yet in the entailment logic of Anderson & Belnap (1975, pp.259, 296–300), the validity of this form of argument is restricted as a consequence of their denial that any proposition is entailed by a contradiction. Their argument was reviewed in [4.2]. However, in Piaget's studies, some version of this argument form is attributed to developing indidividuals.

Here are three cases. The A-not-B error is made by infants who can successfully find a toy hidden at place A, but who continue to search at place A even when the toy is hidden, in full view, at place B. The form of their incorrect response can be re-cast as: $(A \text{ v } B) \& \text{-}A \to A$. By contrast, a better response is one where the infant correctly searches at place *B*: $(A \text{ v } B) \& \text{-}A \to B$ (Piaget, 1937/1954, Obs. 40/53 respectively). Again, in a study of inferential necessity, children were presented with a hidden figure, parts of which could be serially exposed by removing up to 20 (1–20) covers. The task was to decide which one of an available 12 (coded A–L) templates matched the hidden figure. The correct template was G (Piaget, 1983/1987, Chap.8). The findings in a parallel study (Dionnet, 1987, p.139) revealed one child, aged 10 years, who removed four covers (12, 18, 15, 5) as follows:

(12) G, E, D, K, H, L;
(18) D, G, E, I;
(15) E, G, I, not-D;
 (5) G, so not-E, not-I.

The child proposed alternatives which were severally rejected on the basis of the observed information. The form of this reasoning corresponds to the disjunctive syllogism. Another example is provided by the magnet task, where the adolescent Gou, aged 14 years, hypothesised that either content or weight could be responsible for the behaviour of the needle; discounted the latter; hypothesised that content or distance could be responsible; discounted distance; and so concluded that the effect was due to content. This pattern of reasoning is a disjunctive syllogism (Inhelder & Piaget, 1955/1958, p.102).

With these three cases in mind, the tasks used with both the infant and the child have relevant variables. The toy is hidden in one of a pair of places, and one of the twelve templates is correct. Thus successive elimination can lead to a correct deduction. It would be plausible to use entailment logic in the interpretation of such (developmentally primitive) cases. But in the case of Gou, disjunction is used truth-functionally because the task is to ascertain, and then to justify, both which variables could be, and which ones actually are, influential in the magnet task. Of course, Gou's case is not unique, as the subjects are placed in exactly this situation in many of the formal operational tasks, especially where a *ceteris paribus* clause is involved. So in these (developmentally advanced) cases, entailment logic is not similarly applicable. Yet, according to Braine & Rumain (1983, p.319), the use of a strategy for isolating variables in an organised problem-space is "an interesting and important aspect of intellectual development". The use of this strategy could not be explained through entailment logic. It is in this respect that standard logic provides a better instrument, both in accounting for the phenomenon instantiated in Inhelder's tasks, and in Piaget's original description of the subject's mental organisation.

The necessity criterion also poses problems for Piaget's account. First, it is evident that there is considerable complexity, and so disagreement, pertaining to necessity. Several defining criteria, such as analyticity, unrevisability, self-evidence, apriority, have been suggested by philosophers in the absence of common agreement (Grayling, 1982; Haack, 1978). Piaget (1967b, p.91) is aware of this conceptual uncertainty, shown by his review of ten such criteria. Further, Piaget's (1977/1986, pp.301–2; 1983/1987, p.136) own definition of necessity replaces the standard definition (a necessary proposition is one whose negation is impossible) by a non-standard definition, due to Leibniz, whereby a necessary proposition is one whose negation entails contradictions. One advantage of the latter definition is that the denial of necessity entails a contradiction which, in turn, entails any proposition. Modal errors in reasoning lead to any conclusion. Examples in children's reasoning are easy to find, because children attempt to justify the contradictions in their reasoning by appeal to an indefinite stock of situationally specific beliefs. But Piaget's preferred definition of necessity is at variance with the entailment logic of Anderson & Belnap, who specifically deny that a contradiction entails any proposition.

Second, Braine (1979) has argued that systems of modal logic, such as strict implication, are inapplicable to conditionals that are contingent, or causal, or instantiated by arbitrary content. Reasoning on formal operational tasks is similar in this respect. In none of these cases are the conditional propositions logically necessary. By parity of argument, Braine's objection rules out the applicability of entailment logic. Yet modal reasoning is a fact. The major theoretical problem is, in part, to decide which one of the infinitely many modal systems to use in the description of modal reasoning (cf. Johnson-Laird, 1978) and, in part, to show how reasoning in its polymorphous forms (propositional, modal) develops (Braine & Rumain, 1983). This general problem is especially important in relation to Piaget's position, which accords a central role to modality in understanding (Smith, 1987a).

A third problem is that the necessity of a proposition is explicitly tagged in entailment logic. Indeed, the main purpose of that system is to provide a decision procedure for the systematic detection of deducibility. But it was noted in [8.3] that intellectual construction is taken by Piaget not to be a fully conscious process. Further, modal understanding is denied to be tied to its linguistic expression (Gréco, 1959, p.84; Piaget, 1967c, p.271). It follows that problems must arise in using the explicit criteria presupposed by entailment logic in the identification of the modal status of children's beliefs, even in cases of modal success. This difficulty is compounded due to the presence of modal errors (see [25.2]).

A fourth problem follows from this. The suggestion might be that entailment logic is expected to be explanatory not of the individual's understanding of specific propositions—which are often not necessary—but rather of the deductions drawn from (non-necessary) propositions. In a Piagetian approach, understanding becomes necessary (cf. Piaget 1983/1987, p.115) and it is this transition that entailment logic is supposed to explain. But it is precisely this aspect of Piaget's constructivism—the passage from extensional generality to deductive justification (Piaget, 1983/1987, pp.138–9) or the temporal construction of atemporal necessity (Piaget & Garcia, 1983/1989, p.15)—that entailment logic alone could not explain. To see why, consider a paradigm case which is the transition from stage II to stage III in concrete operations. A defining characteristic of a stage II response is its empirical, and so non-necessary, character in contrast to the necessity that is constitutive of a stage III response (see [13.1]). But this is a transition from a contingency to a necessity, and so the underlying relation could not be entailment (Anderson & Belnap, 1975, p.14). A contingency can always be false—witness the presence of stage I (false) responses. Even if a contingency is true, an entailment should not depend on the accidents of an individual psychology.

In short, a choice must be made. If entailment logic is accepted, both its relevance and necessity criteria require modifications to Piaget's accounts of reasoning by infants, children, and adolescents. On the other hand, the retention of any of these Piagetian accounts requires modification of both the relevance and necessity criteria of entailment logic. Although some developmentalists (Overton, 1990; Ricco, 1990) seem attached to the former, others contend that the latter is better suited to Piaget's purposes (Mays, personal communication; cf. Vonèche & Vidal, 1985). This should not be a surprising outcome. It was noted in [4.1] that different logical systems result in different commitments. The conclusion is inescapable that Piaget's prodigal use of different constructivist models can be expected to require adjustments. The aim of this discussion has not been to assign priorities in favour of models based on standard rather than non-standard logic or conversely, but rather to identify questions that merit more attention. Doubtless there are other aspects of the account that require similar scrutiny.

CHAPTER EIGHT

Conclusion—
Necessary Knowledge
and Piagetian Research

"EH: How do you see the future of psychology?
JP: With optimism. We see new problems every day"
(Piaget, 1970, p.32)

[27] OVERVIEW—PIAGETIAN PERSPECTIVES ON NECESSARY KNOWLEDGE

One of Piaget's central problems has been the temporal construction of atemporal knowledge, a principal instance of which is necessary knowledge [1]. This problem has been addressed in his writings during the period 1918–1990. Piaget's answer to this problem sets out to show the respects in which there is a logic of epistemic discovery. An interpretation of Piaget's account is elaborated, according to stated empirically necessary conditions of the understanding of necessity, which occurs as the outcome of a necessary process of construction [25]. This latter process occurs as the differentiation of the defining (necessary) properties of a concept from its non-defining (non-necessary) properties. With respect to knowledge of the actual world, any defining property is always co-instantiated with some set of non-defining properties, whose dissociation is necessary for intellectual growth. Yet dissociation occurs only by virtue of modal knowledge bearing on which properties of that concept can be, and which could not be, transformed.

As the former corresponds to knowledge of possibilities, and the latter to knowledge of necessities, some form of modal knowledge is a condition of knowledge of the actual world. A developmental change is a change in modal knowledge. Although Piaget's account does not provide a complete resolution of his problem, it does have two attractive features. One is that his account does offer an answer to a problem that is frequently ignored despite its outstanding but fundamental status. A second is that his answer characterises some of the internal factors in intellectual growth. Piaget's preoccupation with showing the distinctness of internal factors leaves open the demonstration of their inter-dependency with other plausible, external factors in nature and nurture [23].

An illustrative review of the problems of knowledge and necessity, which have been the preoccupation of philosophers from Plato to Kant, is presented [3.1]. This review has more than historical interest, as the discussion in [20] bears on versions of platonism that are implicated in current psychological perspectives. The philosophical problems are substantive and problematic, but they continue to have a dominating influence. It is commonly assumed in philosophical discussions that a minimally adequate account must do more than show how knowledge of the actual world is acquired and used [25.1]. This is because knowledge inevitably bears on what could be the case, and so on what must be the case in the infinite 'possible worlds'. Piaget's account aspires to be adequate in just this sense [25.2]. This key assumption is illustrated by reference to contemporary discussions, including Popper's philosophy of science and Kripke's philosophical epistemology [3.2]. Thus Piaget's main problem has its basis in philosophy, concerning the fundamental categories of experience and rationality.

The discussion has three strands. One strand is philosophical and concerns the importance of normative issues when epistemological questions arise. A second strand is psychological and concerns the extent to which Piaget's position is vulnerable to psychological challenges. The third strand is epistemological and concerns the respects in which Piaget's position is an intelligible position relevant to his main question.

The philosophical strand is discussed first. Illustration of the general importance of normative issues is provided in [4] and [5]. The specific point to notice concerns the distinctive nature of Piaget's genetic epistemology, which is distinct from both philosophy and psychology. A common argument has been used by Piaget against exclusively normative discussions, namely that epistemological problems have an empirical dimension which has been ignored. This argument is illustrated by reference to traditional and contemporary discussions in epistemology [3]. Realising that the original, normative problems are unamenable to empirical investigation, Piaget's proposal is to change the normative question about the defining conditions of concepts of knowledge and necessity, and substitute in their place the empirical question about how necessary knowledge is constructed. It is in this sense that Piaget's genetic (constructive) epistemology is a *tertium quid* [7].

This position was outlined by Piaget in an early discussion at a conference in 1922 and elaborated in his *chef d'oeuvre* in 1950 some 28 years later. The difference emerges in the typical questions that are addressed in the three approaches. A typical question in philosophical epistemology is "what is the nature of necessary knowledge?". This request for defining conditions is subjected to rational (a priori) investigation. Since empirical investigation is an indispensable feature of genetic epistemology, it is not reducible to philosophical epistemology. Yet the questions addressed in constructivist epistemology are questions taken from philosophy and transformed, such as "how is necessary knowledge constructed?" This question has an epistemological element in that the rationality of necessary knowledge is taken to be a psychological construction with its basis in contingent social contexts. But this question is also amenable to empirical investigation as well. Yet it is not a standard question in (developmental) psychology, whose concern is with questions such as "when and under what conditions do children use their necessary knowledge?". The psychological question is primarily directed on *children* and their necessary knowledge, unlike the question in genetic epistemology which concerns *necessary knowledge* under construction during childhood.

The second strand concerns the psychological assimilation of, and challenge to, Piaget's position. Acute problems of interpretation arise with respect to Piaget's answer to his main question. These problems are due to the vast bulk of his writings; to their vulnerability to mistranslation; to their diversity due to the adoption of multiple models which are put to serial use; and to their complexity whereby novel, empirical findings are accorded distinctive and original construal. Questions of interpretation are, therefore, crucial. Yet these questions have not been given their due importance in Piagetian commentary and research. The suggestion is not that 'Piaget's theory' is right and the critics are not, but rather that Piaget's writings contain multiple positions whose specific character has not always been noticed. One main proposal is that more importance needs to be assigned to the interpretation of Piaget's several positions. The primary reason is not to endorse Piaget's stance, but rather to ascertain the extent to which distinctive elements relevant to the resolution of a complex question concerning the construction of necessary knowledge are given due worth. This proposal is supported in two ways. One is through demonstration that there are alternative interpretations, for example about the status of age and developmental level [18], or about development as a process of differentiation rather than an *ex nihilo* process in [25.1]. The other is a general argument concerning the limits on empirical testability [9].

An account of the development of knowledge must be testable. Yet empirical testing based on falsifiability through *modus tollens* has the weakness that it is indeterminate in cases where the falsified predictions have been extracted from a complex antecedent. However, any account addressing Piaget's main problem will be complex and constituted by several elements. Negative testing indicates that something must be changed, but does not identify which elements are the ones to change. It is at this point that Piaget's position has been subjected to psychological assimilation, whereby the methods, procedures, and tasks that are dominant in research-programmes in psychology are used as the standard by which Piaget's position can be evaluated. Psychological assimilation begs the question about the independent status of questions in genetic epistemology. Three instances of this assimilation concern methods, procedures, and tasks. The common theme to the argument in [10]–[19] is that psychological discussions, of course, have independent interest and interpretive power in relation to psychological questions. But they do not require substantial changes to be made to Piaget's position in relation to the construction of necessary knowledge, which is concerned with a set of questions that are only partially intersecting. This difference is taken up in [25].

One instance of the psychological assimilation concerns empirical methods [10]. The argument is that Piaget's *critical method* is used deliberately and not by default in an attempt to find, so as to check, the specific character of children's natural understanding. This method requires children to demonstrate their understanding in displays of both procedural and declarative knowledge, where attention is given to their reasons for the understanding so displayed [11]. The central reason for the use of this method is that any concept is tied to its defining criteria, which are distinct from the non-defining criteria that happen to be correlated with it. Yet a defining property is a necessary property, which governs the use of the concept not merely in the actual world but also in any-and-all 'possible worlds'. By contrast, a non-defining property is not so tied, not even in the actual world. The differentiation of the former from the latter is a *sine qua non* of intellectual progress. In turn, diagnostic assessment must be sensitive enough to show the extent to which their differentiation has been successfully undertaken—shown by children's demarcation of both relevant from non-relevant, and defining from non-defining, properties of the concepts under investigation. Although some developmentalists have argued that Piaget's method is vulnerable, leading to false-negative attributions of knowledge [12], a counter-argument is elaborated in [13]. The counter-argument is a review of two philosophical accounts—the foundationalist and the causal accounts—which provide alternative proposals as to the defining conditions of knowledge. Both arguments have the consequence that necessary knowledge could not be acquired in the absence of relevant justifications. The counter-argument bears on a methodological issue, which undermines the extensive body of psychological research that has been regarded in the replacement of Piaget's substantive position.

A second instance of psychological assimilation arises with respect to the procedures used in designing assessment tasks [14]. In psychological research-programmes, priority is given to experimental methods. The importance of such methods is not in doubt. What is open to doubt is whether an empirical investigation has to be experimental in the traditional sense.

In a forensic sense, an experimental method does not require the control of antecedent variables, but is instead directed on the identification and stability of an individual's beliefs. It is in this sense that Piaget's critical method is experimental, by virtue of its concern with the individual's ability to use the defining criteria of concepts at their disposal [15]. Studies of conservation provide a *locus classicus*, serving to clarify this point [16]. Conservation is a fundamental property of all concepts by virtue of which a specific concept, rather than any other, can be used consistently in one and the same act of understanding. Just as deductively valid arguments are truth-preserving, so defining criteria permit the coherent use of a concept through transformation of its non-defining properties. In this way is that concept conserved. Further, in this same way is necessity an invariable property tied to the use of concepts. The argument is that many studies of conservation have disregarded the modal character of children's understanding and that procedural changes in assessment tasks have not been systematically carried through by virtue of the neglect of modal understanding.

A third instance of psychological assimilation occurs over the use made of assessment tasks [17]. Such tasks are used for multiple purposes and they provide under-determining evidence for any-and-all substantive positions. This methodological claim is supported by reference to the distinction between theory and observation in scientific contexts. The problematic relation between assessment tasks and postulated models of understanding is shown. The argument is directly relevant to the appraisal of Piaget's position. An assessment task may embody a structure that fails to match the intellectual structure used by the developing individual. Thus the directed search for the latter structures in empirical epistemology is not completely bound by the findings derived from studies based solely on the former structures. Two specific instances that show the scope for mismatching of theoretical interests are reviewed. One concerns the status of age as a criterion of developmental level [18]. The argument is that neither Piaget's writings nor Piagetian research provides an adequate basis for this common claim. Here, as elsewhere, issues pertaining to interpretation and investigation inter-penetrate. The other concerns the psychological status of mental models [19]. The argument is that if mental models are construed to be devoid of mental logic, and so of deductively necessary elements, then findings and positions associated with their use cannot be used to settle problems about the construction of necessary from non-necessary knowledge.

Two further challenges to Piaget's constructivism are reviewed. Their common feature is the implied commitment to platonism. The argument assumes that constructivism and platonism are exclusive alternatives such that a choice has to be made between them. The point of the discussion is to identify the consequences of the two alternatives which evidently could not be combined with Piaget's constructivism [20]. One perspective concerns the social construction of knowledge, which can be interpreted in a weak and a strong sense [21]. The former (socioconstructivism) is shown to be compatible with individual constructivism, although certain claims associated with this position relate to the strong position (social constructionism). The argument is that the strong position is committed to a platonism whereby cultural objects have an independent status that is distinct from their realisation in individual minds. The second perspective concerns the learning paradox. The paradox is a *reductio*, stating that novel concepts and structures are unlearnable and so must be innate [22]. The counter-argument is that this nativist conclusion is incompatible with constructivism because of its explicit commitment to some form of platonism. Further, it embodies the very problem that it was designed to resolve. Problems about the fixation of beliefs to available concepts and structures arise, including the replacement of non-necessary by necessary beliefs.

The third strand concerns Piaget's proposals in answer to his main question. This position is reviewed in five complementary ways.

First, six main claims are extracted from Piaget's early and more recent writings [8]. The aim in this part of the discussion is to identify essential elements in Piaget's account, to provide suitable exegesis sufficient to show their place in Piaget's account, and to offer selective commentary in elucidation of their general acceptability. There is no suggestion that the six claims exhaust Piaget's position, still less that they provide a testable model that provides the clear resolution of the central question. Rather, the intention is to identify some theoretical constructs which are expected to contribute to an interpretive framework for the further investigation of the main question. In essence, the claim is that intellectual construction is a normative process whereby concepts that always have some functional presence in human understanding—from infancy to adult life—are put to differential use in an individual's actions. The different uses are identifiable through Piaget's structuralist models, and correspond to the terms of a process of epistemic change. Piaget has, however, used multiple models, based on category theory and entailment logic, and not merely the familiar models of operational logic. Concepts are used in the judgments made by individuals, which are expressed in actions and beliefs. Structuralist models provide an inventory of the connections that can be made between judgments, and so between beliefs and actions. The individual does not always have conscious access to the web of connections between inter-relatable judgments. In turn, the formation of new judgments requires consistent connections to be made with some system of knowledge. By this very activity are new systems of knowledge generated, because epistemic construction is constrained in two respects. First, the new judgment may not be consistent with the available system. Second, the new judgment may be consistent with a different system under construction through the changes made to an existing system. Epistemic search is a search for coherence, marked by the extent to which a current judgment is consistent with some set of possible alternatives. This search is a characteristic of the epistemic subject, and not the individual person, concerning the development in the use of intellectual values. This process of construction has empirical and normative components related to rational understanding.

Second, Piaget's account must deal with two issues, one about sequence and the other about mechanisms [23]. Although the structuralist models have interpretive scope as descriptions of the terms of the epistemic process, they do not have similar success as models of that process. Although the importance of this distinction is heeded, the argument is that Piaget's account of equilibration does address the latter issue, which is an outstanding one for all constructivist accounts. That account embodies two claims: the weak claim is about the distinctness of equilibration; the strong claim is about its inter-dependent operation with other plausible factors that influence intellectual growth. The suggestion is that Piaget's work is primarily directed on the intelligibility of the weak claim, but that its acceptability is reliant on the strong claim, which has not been made good. Thus Piaget's account of epistemic construction is incomplete. This admission does not, however, warrant the rejection of the weak claim, even though this conclusion is often drawn.

Third, issues concerning sequence and mechanism have been constantly addressed in Piaget's studies. Classification serves as an example [24]. Illustration of the diversity and unity of Piaget's position is provided by reference to his early, operational and constructivist studies. The claim is that these multiple studies are based on different models of intellectual construction, and that they contain inter-dependent positions that are directed on the demarcation of distinct levels in developmental sequences with attention to respects in which they could be an internal source of change. Piaget's position is reviewed together with psychological research on inductive categorisation and on the necessity of class inclusion reasoning.

Fourth, a modal model of construction through differentiation is presented. This model is a denial that intellectual development occurs as an absence-to-presence process [25.1]. Rather, it is the gradual reduction in the multiple and polymorphous occurrence of modal errors [25.2]. Modal errors occur when modal concepts, which are available throughout mental life, are put to incorrect use. Such errors are expressed in two forms and are manifest as 'pseudo-necessity' and as 'necessity blindspots'. Analogous errors occur with respect to possibility. The relevance of this model to Piaget's main question lies in the fact that children's failure to dissociate the defining and non-defining properties of concepts gives rise to modal errors. Their removal is a necessary feature of intellectual progression and can result in necessary knowledge. This process of change is necessary because it consists in the removal of internal constraints on the construction of knowledge.

Finally, it is argued that the consistency of Piaget's constructivism can be questioned [26]. A central feature of the structuralist models is a commitment to the reversible character of rational thought. Because the argument in [23] was that the structuralist models did not contain an adequate mechanism of developmental change, Piaget's account must be supplemented. One supplement is the use of entailment logic, which is stated to be an intensional logic that is distinct from the extensional logic used in the structuralist models. The argument is that the use of entailment logic with the structuralist models creates problems. One problem is that creative search may be viewed extensionally, and so cannot be described through an intensional logic that uses relevance as its criterion. A second problem is that the construction of necessary from non-necessary knowledge could not be described through an intensional logic that uses necessity as a criterion.

[28]   NECESSARY KNOWLEDGE AND CONSTRUCTIVIST RESEARCH

There is an evident omission in the discussion. Although there has been too little research on the development of modal understanding, it has not been completely absent. Indeed, there has recently been a growing interest in this issue. The aim in this final section is to identify and comment on some themes that are characteristic of this research, which can—for convenience—be placed into three, non-exclusive groupings, namely modal understanding, microgenesis, and empirical epistemology.

One grouping is explicitly directed on the development of modal understanding with special attention to Piagetian issues. However, different perspectives guide this research. One is a commitment to some version of constructivsim (Acredolo & O'Connor, 1991; Byrnes & Beilin, 1991; Moshman, 1990; Moshman & Timmons, 1982; Piéraut-Le Bonniec, 1974/1980, 1990; Smith, 1987a, 1992a). A second is a commitment to the dominant view in logical empiricism and analytic philosophy, according to which necessity has its basis in language (Carnap, 1947/1956; Haack, 1978). Note that studies which are compatible with this perspective are also stated to be relevant to Piagetian issues (Braine, 1990; Braine & O'Brien, 1991; Osherson, 1974, 1975; Russell, 1982, 1983). Three main comments arise, concerning the linguistic basis of necessity, psychological assimilation, and epistemic modality.

With respect to the two guiding perspectives, one comment to make is that they are contraries. According to Putnam (1980, p.300), notions such as reflective abstraction and necessity, which are central to constructivism, are ultimately linguistic. A similar position, in which an essential role is accorded to language in propositional reasoning, is elaborated by Braine and O'Brien (1991). But according to Piaget (1979/1980, p.32), these same notions have their basis in action prior to language. Further, errors in human reasoning recur despite the ready availability of appropriate linguistic ability (Byrnes & Duff, 1989; Cummins, 1978; Falmagne, Mawby & Pea, 1989). Thus these perspectives cannot be combined without some modification.

A second comment is that the psychological assimilation of Piagetian epistemology is apparent in many studies (see [9]). One instance of this assimilation is apparent in the concern to set age-norms relevant to the onset of modal understanding. Thus Piéraut-Le Bonniec (1974/1980, p.106) claims that generative understanding of the alethic (possibility, necessity) modalities is not present before the age of 10 years. By contrast, Sophian and Somerville

(1988) claim that a recognitive understanding of possibility is present in children aged four years, and similar age claims are made about the understanding of necessity by Fabricius et al. (1987). Accepting the argument in [18], such disputes do little to settle theoretical questions. Indeed, if the interpretation presented in [25.2] is accepted, some form of modal understanding is always present throughout mental life. Thus the main questions should turn on which modal model to use in empirical research, and on which forms of modal understanding are identified through it. Neither question can be resolved by reference to studies that use discrepant, modal models in relation to different levels of modal understanding (the Aristotelian square of modalities with respect to generative understanding, and the bare notions of possibility and necessity in relation to recognitive understanding and inferential mastery respectively).

A second instance of psychological assimilation concerns the procedures used in the design of assessment tasks. The argument in [16] was that the psychological question "what are the optimal procedures for the design of conservation tasks?" has little bearing on the epistemological question "what is the modality of understanding with respect to any conservation task?". There is some tendency to give more attention to the former than to the latter question in studies of children's operational knowledge (Cormier & Dagenais, 1983; Markman, 1978; Miller, 1986). A related discussion of this point occurs in [24.3].

A third instance of psychological assimilation is shown by the importance assigned to children's judgments, rather than to their justifications. Thus Osherson & Markman (1975) and Russell (1982; 1983) presented children with propositions of different modalities (tautologies, contingencies, contradictions). The justifications that children should be able to offer for their responses, whether correct or not, were not at the forefront of such studies, whose conclusions would be indeterminate through the argument in [13]. An empirical exemplication of the counter-case is provided by Piéraut-Le Bonniec (1990) in relation to Piagetian constructivism.

A third comment concerns the distinction between alethic and epistemic modalities (Piéraut-Le Bonniec, 1974/1980, p.26; von Wright, 1951). Although these modalities are isomorphic, certainty and necessity are independent notions. Wittgenstein (1969) has provided examples of non-necessary propositions that are certain, whereas Kripke (1980) has provided examples of necessary propositions that are known inductively and so are not certain. Further, the Piagetian distinction between 'pseudo-necessity' and 'necessity blindspots' is based on a similar distinction (see [25.2]). Yet children's understanding of certainty and uncertainty is taken to clarify their understanding of necessity and possibility (Acredolo & O'Connor, 1991; Miller, Brownell, & Zukier, 1977). The key issue is whether clarification amounts to explanation, as Byrnes and Beilin (1991) make similar commitments partly through disatisfaction with the Piagetian notion of differentiation, which they regard as a descriptive rather than an explanatory notion.

There are precedents to consider, when independent norms are subjected to joint investigation. With respect to moral and intellectual norms, Kohlberg (1968; cf. Kuhn, Langer, & Haan, 1977) argued that formal operational thinking was a necessary but insufficient condition of advanced moral reasoning. It is an open question as to whether the construction of alethic and epistemic modalities is concurrent or consecutive. Further, construction as a process of differentiation concerns the dissociation of the defining properties relevant to one concept or norm from those relevant to some other. Piaget's (1941) notion of *décalage* was invoked in the identification of the speed with which distinct, but formally similar notions, were constructed. If 'simple' notions such as mass, weight, and volume are dissimilar in just this sense (Piaget & Inhelder 1941/1974), it is not unreasonable to suppose that the more complex norms of alethic and epistemic modalities could be so as well.

A second grouping is a research-programme directed on the psychological subject (Inhelder, 1978). The latter is conceived to be the complement of the epistemic subject [8.6] and is partially constituted by the structural system available to the individual (Inhelder & de Caprona, 1992a, p.21). Thus the intention is not to view one subject as a better psychological successor to the other, but rather to view one as an *alter ego* of the other. There are two reasons for drawing this distinction. One is that a structural description does not provide a model of epistemic transition (Inhelder, 1978, p.101). A second is that psychological functioning is a neglected feature of the research-programme directed on the epistemic subject (Inhelder, 1978, p.102). It is specifically noted that Piaget's model of development as differentiation, conceived as access to new possibilities bound by necessary relations, is intelligible (Inhelder & de Caprona, 1985, p.9). Even so, that model embodies the weakness that there has been neglect of the specific ways in which both access and closure are acquired and used.

The *leitmotif* of this complementary approach is microgenesis, conceived as the study of the individually specific ways in which developing individuals in fact perform on natural tasks (Inhelder & de Caprona, 1992a, p.24). Microgenesis is an attempt to explain human conduct through its function, expressed as the goals to be attained and the concomitant procedural knowledge leading to their attainment. At issue is the extent to which procedural knowledge is tied to its realisation in a specific context or generalisable across contexts (Inhelder & de Caprona, 1992a, p.35). Procedural knowledge that does generalise is not structural knowledge (Inhelder & de Caprona, 1992a, p.49) but the former has two features that are lacking in the latter. One is its individual character, expressed *hic et nunc*. The other is the hypothetical necessity of means–ends relationships. Manifestly, these two features are alien to structural knowledge, which is universal and is categorically necessary. But as the aim in microgenesis is to provide a complementary account to Piagetian constructivism, the strengths of either position can be combined with those of the other. Fifteen studies that correspond to this research-progranmme are reviewed by Inhelder and de Caprona (1992b). Some of these studies are subsumed under related areas of study (Karmiloff-Smith, 1991; Montangero, 1991).

One comment to make about this approach is that it extends the stock of problems in the domain of constructivist theories. Montangero's (1991) comment, that the concern is with the new uses of available structures, has some purchase on the research-programme itself. This is, of course, a welcome extension, the full details of which are beyond the scope of this discussion. Research arising from this approach has its origin in Piagetian positions but it does not exclude their critical re-appraisal, modification, and rejection (Karmiloff-Smith, 1991).

A second comment about microgenesis is that its commitment to functionalism is open to challenge, not least from the philosopher responsible for its application to cognitive science, as he has now changed his mind (Putnam, 1988). Further, this challenge is relevant to the construction of modal understanding. A central argument used by Putnam concerns 'Twin Earth' and the problems of reference arising from changes in the contingent properties of natural kinds, such as water. This argument bears on the problems of trans-world identity and reference. Thus Putnam's argument is analogous to that of Kripke (1980), not least in pointing to a problems arising from 'possible worlds' semantics [3.2]. The comment to make is twofold. One is that the implications of 'possible world' semantics have not been fully appreciated in psychological research on categorisation [24.3], nor in research on structuralist knowledge such as conservation [16]. The second is that the separation of functionalist and structuralist problems becomes impossible to draw, because according to the argument in [25.2], some form of modal understanding (structuralist problem) is implicated in procedural knowledge (functionalist problem) operative *hic et nunc*, and conversely.

The suggestion is not that research on the microgenesis of psychological functioning is misplaced, but rather that the self-imposed limit of addressing complementary questions to structuralism is self-defeating. This is because a functionalist study could lead to one set of interpretations, about the extent to which some forms of knowledge are procedural, and so generalisable, whereas a structuralist study would lead to another set of interpretations, about the extent to which those same forms of knowledge have a modal and systemic character. The general claim that the two sets of interpretations are compatible generates the reasonable expectation that compatibility should be verified in particular cases. This is, of course, a modest suggestion by virtue of the signal contributions made in Inhelder's (1936; 1989) studies of both structuralist and functionalist knowledge.

In fact, microgenesis easily extends into the third grouping, empirical epistemology, directed on questions in both cognitive science and Piagetian epistemology. Into this grouping falls the position outlined by Inhelder & Piaget (1979/1980), where the inter-dependence of structuralist and functionalist approaches was specifically commended. A similar position was endorsed by Chapman (1988, p.364) about the unity of the formal and functional aspects of thinking. Studies of formal operational thought and formal reasoning provide further examples of this commitment (Markovits, 1984, 1992; Markovits & Vachon, 1990; Overton, 1990, 1991; Overton et al., 1987). The specific question of the adequacy of cognitive science from the vantage-point of genetic epistemology has been raised in studies of pathological reasoning, leading to considerations about the affective aspects of structural thought (T. Brown, 1980, 1988; Brown & Weiss, 1987). The implication is that there could be mutual advantage from the convergence between cognitive science and constructivist epistemology (Boden, 1982; Cellérier, 1992a,b). In this context, the detailed case of the development of transitivity sets a clear example (Leiser & Gillièron, 1990). This study has its basis in the claim that intellectual change occurs from action to thought as the differentiation of multiple instantiations of logical principles and systems (Gillièron, 1984). The specific proposal is that structuralist knowledge of transitivity is the outcome of its primitive analogues based in procedural knowledge. This stance makes the assumption that research on procedures (cognitive science) is not merely compatible with, but even made plausible by, research on reversible thought (genetic epistemology) and conversely. The major difficulties are threefold. One is that this proposal could be turned down in principle, if standard review of current research in cognitive science and their scant reference to genetic epistemology are a guide (Hunt, 1989; Johnson-Laird, 1983). A second is that cognitive science is committed to a representational theory of knowledge, but that its working definition of *representation* is radically defective due to unwanted commitments to a correspondence theory of truth (Bickhard & Campbell, 1989). According to their knowing-levels analysis, Piagetian epistemology embodies a better notion of operational knowledge, though one that incompletely acknowledges the interactive character of all knowledge (Bickhard, 1988; Campbell & Bickhard, 1986). The implication is that the convergence of cognitive science and genetic epistemology requires more than their additive composition. A third difficulty is that the importance assigned to modal knowledge in [8.4] and [25.2] creates tension for reconciling attempts to combine the two approaches.

To see the difficulty, consider the reconciling position about adolescent reasoning, that both a Piagetian account and an account in terms of mental models can be combined (see [19]). The proposal is that the former is silent about the procedural aspects in reasoning performance, whereas a mental model approach accords too little importance to the structural aspects of rational competence. So on both theoretical and empirical grounds, it is possible to combine both approaches, as the strength of one compensates for the weakness of the other (Markovits & Vachon, 1990; Overton, 1991). This is an attractive suggestion, especially as specific recognition is accorded to the development of modal understanding in research on the psychological processes in reasoning tasks (Markovits, 1984, p.368; Overton, 1990, p.17). But it leaves unexplained the main question of how model construction, which is logic-free, works inter-dependently with a structural organisation, which embodies a mental logic. How does the non-logical construction of models connect with the construction of logical notions that make up the individual's competence? Two expressions of this general difficulty can be noticed.

Thus it is proposed that the model-builder who is presented with an "if p then q" proposition must spontaneously generate an alternate relation of the form "if A then q" (Markovits & Vachon, 1990, p.943). The reason why the individual must be able to do this is because a false antecedent (materially) implies a true consequent (Quine, 1972). So the individual who realises that A is a substitution instance of the negation of p is in a position to understand the relation of implication. In turn, the individual should be able to combine any possibility that has been generated in this way in a coherent system of thinking (Markovits, 1984, p. 368). The problem is that the processes of generating a new possibility, or of combining any possibility in a coherent system of thought, are guided by a mental logic, according to Piaget (1981/1987), but are not guided by logic at all, according to Johnson-Laird (1990). In the latter position, the initial construction of a possibility is regarded as a psychological process that owes nothing to the rules of logic. But this is a constitutive feature of any mental models approach. As such, it must defeat any reconciling position to combine logic-free and mental logic approaches, including the position where Markovits (1993) sets out to show how "a logically necessary conclusion is one that can be read off from a mental model, the elements of which may differ radically from one level of abstraction to another". But this leaves unexplained the presence and operation of internal constraints on construction due to the use of bounded, logical structures. Thus the extent to which the reconciling position provides a unitary account of the development of reasoning is not completely clear.

Again, Overton et al. (1987) set out to show that conditional reasoning with familiar content has a differential effect on development during adolescence. Their proposal is that the familiar semantic content of certain versions of the selection task interacts with moderating logical processes. But the question about which individuals can succeed on which of eight versions of a reasoning task differs from the question of how an individual's success on any version is due to the inter-connection between the psychological processes of model-building and the logical processes of structural growth. Thus in Noelting's (1980—his Table 3) study of proportionality, the ordered level of responses is taken to have a structural basis in terms of the possible relationships that are elaborated in the account of formal operational thought. The familiar task of sharing drinks is taken to be subject to structural constraints, in which psychological construction is subsumed by the mental logic of operational thought. There is looming gap between such studies, concerning the inter-dependency of internal factors with other plausible factors likely to influence intellectual growth [23].

In sum, there is an ongoing interest in the construction of necessary knowledge. Piaget's central question noted in [1] has had a double influence, one in the identification of an important problem, and the other in providing some answer to it. But the summit has yet to be reached. Indeed, it could only be reached through a joint venture, combining psychological research on the multiple origins of knowledge with epistemological research on its uniform legitimation in the light of the standards of rationality. So the climb will have to continue yet a while with a range of routes on offer, which was Piaget's (1987, p.viii; quoted in Smith, 1992a, p.464) final prophecy about his own achievements.

Jean Piaget *circa* 1978.
From J.J. Ducret (1990) *Jean Piaget: Biographie et parcours intellectuel*,
published by Editions Delachaux et Niestlé, Lausanne.

References

Acredolo, C. & Acredolo, L. (1979). Identity, compensation, and conservation. *Child Development, 50,* 524–35.

Acredolo, C. & O'Connor, J. (1991). On the difficulty of detecting uncertainty. *Human Development, 34,* 204–23.

Anderson, A.R. & Belnap, N. (1975). *Entailment: The logic of relevance and necessity.* Princeton, NJ: Princeton University Press.

Apostel, L. (1982). The future of Piagetian logic. *Revue Internationale de Philosophie, 142–3,* 612–35. Reprinted in L. Smith (1992a) *Jean Piaget: Critical assessments.* London: Routledge.

Apostel, L., Mays, W., Morf, A., Piaget, J. (1957). *Les liaisons analytiques et synthétiques.* Paris: Presses Universitaires de France.

Aristotle (nd/1975). *Posterior analytics.* Oxford: Oxford University Press.

Ayer, A.J. (1956). *The problem of knowledge.* Harmondsworth: Penguin.

Baldwin, J.M. (1911). *Thought and thinking.* London: George Allen.

Beilin, H. (1985). Dispensable and core elements in Piaget's research program. *The Genetic Epistemologist, 13,* 1–16. Reprinted in L. Smith (1992a) *Jean Piaget: Critical assessments.* London: Routledge.

Beilin, H. (1989). Piagetian theory. *Annals of Child Development, 6,* 85–131

Bereiter, C. (1985). Toward a solution of the learning paradox. *Review of Educational Research, 55,* 201–26.

Bereiter, C. (1991). Commentary. *Human Development, 34,* 294–98

Bergson, H. (1907/1911). *Creative evolution.* London: Macmillan.

Bickhard, M. (1988). Piaget on variation and selection models: Structuralism, logical necessity, and interactivism. *Human Development, 31,* 274–312. Reprinted in L. Smith (1992a) *Jean Piaget: Critical assessments.* London: Routledge.

Bickhard, M. & Campbell, R. (1989). Interactivism and genetic epistemology. *Archives de Psychologie, 57,* 99–121

Boden, M. (1979). *Piaget.* Brighton, UK: Harvester Press.

Boden, M. (1982). Is equilibration important? A view from artificial intelligence. *British Journal of Psychology, 73,* 165–73.

Bond, T. & Jackson, I. (1991). The Gou protocol revisited: A Piagetian contextualisation of critique. *Archives de Psychologie, 59,* 31–53. Reprinted in L. Smith (1992a) *Jean Piaget: Critical assessments.* London: Routledge.

Bond, T. & Shayer, M. (1991) *Piaget's logical model of formal operations and the selection task: A test of their relationship.* Unpublished paper.

Boom, J. (1991). Collective development and the learning paradox. *Human Development, 34,* 273–87.

Bornstein, M. & Bruner, J. (1989). *Interaction in human development.* Hillsdale, NJ: Lawrence Erlbaum Associates Inc.

Bovet, M., Parrat-Dayan, S., & Deshusses-Addor, D. (1981). Peut-on parler de précocité et de regression dans la conservation? I. Précocité. *Archives de Psychologie, 49,* 289–303.

Bovet, M., Parrat-Dayan, S., & Kamii, C. (1986). Early conservation: What does it mean? *The Journal of Psychology, 120,* 21–35.

Bradley, R. & Swartz, N. (1979). *Possible worlds: An introduction to logic and its philosophy.* Oxford: Blackwell.

Braine, M. (1959). The ontogeny of certain logical operations. *Psychological Monographs: General and Applied, 73,* 1–43. Reprinted in L. Smith (1992a) *Jean Piaget: Critical assessments.* London: Routledge.

Braine, M. (1990). The "natural approach" to reasoning. In W. Overton (Ed.), *Reasoning, necessity and logic.* Hillsdale, NJ: Lawrence Erlbaum Associates.

Braine, M. & O'Brien, D. (1991). A theory of if: A lexical entry, reasoning program, and pragmatic principles. *Psychological Review, 98,* 182–203.

Braine, M. & Rumain, B. (1983). Logical reasoning. In P. Mussen (Ed.), *Handbook of child psychology. Vol. 3.* New York: Wiley.

Brainerd, C. (1973). Judgements and explanations as criteria for the presence of cognitive structures. *Psychological Bulletin, 79,* 172–179. Reprinted in L. Smith (1992a) *Jean Piaget: Critical assessments.* London: Routledge.

Brainerd, C. (1978). *Piaget's theory of intelligence.* Engelwood Cliffs, NJ: Prentice Hall.

Brown, A., Bransford, J., Ferrara, R. & Campione, J. (1983). Learning, remembering and understanding. In P. Mussen (Ed.), *Handbook of child psychology, Vol. 3.* New York: Wiley.

Brown, G. & Desforges, C. (1980). *Piaget's theory: A psychological critique.* London: Routledge & Kegan Paul.

Brown, H.I. (1988). *Rationality.* London: Routledge.

Brown, T. (1980). The microgenesis of schizophrenic thought. *Archives de Psychologie, 48,* 215–37.

Brown, T. (1988). Ships in the night: Piaget and American cognitive science. *Human Development, 31,* 60–64.

Brown, T. & Weiss, L. (1987). Structures, procedures, heuristics and affectivity. *Archives de Psychologie, 55,* 59–94 Reprinted in L. Smith (1992a) *Jean Piaget: Critical assessments.* London: Routledge.

Bruner, J., Olver, R., & Greenfield, P. (1966). *Studies in cognitive growth*. New York: Wiley.

Bryant, P. (1974). *Perception and understanding in young children*. London: Methuen.

Bryant, P. (1985). Parents, children and cognitive development. In R. A. Hinde, A.N. Perret-Clermont, & J. Stevenson-Hinde (Eds.), *Social relationships and cognitive development*. Oxford: Oxford University Press.

Bryant, P. (1989). Commentary. *Human Development, 32*, 369–74.

Bryant, P. & Trabasso, T. (1971). Transitive inferences and memory in young children. *Nature, 232*, 456–58. Reprinted in L. Smith (1992a) *Jean Piaget: Critical assessments*. London: Routledge.

Bynum, T., Thomas, J., & Weitz, L. (1972). Operational thinking: Inhelder and Piaget's evidence. *Developmental Psychology, 7*, 129–32. Reprinted in L. Smith (1992a) *Jean Piaget: Critical assessments*. London: Routledge.

Byrnes, J. (1988). Formal operations: A systematic reformulation. *Developmental Review, 8*, 1–22.

Byrnes, J. & Beilin, H. (1991). The cognitive basis of uncertainty. *Human Development, 34*, 189–203.

Byrnes, J. & Duff, M. (1989). Young children's comprehension of modal expressions. *Cognitive Development, 4*, 369–87.

Callebaut, W. & Pinxten, R. (1987). *Evolutionary epistemology*. Dordrecht: Reidel.

Campbell, R. (1991). Does class inclusion have mathematical prerequisites? *Cognitive Development, 6*, 169–94.

Campbell, R. & Bickhard, M. (1986). *Knowing levels and developmental stages*. Basel: Karger.

Campbell, R. & Bickhard, M. (1987). A deconstruction of Fodor's anticonstructivism. *Human Development, 30,* 48–59. Reprinted in L. Smith (1992a) *Jean Piaget: Critical assessments*. London: Routledge.

Carey, S. (1985). *Conceptual change in childhood*. Cambridge, MA: MIT Press.

Carnap, R. (1947/1956). *Meaning and necessity*. Second Edition. Chicago: University of Chicago Press.

Carraher, D. (1991). Mathematics in and out of schools. In M. Harris (Ed.), *Schools mathematics and work*. London: Falmer.

Case. R. (1985). *Intellectual development*. London: Academic Press.

Cellérier, G. (1980). Cognitive strategies in problem solving. In M. Piattelli-Palmarini (Ed.), *Language and learning*. London: Routledge.

Cellérier, G. (1992a). Le constructivisme génétique aujourd'hui. In B. Inhelder & G. Cellérier (Eds.), *Le cheminement des découvertes de l'enfant*. Lausanne: Delachaux et Niestlé.

Cellérier, G. (1992b). Organisation et fonctionnement des schèmes. In B. Inhelder & G. Cellérier (Eds.), *Le cheminement des découvertes de l'enfant*. Lausanne: Delachaux et Niestlé.

Chalmers, M. & McGonigle, B. (1984). Are children more logical than monkeys on the five-term series problem? *Journal of Experimental Child Psychology, 37*, 355–77. Reprinted in L. Smith (1992a) *Jean Piaget: Critical assessments*. London: Routledge.

Chapman, M. (1986). The structure of exchange: Piaget's sociological theory. *Human Development, 29*, 181–94.

Chapman, M. (1987). Inner processes and outward criteria: Wittgenstein's importance to psychology. In M. Chapman & R. Dixon (Eds.), *Meaning and the growth of understanding: Wittgenstein's significance for developmental psychology.* Berlin: Springer-Verlag.

Chapman, M. (1988). *Constructive evolution.* Cambridge: Cambridge University Press.

Chapman, M. (1991). The epistemic triangle: Operative and communicative components of cognitive competence. In M. Chandler & M. Chapman (Eds.), *Criteria for competence.* Hillsdale, NJ: Lawrence Erlbaum Associates Inc.

Chapman, M. & Lindenberger, U. (1988). Functions, operations and *décalage* in the development of transitivity. *Developmental Psychology, 24,* 542–51. Reprinted in L. Smith (1992a) *Jean Piaget: Critical assessments.* London: Routledge.

Cherniak, C. (1986). *Minimal rationality.* Cambridge, MA: MIT Press.

Chisholm, R. (1977). *Theory of knowledge.* Second edition. Engelwood Cliffs, NJ: Prentice Hall.

Chisholm, R. (1982). *The foundations of knowledge.* Brighton, UK: Harvester.

Chomsky, N. (1980). On cognitive structures and their development: A reply to Piaget. In M. Piattelli-Palmarini (Ed.), *Language and learning.* London: Routledge & Kegan Paul.

Cohen, L.J. (1986). *The dialogue of reason.* Oxford: Oxford University Press.

Cole, M. & Bruner, J. (1971). Cultural differences and inferences about psychological processes. *American Psychologist, 26,* 867–76. Reprinted in L. Smith (1992a) *Jean Piaget: Critical assessments.* London: Routledge.

Cormier, P. & Dagenais, Y. (1983). Class inclusion developmental levels and logical necessity. *International Journal of Behavioural Development, 6,* 1–14. Reprinted in L. Smith (1992a) *Jean Piaget: Critical assessments.* London: Routledge.

Couturat, L. (1914). *L'algèbre de la logique.* Reprinted 1965. Hildesheim: Georg Olms

Cummins, J. (1978). Language and children's ability to evaluate contradictions and tautologies: A critique of Osherson and Markman's findings. *Child Development, 49,* 895–97

Davidson, D. (1981). *Actions and events.* Oxford: Oxford University Press.

Davidson, P. M. (1988). Piaget's category-theoretic interpretation of cognitive development: A neglected contribution. *Human Development, 31,* 225–44. Reprinted in L. Smith (1992a) *Jean Piaget: Critical assessments.* London: Routledge.

Demetriou, A. & Efklides, A. (1979). Formal operations in young adults as a function of education and sex. *International Journal of Psychology, 14,* 241–53.

Demetriou, A. & Efklides, A. (1988). *The neo-Piagetian theories of cognitive development.* Amsterdam: North Holland Press.

de Ribaupierre, A. (1989). On the use of longitudinal research in developmental psychology. In A. de Ribaupierre (Ed.), *Transition mechanisms in child development.* Cambridge: Cambridge University Press.

Descartes, R. (1637/1931). Discourse on method. In *Philosophical works. Vol.1.* New York: Dover.

Dionnet, S. (1987). *Aspects développementaux des Processus de Reconnaissance dans une tache d'identification de forme.* Thèse Doctorale, Université de Genève.

Doise, W. (1989). Constructivism in social psychology. *European Journal of Social Psychology, 19,* 389–400.

Doise, W. & Hanselmann, C. (1991). Conflict and social marking in the acquisition of operational thinking. *Learning and Instruction, 1,* 119–27.

Doise, W. & Mugny, G. (1981/1984). *Le développment social de l'intelligence.* Paris: Intereditions/*The social development of the intellect.* Oxford: Pergamon Press.

Donaldson, M. (1978). *Children's minds.* London: Fontana.

Donaldson, M. (1983). Justifying conservation: Comments on Neilson et al. *Cognition, 15,* 293–95.

Donaldson, M., Grieve, R., & Pratt, C. (1983). Introduction. *Early childhood development and education.* Oxford: Blackwell.

Droz, R. (1972). Psychologie de la recherche et recherche en psychologie. *Revue Européenne des Sciences Sociales et Cahiers Vilfedo Pareto, 10,* 25–41.

Droz, R., Berthoud, S., Calpini, J-C., Dallenbach, J-F., & Michiels, M-P. (1976). Méthode expérimentale—méthode clinique. *Revue Européenne des Sciences Sociales et Cahiers Vilfredo Pareto, 14,* 305–24.

Droz, R. & Volken, H. (1991). L'équilibration Piagétienne: portée heuristique et devenir d'un concept utopique. *Revue Européenne des Sciences Sociales, 89,* 55–73.

Eames, D., Shorrocks, D., & Tomlinson, P. (1990). Naughty animals or naughty experimenters? Conservation accidents re-visited with video-stimulated commentary. *British Journal of Developmental Psychology, 8,* 25–37. Reprinted in L. Smith (1992a) *Jean Piaget: Critical assessments.* London: Routledge.

Edwards, D. & Mercer, N. (1987). *Common knowledge.* London: Methuen.

Elkind, D. (1961). The development of quantitative thinking: A systematic replication of Piaget's studies. *The Journal of Genetic Psychology, 98,* 37–46. Reprinted in L. Smith (1992a) *Jean Piaget: Critical assessments.* London: Routledge.

Elkind, D. (1967). Piaget's conservation problems. *Child Development, 38,* 15–27.

Ennis, R.H. (1976). Children's ability to handle Piaget's propositional logic: A conceptual critique. *Review of Educational Research, 45,* 1–41. Reprinted in L. Smith (1992a) *Jean Piaget: Critical assessments.* London: Routledge.

Fabricius, W., Sophian, C. & Wellman, H. (1987). Young children's sensitivity to logical necessity in their inferential search behaviour. *Child Development, 58,* 409423.

Falmagne, R., Mawby, R., & Pea, R. (1989). Linguistic and logical factors in recognition of indeterminacy. *Cognitive Development, 4,* 141–76.

Feuerstein, R. (1980). *Instrumental enrichment.* Baltimore: University Parks Press.

Figurelli, J. & Keller, H. (1972). The effects of training and socio-economic class upon the acquisition of conservation concepts. *Child Development, 43,* 293–332.

Fischer, K.W. (1980). A theory of cognitive development: The control and construction of hierarchies of skills. *Psychological Review, 87,* 477–31.

Flavell, J. (1982). On cognitive development. *Child Development, 53,* 1–10. Reprinted in L. Smith (1992a) *Jean Piaget: Critical assessments.* London: Routledge.

Flavell, J. & Wohlwill, J. (1969). Formal and functional aspects of cognitive development. In D. Elkind & J. Flavell (Eds.), *Studies in cognitive development.* Oxford: Oxford University Press.

Fodor, J. (1976). *The language of thought.* Brighton, UK: Harvester Press.

Fodor, J. (1980). Fixation of belief and concept acquisition. In M. Piattelli-Palmarini (Ed.), *Language and learning.* London: Routledge & Kegan Paul.

Fondation Archives Jean Piaget. (1989). *Bibliographie Jean Piaget.* Geneva: Fondation Archives Jean Piaget, Université de Geneva.

Frege, G. (1888/1980). *The foundations of arithmetic.* Oxford: Oxford University Press.

Frege, G. (1980). On sense and reference. In P. Geach & M. Black (Eds.), *Translations from the philosophical writings of Gottlob Frege.* 3rd Edition. Oxford: Blackwell.

Gallagher, J. & Reid, D. (1981). *The learning theory of Piaget and Inhelder.* Monterey, CA: Brooks/Cole.

Gellatly, A. (1989). The myth of cognitive diagnosis. In A. Gellatly, D. Rogers, J. Sloboda (Eds.), *Cognition and social worlds.* Oxford: Oxford University Press.

Gelman, R. (1972). Logical capacity of very young children: Number invariance rules. *Child Development, 43,* 371–83. Reprinted in L. Smith (1992a) *Jean Piaget: Critical assessments.* London: Routledge.

Gelman, R. (1978). Cognitive development. *Annual Review of Psychology, 29,* 297–332.

Gelman, R. & Baillargeon, R. (1983). A review of some Piagetian concepts. In P. Mussen (Ed.), *Handbook of child psychology. Vol. 3.* New York: Wiley.

Gelman, R. & Gallistel, R. (1978). *The child's understanding of number.* Cambridge, MA: Harvard University Press.

Gelman, S.A. & Markman, E.M. (1987). Young children's inductions from natural kinds: The role of categories and appearances. *Child Development, 58,* 1532–41.

Gelman, S.A. & O'Reilly, A.W. (1988). Children's inductive inferences within superordinate categories: The role of language and category structure. *Child Development, 59,* 876–877.

Gelman, S.A. & Wellman, H. (1991). Insides and essences: Early understanding of the non-obvious. *Cognition, 38,* 213–44.

Gettier, E. (1963). Is justified true belief knowledge? *Analysis, 23,* 121–23.

Gillièron, C. (1980). Réflexions sur le problème des décalages: A propos de l'article de Montangero. *Archives de Psychologie, 48,* 283–32.

Gillièron, C. (1984). Réflexions préliminaires à une étude de la négation. *Archives de Psychologie, 52,* 231–53.

Gillièron, C. (1987). Is Piaget's 'Genetic Epistemology' evolutionary? In W. Callebaut & R. Pinxten (Eds.), *Evolutionary Epistemology.* Dordrecht: Reidel.

Gillièron, C. & Leiser, D. (1991). Les quatres piliers d'une (bonne) procédure, ou: Les petits-enfants de la structure. In J. Montangero & A. Tryphon (Eds.), *Psychologie génétique et sciences cognitives.* Genève: Fondation Archives Jean Piaget.

Glaser, R. (1988). Cognitive science and education. *International Social Science Journal, 115,* 21–44.

Goldman, A. (1978). Epistemics: The regulative theory of cognition. *Journal of Philosophy, 75*, 509–523.

Goldman, A. (1979). What is justified belief? In G. Pappas (Ed.), *Justification and knowledge*. Dordrecht: Reidel.

Gould, S.J. (1989). *Wonderful life*. London: Hutchinson Radius.

Gray, W.M. (1978). A comparison of Piaget's theory and criterion referenced measurement. *Review of Educational Research, 48*, 223–49.

Gray, W.M. (1990). Formal operational thought. In W. Overton (Ed.), *Reasoning necessity and logic*. Hillsdale, NJ: Lawrence Erlbaum Associates Inc.

Grayling, A.C. (1982). *An introduction to philosophical logic*. Brighton, UK: Harvester Press.

Gréco, P. (1959). Apprentissage et connaissance opératoire. In P. Gréco & J. Piaget. *Apprentissage et connaissance*. Paris: Presses Universitaires de France.

Grize, J-B. (1962). Note sur l''étude génétique de l'implication" de B. Matalon. In E. Beth, J-B Grize, R. Martin, B. Matalon, A. Naess, & J. Piaget. (Eds.), *Implication, formalisation et logique naturelle*. Paris: Presses Universitaires de France.

Grize, J-B. (1987). Operatory logic. In B. Inhelder, D. de Caprona, A. Cornu-Wells (Eds.), *Piaget today*. Hove, UK: Lawrence Erlbaum Associates Ltd.

Gruber, H. & Barrett, P. (1974). *Darwin on man*. London: Wildwood House Ltd.

Gruber, H. & Vonèche, J-J. (1977). *The essential Piaget*. London: Routledge & Kegan Paul.

Guttenplan, S. (1986). *The languages of logic*. Oxford: Blackwell.

Haack, S. (1978). *Philosophy of logics*. Cambridge: Cambridge University Press.

Haack, S. (1990). Recent obituaries of epistemology. *American Philosophical Quarterly, 27*, 199212.

Hale, B. (1987). *Abstract objects*. Oxford: Blackwell.

Halford, G. (1982). *The development of thought*. Hillsdale, NJ: Lawrence Erlbaum Associates Inc.

Halford, G. (1989). Reflections on 25 years of Piagetian cognitive-developmental psychology, 1963–1988. *Human Development, 32*, 325–57.

Hall, V. & Kaye, D. (1978). The necessity of logical necessity in Piaget's theory. In L. Siegel & C. Brainerd (Eds.), *Alternatives to Piaget*. London: Academic Press.

Hamlyn, D.W. (1978). *Experience and the growth of understanding*. London: Routledge & Kegan Paul.

Hamlyn, D.W. (1982). What exactly is social about the origin of understanding? In P. Light & G. Butterworth (Eds.), *Social cognition*. Brighton, UK: Harvester Press.

Hardy, G. H. (1959). *Ramanujan*. New York: Chelsea Publishing Company.

Harré, R. (1986a). Social sources of mental content and order. In J. Margolis, P. Mancias, R. Harré, P. Secord (Eds.), *Psychology: Designing the discipline*. Oxford: Blackwell.

Harré, R. (1986b). The step to social constructionism. In M. Richards & P. Light (Eds.), *Children of social worlds*. Cambridge: Polity Press.

Harré, R. (1987). Enlarging the paradigm. *New Ideas in Psychology, 5*, 3–12.

Harris, P. (1983). Infant cognition. In P. Mussen (Ed.), *Handbook of child psychology. Vol 2*. New York: Wiley

Hart, K. (1981). *Children's understanding mathematics: 11–16*. London: Murray.

Hawking, S. (1988). *A brief history of time*. London: Bantam Press.

Henriques, G. (1977). La nécessité dans le développement cognitif: Préalable ou achèvement? *Archives de Psychologie, 45,* 253–65.

Hintikka, J. (1962). *Knowledge and belief*. Ithaca, NY: Cornell University Press.

Hintikka, J. & Hintikka, M. (1989). *The logic of epistemology and the epistemology of logic*. Dordrecht: Kluwer.

Hudson, W.D. (1983). *Modern moral philosophy*. (2nd ed.). London: Macmillan.

Hughes, G. & Cresswell, M. (1972). *An introduction to modal logic*. Second edition. London: Methuen.

Hughes, M. (1986). *Children and number*. Oxford: Blackwell.

Hume, D. (1739/1965). *A treatise of human nature*. Oxford: Oxford University Press.

Hume, D. (1777/1966). *Enquiries concerning the human understanding*. Oxford: Oxford University Press.

Hunt, E. (1989). Cognitive science: Definition, status, and questions. *Annual review of psychology, 40,* 603–30.

Hunt, J.McV. (1969). The impact and limitations of the giant of developmental psychology. In D. Elkind & J. Flavell (Eds.), *Studies in cognitive development*. New York: Oxford University Press.

Inhelder, B. (1936). Observations sur le principe de conservation dans la physique de l'enfant. *Cahiers de pédagogie expérimentale et de psychologie de l'enfant. 9,* 1–16.

Inhelder, B. (1956). Criteria of the stages of mental development. In J. Tanner & B. Inhelder (Eds.), *Discussions on child development ,Vol. 1*. London: Tavistock.

Inhelder, B. (1978). *De l'approche structurale à l'approche procédurale: Introduction à l'étude des stratégies*. Acta XXI Congrès Internationale de Psychologie, Paris.

Inhelder, B. (1982). Outlook. In S. Modgil & C. Modgil (Eds.), *Jean Piaget: Consensus and controversy*. London: Holt, Rinehart & Winston.

Inhelder, B. (1989). Bärbel Inhelder. In G. Lindzey (Ed.), *A history of psychology in autobiography. Vol. VIII*. Stanford, CA: Stanford University Press.

Inhelder, B., Blanchet, A., Sinclair, A., & Piaget, J. (1975). Relations entre les conservations d'ensemble d'éléments discrets et celles de quantités continues. *Année Psychologique, 75,* 23–60.

Inhelder, B. & de Caprona, D. (1985). Introduction. Constructivisme et création des nouveautés. *Archives de Psychologie, 53,* 7–17.

Inhelder, B. & de Caprona, D. (1992a). Vers le constructivisme psychologique. Structures? Procédures? Les deux indissociables. In B. Inhelder & G. Cellérier (Eds.), *Le cheminement des découvertes de l'enfant*. Lausanne: Delachaux et Niestlé.

Inhelder,B. & de Caprona, D. (1992b). Un parcours de recherche. In B. Inhelder & G. Cellérier (Eds.), *Le cheminement des découvertes de l'enfant*. Lausanne: Delachaux et Niestlé.

Inhelder, B. & Piaget, J. (1955/1958). *De la logique de l'enfant à la logique de l'adolescent*. Paris: Presses Universitaires de France/*Growth of logical thinking*. London: Routledge & Kegan Paul.

Inhelder, B. & Piaget, J. (1959/1964). *La Genèse des structures logiques élémentaires*. Neuchatel: Delachaux et Niestlé/*Early growth of logic in the child*. London: Routledge & Kegan Paul.

Inhelder, B. & Piaget, J. (1979/1980). Procédures et structures. *Archives de psychologie, 47,* 165–76/ Procedures and structures. In D. Olson (Ed.), *The social foundations of language.* New York: Norton.

Inhelder, B. & Sinclair, H. (1969). Learning cognitive structures. In P. Mussen, J. Langer, & M. Covington (Eds.), *Trends and issues in developmental psychology.* New York: Holt, Rinehart & Winston.

Inhelder, B., Sinclair, H., & Bovet, M. (1974). *Learning and the development of cognition.* London: Routledge & Kegan Paul.

Isaacs, N. (1951). Critical notice: *Traité de logique. British Journal of Psychology, 42,* 185–88. Reprinted in L. Smith (1992a) *Jean Piaget: Critical assessments.* London: Routledge.

Iseminger, G. (1980). Is relevance necessary for validity? *Mind, 89,* 196–213.

Johnson-Laird, P.N. (1978). The meaning of modality. *Cognitive Science, 2,* 17–26.

Johnson-Laird, P.N. (1980). Mental models in cognitive science. *Cognitive Science, 4,* 71–115.

Johnson-Laird, P.N. (1983). *Mental Models.* Cambridge: Cambridge University Press.

Johnson-Laird, P.N. (1990). The development of reasoning ability. G. Butterworth & P. Bryant (Eds.), *Causes of development.* New York: Harvester Wheatsheaf.

Johnson-Laird, P.N. & Bara, B.G. (1984). Syllogistic inference. *Cognition, 16,* 1–61.

Johnson-Laird, P.N., Byrne, R. (1990). *Deduction.* Hove, UK: Lawrence Erlbaum Associates Ltd.

Johnson-Laird, P.N., Byrne, R., & Tabossi, P. (1989). Reasoning by model: The case of multiple quantification. *Psychological Review, 96,* 658–73.

Johnson-Laird, P.N. & Wason, P.C. (1977). *Thinking: Readings in cognitive science.* Cambridge: Cambridge University Press.

Juckes, T.J. (1991). Equilibration and the learning paradox. *Human Development, 34,* 261–72.

Kant, I. (1783/1953). *Prolegomena to any future metaphysics.* Manchester: Manchester University Press.

Kant, I. (1787/1933). *Critique of pure reason.* Second edition. London: Macmillan.

Kant, I. (1800/1963). *Introduction to logic.* Westport, Conn: Greenwood Press.

Karmiloff-Smith, A. (1978). Open Peer Commentary. *The Behavioural and Brain Sciences, 2,* 188–90.

Karmiloff-Smith, A. (1990). Un cas particulier de symmétrie inférentielle. In J. Piaget, G. Henriques & E. Ascher (Eds.), *Morphismes et Catégories.* Lausanne: Delachaux et Niestlé.

Karmiloff-Smith, A. (1991). Beyond modularity: Innate constraints and developmental change. In S. Carey & R. Gelman (Eds.), *The epigenesis of mind: Essays on biology and cognition.* Hillsdale, NJ: Lawrence Erlbaum Associates Inc.

Karmiloff-Smith, A. & Inhelder, B. (1975). If you want to get ahead, get a theory. *Cognition, 3,* 195–212. Reprinted in L. Smith (1992a) *Jean Piaget: Critical assessments.* London: Routledge.

Karplus, R. (1981). Education and formal thought: A modest proposal. In I. Sigel, D. Brodzinsky, & R. Golinkoff (Eds.), *New directions in Piagetian theory and practice.* Hillsdale, NJ: Lawrence Erlbaum Associates Inc. Reprinted in L. Smith (1992a) *Jean Piaget: Critical assessments.* London: Routledge.

Keating, W.P. (1990). Structuralism, deconstruction, reconstruction: The limits of reasoning. In W. Overton (Ed.), *Reasoning necessity and logic*. Hillsdale, NJ: Lawrence Erlbaum Associates Inc.

Kingma, J. & Koops, W. (1983). Piagetian tasks, traditional intelligence and achievement tests. *British Journal of Educational Psychology, 53*, 278–90.

Kirkham, R. (1984). Does the Gettier problem rest on a mistake? *Mind, 93*, 501–513.

Kitchener, R. (1981). Piaget's social psychology. *Journal for the Theory of Social Behaviour, 11*, 253–77.

Kitchener, R. (1986). *Piaget's theory of knowledge*. New Haven: Yale University Press.

Kitchener, R. (1987). Is genetic epistemology possible? *British Journal for the Philosophy of Science, 38*, 283–299.

Kohlberg, L. (1968). Moral development. In D. Sills (Ed.), *International encyclopedia of the social sciences, Vol.10*. New York: Macmillan Company. Reprinted in L. Smith (1992a) *Jean Piaget: Critical assessments*. London: Routledge.

Kohlberg, L. (1987). *Child psychology and childhood education*. London: Longman.

Kohnstamm, G.A. (1963). An evaluation of part of Piaget's theory. *Acta Psychologica, 21*, 313–56.

Kornblith, H. (1985) *Naturalizing epistemology*. Cambridge, MA: MIT Press.

Kripke, S. (1963). Sematical considerations on modal logic. *Acta Philosophica Fennica, 16*, 83–94.

Kripke, S. (1980). *Naming and necessity*. Oxford: Blackwell.

Kuhn, D. (1974). Inducing development experimentally: Comments on a research paradigm. *Developmental Psychology, 10*, 590–600.

Kuhn, D. (1979). The application of Piaget's theory of cognitive development to education. *Harvard Educational Review, 49*, 340-60.

Kuhn, D., Langer, J., & Haan, N. (1977). The development of formal operations in logical and moral judgment. *Genetic Psychology Monographs, 95*, 97–188.

Kuhn, T.S. (1970). *The structure of scientific revolutions*. Second edition. Chicago: University of Chicago Press.

Kuhn, T.S. (1977). *The essential tension*. Chicago: University of Chicago Press.

Lakatos, I. (1974). Falsification and the logic of scientific research programmes. In I. Lakatos & A. Musgrave (Eds.), *Criticism and the growth of the knowledge*. Corrected edition. Cambridge: Cambridge University Press.

Laudan, L. (1977). *Progess and its problems*. Berkeley, CA: University of California Press.

Laudan, L. (1984). *Science and values*. Berkeley, CA: University of California Press.

Lawson, A.E., Karplus, R., & Adi, H. (1978). The acquisition of propositional logic and formal operational schemata. *Journal of Research in Science Teaching, 15*, 465–78. Reprinted in L. Smith (1992a) *Jean Piaget: Critical assessments*. London: Routledge.

Lawson, A.E. (1987). The four-card problem resolved? Formal operational reasoning and reasoning to a contradiction. *Journal of Research in Science Teaching, 24*, 611–27.

Lawson, A.E. (1989). Research on advanced reasoning, concept acquisition, and a theory of science instruction. In P. Adey (Ed.), *Adolescent development and school science*. London: Falmer.

Lawson, A.E. & Staver, J.R. (1989). Toward a solution of the learning paradox: Emergent properties and neurological principles of constructivism. *Instructional Science, 18,* 169–77.

Leibniz, G.W. (1686/1973). Necessary and contingent truths. In G. Parkinson (Ed.), *Leibniz: Philosophical writings*. London: Dent.

Leibniz, G.W. (1765/1981). *New essays on human understanding*. Cambridge: Cambridge University Press.

Leiser, D. & Gillièron, C. (1990). *Cognitive science and genetic epistemology*. New York: Plenum Press

Lemmon, E.J. (1966). *Beginning logic*. London: Nelson.

Lewis, C.I. & Langford, C. (1932/1959). *Symbolic logic*. Second Edition. New York: Dover Publications.

Lewis, D.K. (1986). *On the plurality of possible worlds*. Oxford: Blackwell.

Light, P. (1986). Context, conservation and conversation. In M. Richards & P. Light (Eds.), *Children of social worlds*. Cambridge: Polity Press.

Light, P. , Buckingham, N., & Robbins, H. (1979). The conservation task as an interactional setting. *British Journal of Educational Psychology, 49,* 304–10.

Light, P. & Perret-Clermont, A-N. (1989). Social context effects in learning and testing. In A. Gellatly, D. Rogers, & J. Sloboda (Eds.), *Cognition and social worlds*. Oxford: Oxford University Press.

Linksy, L. (1971). *Semantics and the philosophy of language*. Oxford: Oxford University Press.

Lipschutz, S. (1964). *Set theory and related topics*. New York: McGraw Hill.

Loux, M. (1979). *The possible and the actual: Readings in the metaphysics of modality*. Ithaca, NY: Cornell University Press.

Lovell, K., Mitchell, B., & Everett, I. (1962). An experimental study of the growth of some logical structures. *British Journal of Psychology, 53,* 175–88. Reprinted in L. Smith (1992a) *Jean Piaget: Critical assessments*. London: Routledge.

Lysnychuk, L., Pressley, M., & Vye, N. (1990). Reciprocal teaching improves standardized reading–comprehension performance in poor comprehenders. *The Elementary School Journal, 90,* 469–84.

Maffie, J. (1990). Recent work on naturalized epistemology. *American Philosophical Quarterly, 27,* 281293.

Markman, E.M. (1978). Empirical versus logical solutions to part–whole comparison problems concerning classes and collections. *Child Development, 49,* 168–177.

Markman, E.M. (1989). *Categorization and naming in children: Problems of induction*. Cambridge, MA: MIT Press.

Markovits, H. (1984). Awareness of the 'possible' as a mediator of formal thinking in conditional reasoning problems. *British Journal of Psychology, 75,* 367–76.

Markovits, H. (1991). Personal communication.

Markovits, H. (1993). The development of conditional reasoning: A Piagetian reformulation of mental models theory. *Merrill-Palmer Quarterly, 39,* 131–58.

Markovits, H. & Vachon, R. (1990). Conditional reasoning, representation, and level of abstraction. *Developmental Psychology, 26,* 942–51.

Matalon, B. (1962/1990). A genetic study of implication. In W. Overton (Ed.), *Reasoning, necessity and logic: Developmental perspectives.* Hillsdale, NJ: Lawrence Erlbaum Associates Inc.

Mays, W. (1982). Piaget's sociological theory. In S. Modgil & C. Modgil (Eds.),. *Jean Piaget: Consensus and controversy.* London: Holt, Rinehart & Winston. Reprinted in L. Smith (1992a) *Jean Piaget: Critical assessments.* London: Routledge.

Mays, W. (1992) Piaget's logic. *Archives de Psychologie, 60,* 45–70.

McCloskey, M. (1983). Naive theories of motion. In D. Gentner & A. Stevens (Eds.), Mental models. Hillsdale, NJ: Lawrence Erlbaum Associates Inc.

McGarrigle, J. & Donaldson, M. (1974). Conservation accidents. *Cognition, 3,* 341–50. Reprinted in L. Smith (1992a) *Jean Piaget: Critical assessments.* London: Routledge.

McGinn, C. (1991). *The problem of consciousness: Essays towards a resolution.* Oxford: Blackwell.

Miller, S. (1978). Identity conservation and equivalence conservation: A critique of Brainerd and Hooper. *Psychological Bulletin, 85,* 58–69.

Miller, S. (1986). Certainty and necessity in the understanding of Piagetian concepts. *Developmental Psychology, 22,* 3–18. Reprinted in L. Smith (1992a) *Jean Piaget: Critical assessments.* London: Routledge.

Miller, S., Brownell, C., & Zukier, H. (1977). Cognitive certainty in children: Effects of concept, developmental level, and method of assessment. *Developmental Psychology, 13,* 236–45.

Moessinger, P. (1978). Piaget on equilibration. *Human Development, 21,* 255–67. Reprinted in L. Smith (1992a) *Jean Piaget: Critical assessments.* London: Routledge.

Montangero, J. (1980). The various aspects of horizontal décalage. *Archives de Psychologie, 48,* 259–82. Reprinted in L. Smith (1992a) *Jean Piaget: Critical assessments.* London: Routledge.

Montangero, J. (1991). A constructivist framework for understanding early and late-developing psychological competence. In M. Chandler & M. Chapman (Eds.), *Criteria for competence,* Hillsdale, NJ: Lawrence Erlbaum Associates Inc.

Morf, A. (1957). Les relations entre la logique et le langage lors du passage du raisonment concrèt au raisonment formel. In L. Apostel, B. Mandelbrot, & A. Morf. *Logique, langage, et théorie de l'information.* Paris: Presses Universitaires de France.

Moshman, D. (1990). The development of metalogical understanding. In W. Overton (Ed.), *Reasoning, necessity and logic.* Hillsdale, NJ: Lawrence Erlbaum Associates Inc.

Moshman, D. & Timmons, M. (1982). The construction of logical necessity. *Human Development, 25,* 309–23.

Murray, F. (1972). Acquisition of conservation through social interaction. *Developmental Psychology, 6,* 1–6.

Murray, F. (1978). Teaching strategies and conservation training. In A. Lesgold, J. Pellegrino, S. Fokkema, & R. Glaser (Eds.), *Cognitive psychology and instruction.* New York: Plenum Press. Reprinted in L. Smith (1992a) *Jean Piaget: Critical assessments.* London: Routledge.

Murray, F. (1981). The conservation paradigm: The conservation of conservation research. In I. Sigel, D. Brodzinsky, & R. Golinkoff (Eds.), *New directions in Piagetian theory and practice.* Hillsdale, NJ: Lawrence Erlbaum Associates Inc.

Murray, F. (1990). The conversion of truth into necessity. In W. Overton (Ed.), *Reasoning, necessity and logic.* Hillsdale, NJ: Lawrence Erlbaum Associates Inc.

Nagel, E. (1961). *The structure of science.* New York: Routledge & Kegan Paul.

Neimark, E. (1975). Intellectual development during adolescence. In F. Horowitz (Ed.), *Review of child development research. Vol. 4.* Chicago: University of Chicago Press.

Neimark, E. (1985). Moderators of competence. In E. Neimark, R. DeLisi, & J. Newman (Eds.), *Moderators of competence.* Hillsdale, NJ; Lawrence Erlbaum Associates Inc.

Nesselroade, J. & Baltes, P. (1979). *Longitudinal research in the study of behavioural development.* London: Academic Press.

Newman, D., Griffin, P., & Cole, M. (1989). *The construction zone: Working for cognitive change in school.* Cambridge: Cambridge University Press.

Nitko, A. (1983). *Educational tests and measurement.* New York: Harcourt.

Noelting, G. (1980). The development of proportional reasoning and the ratio concept. Part I—differentiation of stages. *Educational Studies in Mathematics, 11,* 217–53. Reprinted in L. Smith (1992a) *Jean Piaget: Critical assessments.* London: Routledge.

Osherson, D. (1974). *Logical abilities in children. Vol. 1.* Hillsdale, NJ:: Lawrence Erlbaum Associates Inc.

Osherson, D. (1975). *Logical abilities in children. Vol. III.* Hillsdale, NJ: Lawrence Erlbaum Associates Inc.

Osherson, D. & Markman, E.M. (1975). Language and the ability to evaluate contradictions and tautologies. *Cognition, 3,* 213–26.

Overton, W. (1990). Competence and procedures: Constraints on the development of logical reasoning. In W. Overton (Ed.), *Reasoning, necessity and logic.* Hillsdale, NJ: Lawrence Erlbaum Associates Inc.

Overton, W. (1991). Competence procedures and hardware: Conceptual and empirical considerations. In M. Chandler & M. Chapman (Eds.), *Criteria for competence.* Hillsdale, NJ: Lawrence Erlbaum Associates Inc.

Overton, W., Ward, S., Noveck, I., Black, J., & O'Brien, D. (1987). Form and content in the development of deductive reasoning. *Developmental Psychology, 23,* 22–30. Reprinted in L. Smith (1992a) *Jean Piaget: Critical assessments.* London: Routledge.

Palincsar, A. & Brown, A. (1984). Reciprocal teaching of comprehension-fostering and comprehension-monitoring. *Cognition and Instruction, 1,* 117–75.

Papert, S. (1963). Sur la logique Piagétienne. In L. Apostel, J-B. Grize, S. Papert, & J. Piaget. *La filiation des structures.* Paris: Presses Universitaires de France.

Parrat-Dayan, S. & Bovet, M. (1982). Peut-on parler de précocité et de regression dans la conservation? II. *Archives de Psychologie, 50,* 237–249.

Parsons, C. (1960). Inhelder and Piaget's "The growth of logical thinking". *British Journal of Psychology, 51,* 75–84.

Pascual-Leone, J. (1987). Organismic processes for neo-Piagetian theories: A dialectical causal account of cognitive development. *International Journal of Psychology, 22,* 531–70, Reprinted in L. Smith (1992a) *Jean Piaget: Critical assessments.* London: Routledge.

Pascual-Leone, J. & Bovet, M. (1967). L'apprentissage de la quantification de l'inclusion et la théorie opératoire. *Acta Psychologica, 25,* 334–56.

Pears, R. & Bryant, P. (1990). Transitive inferences about spatial position by young children. *British Journal of Psychology, 81,* 497–510. Reprinted in L. Smith (1992a) *Jean Piaget: Critical assessments.* London: Routledge.

Perret-Clermont,   A-N. (1979/1980). *Social   interaction   and   cognitive development in children.* London: Academic Press.

Perret-Clermont, A-N. (1979/1988a). Introduction pour l'édition en langue russe. *La construction de l'intelligence dans l'interaction sociale.* Berne: Peter Lang.

Perret-Clermont, A-N. (1979/1988b). Postface pour l'édition en langue russe. *La construction de l'intelligence dans l'interaction sociale.* Berne: Peter Lang.

Piaget, J. (1918). *Recherche.* Lausanne: La Concorde.

Piaget, J. (1920). La psychoanalyse dans ses rapports avec la psychologie de l'enfant. *Bulletin Mensuel, Société Alfred Binet, 20,* 18–34, 41–58.

Piaget, J. (1921a). Essai sur quelques aspects du développement de la notion de partie chez l'enfant. *Journal de Psychologie Normale et Pathélogique, 18,* 449–80.

Piaget, J. (1921b). Une forme verbale de la comparaison chez l'enfant. *Archives de Psychologie, 18,* 141–72.

Piaget, J. (1922). Essai sur la multiplication logique et les débuts de la pensée formelle chez l'enfant. *Journal de Psychologie Normale et Pathélogique, 19,* 222–61.

Piaget, J. (1923). La psychologie et les valeurs religieuses. In Association Chrétienne d'Etudiants de la Suisee Romande (Ed.), *Sainte-Croix 1922,* pp.38–82.

Piaget, J. (1923/1959). *Le langage et la pensée chex l'enfant.* Neuchatel: Delachaux et Niestlé/ *Language and thought of the child.* (3rd ed.). London: Routledge & Kegan Paul.

Piaget, J. (1924/1928). *Le Jugement et le raisonnement chez l'enfant.* Neuchatel: Delachaux et Niestlé/*Judgment and reasoning in the child.* London: Routledge & Kegan Paul.

Piaget, J. (1924/1947). Avant-Propos de la Troisième Edition. *Le Jugement et le raisonnement chez l'enfant.* Neuchatel: Delachaux et Niestlé.

Piaget, J. (1925). Psychologie et critique de la connaissance. *Archives de Psychologie, 19,* 193–210.

Piaget, J. (1926/1929). *La représentation du monde chez l'enfant.* Paris: Alcan/*The child's conception of the world.* London: Routledge & Kegan Paul.

Piaget, J. (1928). Les trois systèmes de la pensée de l'enfant. *Bulletin de la Société Française de Philosophie, 28,* 97–141.

Piaget, J. (1931). Le développement intellectuel chez les jeunes enfants. *Mind, 40,* 137–60.

Piaget, J. (1932/1932). *Le jugement moral chez l'enfant.* Paris: Presses Universitaires de France/*The moral judgment of the child.* London: Routledge & Kegan Paul.

Piaget, J. (1936). La genèse des principes de conservation dans la physique de l'enfant. *Annuaire de l'Instruction Publique en Suisse, 27,* 31–44.

Piaget, J. (1936/1953). *La naissance de l'intelligence chez l'enfant.* Neuchatel: Delachaux et Niestlé/*The origins of intelligence in the child.* London: Routledge & Kegan Paul.

Piaget, J. (1937/1954). *La construction du réel chez l'enfant.* Neuchatel: Delachaux et Niestlé/*The construction of reality in the child.* New York: Basic Books.

Piaget, J. (1939). Les groupes de la logistique et la réversibilité de la pensée. *Revue de Théologie et de Philosophie, 27,* 291–92.

Piaget, J. (1941). Le mécanisme du développement mental et les lois du groupement des opérations: Esquisse d'une théorie opératoire de l'intelligence. *Archives de Psychologie, 28,* 215–85.

Piaget, J. (1947/1950). *La psychologie de l'intelligence.* Paris: Colin/*The psychology of intelligence.* London: Routledge & Kegan Paul.

Piaget, J. (1949). *Traité de logique.* Paris: Colin.

Piaget, J. (1950). *Introduction à l'épistémologie génétique. Vol. 1. La pensée mathématique.* Paris: Presses Universitaires de France.

Piaget, J. (1950/1973). Préface de la seconde édition. *Introduction à l'épistémologie génétique. Vol. 1. La pensée mathématique.* Paris: Presses Universitaires de France.

Piaget, J. (1951a). L'utilité de la logistique en psychologie. *L'Année Psychologique, 50,* 27–38.

Piaget, J. (1951b). La réversibilité de la pensée et les opérations logiques. *Bulletin de la Société Française de Philosophie, 44,* 137–64.

Piaget, J. (1952/1976). Autobiography. In E. Boring (Ed.), *A history of psychology in autobiography. Vol. 4.* Worcester, MA: Clark University Press/Autobiographie. (Extended to 1976). *Cahiers Vilfredo Pareto: Revue Européenne d'Histoire des Sciences Sociales, 14,* 1–43.

Piaget, J. (1953). *Logic and psychology.* Manchester: Manchester University Press.

Piaget, J. (1954). The problem of consciousness in child psychology: Developmental changes in awareness. In H. Abramson (Ed.), *Problems of consciousness.* New York: J. Macy.

Piaget, J. (1954b). La période des opérations formelles et le passage de la logique de l'enfant à celle de l'adolescent. *Bulletin de Psychologie, 7,* 247–53.

Piaget, J. (1957a). Epistémologie génétique, programme et méthodes. In W. Beth, W. Mays, & J. Piaget. *Epistémologie génétique et recherche psychologique.* Paris: Presses Universitaires de France.

Piaget, J. (1957b). Logique et équilibre dans les comportements du sujet. In L. Apostel, B. Mandelbrot, & J. Piaget. *Logique et équilibre.* Paris: Presses Universitaires de France.

Piaget, J. (1959). Apprentissage et connaissance. Première partie. In P. Gréco & J. Piaget (Eds.), *Apprentissage et connaisance.* Paris: Presses Universitaires de France.

Piaget, J. (1960). The general problems of the psychobiological development of the child. In J. Tanner & B. Inhelder (Eds.), *Discussions on child development. Vol.4.* London: Tavistock.

Piaget, J. (1961/1966). Part II. In E. Beth & J. Piaget *Epistémologie mathématique et psychologie.* Paris: Presses Universitaires de France/*Mathematical epistemology and psychology.* Dordrecht: Reidel.

Piaget, J. (1962/1985). Comments on Vygotsky's critical remarks concerning *The language and thought of the child* and *Judgment and reasoning in the child.* Cambridge, MA: MIT Press/Commentaire sur les remarques critiques de Vygotski concernant le *Langage et la pensée chez l'enfant* et le *Jugement et le raisonnement chez l'enfant.* In L.S Vygotski. *Pensée et langage.* Paris: Messidor/Editions Sociales.

Piaget, J. (1963). Preface. In J. Flavell *The developmental psychology of Jean Piaget.* New York: Van Nostrand.

Piaget, J. (1964). Development and learning. *Journal of Research in Science Teaching, 2,* 176–86.

Piaget, J. (1964/1968). *Six études de psychologie.* Paris: Denoel-Gonthier/*Six psychological studies.* London: University of London Press.

Piaget, J. (1965/1972). *Sagesse et illusions de la philosophie.* Paris: Presses Universitaires de France/*Insights and illusions in philosophy.* London: Routledge & Kegan Paul.

Piaget, J. (1967a). Epistémologie de la logique. In J. Piaget (Ed.), *Logique et connaissance scientifique.* Paris: Gallimard.

Piaget, J. (1967b). Epistémologie, nature et méthodes. In J. Piaget (Ed.), *Logique et connaissance scientifique.* Paris: Gallimard.

Piaget, J. (1967c). Logique formelle et psychologie génétique. In CNRS (Ed.), *Les modèles et la formalisation du comportement.* Paris: Centre National de la Recherche Scientifique.

Piaget, J. (1967/1971). *Biologie et connaissance.* Paris: Gallimard/*Biology and knowledge.* Edinburgh, UK: Edinburgh University Press.

Piaget, J. (1968). Quantification, conservation, and nativism. *Science, 162,* 976–79.

Piaget, J. (1968/1971). *Le structuralisme.* Paris: Presses Universitaires de France/*Structuralism.* London: Routledge & Kegan Paul.

Piaget, J. (1969/1970). *Psychologie et pédagogie.* Paris: Denoel/*Science of education and psychology of the child.* London: Longman.

Piaget, J. (1970). A conversation with Jean Piaget. *Psychology Today, 3,* 25–32.

Piaget, J. (1970/1972). *L'épistémologie génétique.* Paris: Presses Universitaires de France/*Principles of genetic epistemology.* London: Routledge & Kegan Paul.

Piaget, J. (1970/1977). *Psychologie et epistémologie.* Paris: Gonthier-Denoel/*Psychology and epistemology.* Harmondsworth, UK: Penguin

Piaget, J. (1970/1983). Piaget's theory. In P. Mussen (Ed.), *Handbook of child psychology. Vol. 1.* New York: Wiley.

Piaget, J. (1971). The theory of stages in cognitive development. In D.R. Green (Ed.), *Measurement and Piaget.* New York: McGraw Hill.

Piaget, J. (1972). *Essai de logique opératoire.* Paris: Dunod.

Piaget, J. (1972/1973). *Epistémologie des sciences de l'homme.* Paris: Gallimard/*Main trends in psychology.* London: Allen & Unwin.

Piaget, J. (1974/1977). *La prise de conscience.* Paris: Presses Universitaires de France/*The grasp of consciousness.* London: Routledge & Kegan Paul.

Piaget, J. (1974/1978). *Réussir et comprehendre.* Paris: Presses Universitaires de France/*Success and understanding.* London: Routledge & Kegan Paul.

Piaget, J. (1974/1980). *Recherches sur la contradiction.* Paris: Presses Universitaires de France/*Experiments in contradiction.* Chicago: University of Chicago Press.

Piaget, J. (1975a). Introduction générale au dialogue connaissance scientifique et philosophie. In *Connaissance scientifique et philosophie.* Bruxelles: Académie Royale de Belgique.

Piaget, J. (1975b). L'intelligence, selon Alfred Binet. *Bulletin de la société Alfred Binet et Théodore Simon, 75, 544,* 106–119.

Piaget, J. (1975/1978). *L'équilibration des structures cognitives.* Paris: Presses Universitaires de France/*The development of thought.* Oxford: Blackwell.

Piaget, J. (1975/1985). *L'équilibration des structures cognitives*. Paris: Presses Universitarires de France/*Equilibration of cognitive structures*. Chicago: University of Chicago Press.

Piaget, J. (1976a). Postface. *Archives de Psychologie, 44*, 223–28.

Piaget, J. (1976b). Le possible, l'impossible et le nécessaire. *Archives de Psychologie, 54*, 281–239.

Piaget, J. (1977a). *Etudes sociologiques*. Second edition. Geneva: Droz.

Piaget, J. (1977b). *Recherches sur l'abstraction réfléchisante*. Paris: Presses Universitaires de France.

Piaget, J. (1977/1986). Essai sur la nécessité. *Archives de Psychologie, 45*, 235–51/Essay on necessity. *Human Development, 29*, 301–14.

Piaget, J. (1978). *Recherches sur la généralisation*. Paris: Presses Universitaires de France.

Piaget, J. (1979). Relations between psychology and other sciences. *Annual Review of Psychology, 30*, 1–8.

Piaget, J. (1979/1980). The psychogenesis of knowledge and its epistemological significance. In M. Piattelli-Palmarini (Ed.), *Language and learning*. London: Routledge & Kegan Paul.

Piaget, J. (1980a). Recent studies in genetic epistemology. *Cahiers de la Fondation Archives Jean Piaget, No.1*.

Piaget, J. (1980b). *La raison en tant qu'objectif de la compréhension*. Unpublished paper, Centre International d'Epistémologie Génétique, Geneva.

Piaget, J. (1980c). *Recherches sur les correspondences*. Paris: Presses Universitaires de France.

Piaget, J. (1981/1987). *Possibility and necessity. Vol.1*. Minneapolis: University of Minnesota Press.

Piaget, J. (1983/1987). *Possibility and necessity. Vol.2*. Minneapolis: University of Minnesota Press.

Piaget, J. (1987). Préface. In J. Piaget, P. Mounoud, & J-P. Bronkart (Eds.), *Psychologie*. Paris: Gallimard.

Piaget, J. & Garcia, R. (1983/1989). *Psychogenesis and the history of science*. New York: Columbia University Press.

Piaget, J. & Garcia, R. (1987/1991). *Vers une logique des significations*. Geneva: Murionde/*Toward a logic of meanings*. Hillsdale, NJ: Lawrence Erlbaum Associates Inc.

Piaget, J., Grize, J-B., Szeminska, A., Vinh Bang. (1968/1977). *Epistémologie et psychologie de la fonction*. Paris: Presses Universitaires de France/*Epistemology and psychology of functions*. Dordrecht: Reidel.

Piaget, J., Henriques, G., & Ascher, E. (1990). *Morphismes et catégories*. Lausanne: Delachaux et Niestlé.

Piaget, J. & Inhelder, B. (1941/1974). *Le développement des quantités physiques chez l'enfant*. Neuchatel: Delachaux et Niestlé/*The child's construction of quantities*. London: Routledge & Kegan Paul.

Piaget, J. & Inhelder, B. (1951/1975). *The origin of the idea of chance in children*. London: Routledge & Kegan Paul.

Piaget, J. & Inhelder, B. (1961/1968). Introduction à la séconde édition. *Le développement des quantités physiques chez l'enfant*. Neuchatel: Delachaux et Niestlé.

Piaget, J. & Inhelder, J. (1966/1969). *La psychologie de l'enfant*. Paris: Presses Universitaires de France/*The psychology of the child*. London: Routledge & Kegan Paul.

Piaget, J. & Szeminska, A. (1941/1952). *The child's conception of number*. London: Routledge & Kegan Paul.

Piaget, J. & Voyat, G. (1968). Recherche sur l'identité d'un corps en développement et sur celle du mouvement transitif. In J. Piaget, H. Sinclair, & Vinh Bang. *Epistémologie et psychologie de l'identité*. Paris: Presses Universitaries de France.

Piéraut-Le Bonniec, G. (1974/1980) *The development of modal reasoning*. New York: Academic Press.

Piéraut-Le Bonniec, G. (1990). The logic of meaning and meaningful implication. In W. Overton (Ed.), *Reasoning, necessity and logic*. Hillsdale, NJ: Lawrence Erlbaum Associates Inc. Reprinted in L. Smith (1992a) *Jean Piaget: Critical assessments*. London: Routledge.

Pinard, A. (1981). *The conservation of conservation*. Chicago: University of Chicago Press.

Pinard, A. (1986). 'Prise de conscience' and taking charge of one's own cognitive functioning. *Human Development, 29*, 341–54. Reprinted in L. Smith (1992a) *Jean Piaget: Critical assessments*. London: Routledge.

Plato (nd/1935). *Theaetetus*. In F. Cornford (Ed.), *Plato's theory of knowledge*. London: Routledge & Kegan Paul.

Plato (nd/1941). *Republic*. Oxford: Oxford University Press.

Plato (nd/1956). *Meno*. Harmondsworth: Penguin.

Poincaré, H. (1902/1905). *Science and hypothesis*. London: Walter Scott Publishing Co.

Popper, K.R. (1934/1968). *The logic of scientific discovery*. London: Hutchinson.

Popper, K.R. (1979). *Objective knowledge*. Second Edition. Oxford: Oxford University Press.

Porpodas, C.D. (1987). The one-question conservation experiment reconsidered. *Journal of Child Psychology and Psychiatry, 28*, 343–49. Reprinted in L. Smith (1992a) *Jean Piaget: Critical assessments*. London: Routledge.

Putnam, H. (1980). What is innate and why: Comments on the debate. In M. Piattelli-Palmarini (Ed.), *Language and learning*. London: Routledge & Kegan Paul.

Putnam, H. (1988). *Representation and reality*. Cambridge, MA: MIT Press.

Quine, W.V. (1960). *Word and object*. New York: Wiley.

Quine, W.V. (1961). *From a logical point of view*. New York: Harper.

Quine, W.V. (1972). *Methods of logic*. Third edition. London: Routledge & Kegan Paul

Radnitzky, G. & Bartley, W (1987). *Evolutionary epistemology, rationality and the sociology of knowledge*. La Salle, IL: Open Court.

Reichenbach, H. (1938/1961). *Experience and prediction*. Chicago: University of Chicago Press.

Ricco, R.B. (1990). Necessity and the logic of entailment. In W. Overton (Ed.), *Reasoning necessity and logic*. Hillsdale, NJ: Lawrence Erlbaum Associates Inc.

Rosch, E., Mervis, C., Gray, W., Johnson, D., & Boyes-Braem, P. (1976). Basic objects in natural categories. *Cognitive Psychology, 8*, 382–439.

Rose, S. & Blank, M. (1974). The potency of context in children's cognition: An illustration through conservation. *Child Development, 45,* 499–502. Reprinted in L. Smith (1992a) *Jean Piaget: Critical assessments.* London: Routledge.

Royon, A. (1940). Construction perceptive et construction logico-mathématique de la pensée. *Archives de Psychologie, 28,* 82–142.

Russell, B. (1919). *Introduction to mathematical philosophy.* London: George Allen & Unwin.

Russell, B. (1959). *My philosophical development.* London: Unwin Books.

Russell, J. (1982). The child's appreciation of the necessary truth and necessary falseness of propositions. *British Journal of Psychology, 73,* 253–66.

Russell, J. (1983). Children's ability to discriminate between different types of proposition. *British Journal of Developmental Psychology, 1,* 259–268.

Russell, J. (1987). Rule-following, mental models, and the developmental view. In M. Chapman & R. Dixon (Eds.), *Meaning and the growth of understanding.* New York: Springer-Verlag.

Russell, J., Mills, I., & Reiff-Musgrove, P. (1990). The role of symmetrical and asymmetrical social conflict in cognitive change. *Journal of Experimental Child Psychology, 49,* 58–78. Reprinted in L. Smith (1992a) *Jean Piaget: Critical assessments.* London: Routledge.

Ryle, G. (1949). *The concept of mind.* London: Hutchinson.

Sainsbury, M. (1991). *Logical forms.* Oxford: Blackwell.

Samuel, J. & Bryant, P. (1984). Asking only one question in the conservation experiment. *Journal of Child Psychology and Psychiatry, 25,* 315–18.

Saxe, G. (1991). *Culture and cognitive development.* Hillsdale, NJ: Lawrence Erlbaum Associates Inc.

Scholnick, E.K. (1983). The implications of semantic theory for the development of class logic. In L. Liben (Ed.), *Piaget and the foundations of knowledge.* Hillsdale, NJ: Lawrence Erlbaum Associates Inc.

Schröder, E. & Edelstein, W. (1991). Intrinsic and extrinsic constraints on developing psychological competencies. In M. Chandler & M. Chapman (Eds.), *Criteria for competence.* Hillsdale, NJ: Lawrence Erlbaum Associates Inc.

Schubauer-Leoni, M-l., Bell, N., Grossen, M., & Perret-Clermont, A-N. (1989). Problems in assessment of learning: The social construction of questions and answers in the scholastic context. *International Journal of Educational Research, 13,* 671–84. Reprinted in L. Smith (1992a) *Jean Piaget: Critical assessments.* London: Routledge.

Shayer, M. & Adey, P. (1981). *Towards a science of science teaching.* London: Heinemann.

Shayer, M., Demetriou, A., & Pervez, M. (1988). The structure and scaling of concrete operational thought: Three studies in four countries. *Genetic, Social and General Psychology Monographs, 114,* 309–75. Reprinted in L. Smith (1992a) *Jean Piaget: Critical assessments.* London: Routledge.

Shayer, M., Küchemann, D., & Wylam, H. (1976). The distribution of Piagetian stages of thinking in British middle and secondary school children. *British Journal of Educational Psychology, 46,* 164–73. Reprinted in L. Smith (Ed.), *Jean Piaget: Critical assessments.* London: Routledge.

Siegler, R.S. (1981). Developmental sequences within and betwen concepts. *Monographs of the Society for Research on Child Development, 46,* 189.

Smedslund, J. (1969). Psychological diagnostics. *Psychological Bulletin, 71,* 237–48.

Smith, L. (1981). Piaget mistranslated. *Bulletin of the British Psychological Society, 34,* 1–3.

Smith, L. (1982a). Class inclusion and conclusions about Piaget's theory. *British Journal of Psychology, 73,* 267–76.

Smith, L. (1982b). Piaget and the solitary knower. *Philosophy of the Social Sciences, 12,* 173–82.

Smith, L. (1985). Making educational sense of Piaget's psychology. *Oxford Review of Education, 11.* 181–91.

Smith, L. (1986a). Children's knowledge: A meta-analysis of Piaget's theory. *Human Development, 29,* 195–208.

Smith, L. (1986b). From psychology to instruction In J. Harris (Ed.), *Child psychology in action.* London: Croom Helm.

Smith, L. (1986c). General transferable ability: An interpretation of formal operational thinking. *British Journal of Developmental Psychology, 4,* 377–87.

Smith, L. (1987a). On Piaget on necessity. In J. Russell (Ed.), *Philosophical perspectives on developmental psychology.* Oxford: Blackwell. Reprinted in L. Smith (1992a) *Jean Piaget: Critical assessments.* London: Routledge.

Smith, L. (1987b).The infant's Copernican revolution. *Human Development, 30,* 210–24.

Smith, L. (1987c). A constructivist interpretation of formal operations. *Human Development, 30,* 341–54.

Smith, L. (1989). Changing perspectives in developmental psychology. In C. Desforges (Ed.), *Early childhood education.* Edinburgh, UK: Scottish Academic Press.

Smith, L. (1991). Age, ability and intellectual development in Piagetian theory. In M. Chandler & M. Chapman (Eds.), *Criteria for competence.* Hillsdale, NJ: Lawrence Erlbaum Associates Inc.

Smith, L. (1992a). *Jean Piaget: Critical assessments, Vols. I–IV.* London: Routledge.

Smith, L. (1992b) Judgments and justifications: Criteria for the attribution of children's knowledge in Piagetian research. *British Journal of Developmental Psychology, 10,* 1–23.

Smith, L. (in press). Reasoning models and intellectual development. In A. Demetriou & A. Efklides (Eds.), *Mind, reasoning and intelligence: Structure and development.* Amsterdam: Elsevier. (in press)

Smith, L. & Knight, P. (1992). Adolescent reasoning tests with history content. *Archives de Psychologie, 60,* 225–42.

Sophian, C. & Somerville, S. (1988). Early developments in logical reasoning. *Cognitive Development, 3,* 183–222.

Sperber, D. & Wilson, D. (1986). *Relevance.* Oxford: Blackwell.

Spinoza, B. (1660/1963). In A. Wolf (Ed.), *Short Treatise.* New York: Russell & Russell.

Spinoza, B. (1670/1959). *Ethics.* London: Dutton.

Sternberg, R. J. (1985). *Beyond IQ.* Cambridge: Cambridge University Press

Sternberg, R. J. (1987). A day at the developmental downs: Sportscast for race #2—neo-Piagetian theories. *International Journal of Psychology, 22,* 507–29.

Strauss, S. (1988). *Ontogeny, phylogeny and historical development.* Norwood, NJ: Ablex.

Strawson, P. F. (1952). *An introduction to logical theory*. London: Methuen.

Stroud, B. (1979). Inference, belief and understanding. *Mind, 88,* 179–96.

Subbotskii, E. (1991a). Existence as a psychological problem: Object permanence in adults and preschool children. *International Journal of Behavioral Development, 14,* 67–82.

Subbotskii, E. (1991b). A life span approach to object permanence. *Human Development, 34,* 125–37.

Sugarman, S. (1987). The primacy of description in developmental psychology. *International Journal of Behavioural Development, 10,* 391–414.

Szeminska, A. (1935). Essai d'analyse psychologique du raisonnement mathématique. *Cahiers de pédagogie expérimentale et de psychologie de l'enfant, 7,* 1–18.

Tizard, B. & Hughes, M. (1984). *Young children learning*. London: Fontana.

Toulmin, S. (1953). *The philosophy of science*. London: Hutchinson.

Tudge, J. (1989). When collaboration leads to regression: Some negative consequences of socio-cognitive conflict. *European Journal of Social Psychology, 19,* 123–38.

Uzgiris, I. & Hunt, J.McV. (1975). *Assessment and infancy*. Chicago: University of Chicago Press.

Valsiner, J. (1987). *Culture and the development of children's actions*. Chichester: Wiley.

van Haften, W. (1990). The justification of conceptual development claims. *Journal of Philosophy of Education, 24,* 51–69.

Vinh Bang (1966). La méthode clinique et la recherche en psychologie de l'enfant. In F. Bresson & M. de Montmollin (Eds.), *Psychologie et épistémologie génétique*. Paris: Dunod.

Vonèche, J-J. (1982). Has conservation been conserved? *Contemporary Psychology, 27,* 863–65.

Vonèche, J-J. & Vidal, F. (1985). Jean Piaget and the child psychologist. *Synthèse, 65,* 121–38.

von Wright, G.H. (1951). *An essay in modal logic*. Amsterdam: North-Holland.

von Wright, G.H. (1957). *Logical studies*. London: Routledge & Kegan Paul.

von Wright, G.H. (1971). *Explanation and understanding*. London: Routledge & Kegan Paul.

Voyat, G. (1982). *Piaget systematised*. Hillsdale, NJ: Lawrence Erlbaum Associates Inc.

Vuyk, R. (1981). *Overview and critique of Piaget's genetic epistemology, 1965–1980*. New York: Academic Press.

Vygotsky, L. (1934/1962). *Thought and language*. Cambridge, MA: MIT Press.

Vygotsky, L. (1934/1978). *Mind in society*. Cambridge, MA: Harvard University Press.

Walkerdine, V. (1988). *The mastery of reason*. London: Routledge & Kegan Paul.

Wason, P. C. (1966). Reasoning. In B. Foss (Ed.), *New horizons in psychology*. Harmondsworth, UK: Penguin Books.

Wason, P. C. (1977). The theory of formal operations—a critique. In B. Geber (Ed.), *Piaget and knowing: Studies in genetic epistemology*. London: Routledge & Kegan Paul. Reprinted in L. Smith (1992a) *Jean Piaget: Critical assessments*. London: Routledge.

Wason, P.C. & Johnson-Laird, P.N. (1972). *Psychology of reasoning.* London: Batsford.

Wellman, H., Cross, D., & Bartsch, K. (1986). Infant search and object permanence: A meta-analysis of the A-not-B error. *Monographs of the Society for Research in Child Development. Serial no. 214, vol. 51, no. 3.*

Wermus, H. (1971). Formalisation de quelques structures initiales de la psychogenèse. *Archives de Psychologie, 41,* 271–88.

Wertsch. J. (1985). *Culture, communication and cognition.* Cambridge: Cambridge University Press.

Wesley, F. (1989). Developmental cognition before Piaget: Alfred Binet's pioneering experiments. *Developmental Review, 9,* 58–63.

Wheldall, K. (1985). The new "Developmental Psychology" and education. *Educational Psychology, 5,* 199–201.

Winer, G.A. (1980). Class inclusion reasoning in children: A review of the empirical literature. *Child Development, 51,* 309–29.

Wittgenstein, L. (1958a). *Blue and brown books.* Oxford: Blackwell.

Wittgenstein, L. (1958b). *Philosophical investigations.* Second edition. Oxford: Blackwell.

Wittgenstein, L. (1969). *On certainty.* Oxford: Blackwell.

Wittgenstein, L. (1978). *Remarks on the foundations of mathematics.* Third edition. Oxford: Blackwell.

Wolfram, S. (1989). *Philosophical logic.* London: Routledge.

Wood, D. (1980). Teaching the young child: Some relationships between social interaction, language and thought. In D. Olson (Ed.), *The social foundation of language.* New York: Norton.

Wood, D. (1988). *How children think and learn.* Oxford: Blackwell.

Wood, R. & Power, C. (1987). Aspects of the competence-performance distinction: Educational, psychological and meaurement issues. *Journal of Curriculum Studies, 19,* 409–24.

Wright, D.S. (1982). Piaget's theory of practical morality. *British Journal of Psychology, 73,* 279–83.

Author Index

Subject Index

Titles in the Series
Essays in Developmental Psychology
Series Editors: Peter Bryant, George Butterworth, Harry McGurk

PUBLISHED TITLES

Cox: Children's Drawings of the Human Figure
0-86377-268-4 1993 168pp. $36.95 £19.95 HB

Forrester: The Development of Young Children's
Social-Cognitive Skills
0-86377-232-3 1992 216pp. $37.50 £19.95 HB

Garton: Social Interaction and the Development of
Language and Cognition
0-86377-227-7 1992 168pp. $37.50 £19.95 HB

Goodnow/Collins: Development According to Parents: The Nature,
Sources and Consequences of Parents' Ideas
0-86377-160-2 1990 200pp. $31.95 £19.95 HB / 0-86377-161-0 $15.95 £8.95 PB

Goswami: Analogical Reasoning in Children
0-86377-226-9 1992 156pp. $28.50 £14.95 HB

Goswami/Bryant: Phonological Skills and
Learning to Read
0-86377-150-5 1990 174pp. $33.95 £19.95 HB / 0-86377-151-3 $16.95 £8.95 PB

Harris: Language Experience and Early Language Development:
From Input to Uptake
0-86377-231-5 1992 160pp. $35.95 £19.95 HB / 0-86377-238-2 $16.50 £8.95 PB

Siegal: Knowing Children: Experiments in
Conversation and Cognition
0-86377-158-0 1991 128pp. $31.95 £19.95 HB / 0-86377-159-9 $14.50 £7.95 PB

Smith: Necessary Knowledge: Piagetian Perspectives
on Constructivism
0-86377-270-6 1993 256pp. $46.50 £24.95 HB

Sonuga-Barke/Webley: Children's Saving: A Study in the
Development of Economic Behaviour
0-86377-233-1 1993 168pp. $28.50 £14.95 HB

For UK/Europe, please send orders to: Lawrence Erlbaum Associates Ltd., Mail Order Department, 27 Church Road, Hove, East Sussex, BN3 2FA, England. Note, prices shown here are correct at time of going to press, but may change. Prices outside Europe may differ from those shown. Please send USA & Canadian orders to: Lawrence Erlbaum Associates Inc., 365 Broadway, Hillsdale, New Jersey, NJ07642, USA.